Mischief *in* High Places

The Life and Times of
Sir Richard Squires

TED ROWE

BREAKWATER
P.O. Box 2188, St. John's, NL, Canada, A1C 6E6
WWW.BREAKWATERBOOKS.COM

COPYRIGHT © 2023 Ted Rowe
Library and Archives Canada Cataloguing in Publication
Title: Mischief in high places : the life and times of Sir Richard Squires / Ted Rowe.
Names: Rowe, Ted, author.
Identifiers: Canadiana 2023018362X | ISBN 9781550819816 (softcover)
Subjects: LCSH: Squires, Richard, 1880-1940. | LCSH: Premiers (Canada)—
Newfoundland and Labrador—Biography. | LCSH: Politicians—Newfoundland and
Labrador—Biography. | LCSH: Political corruption—Newfoundland and Labrador. |
CSH: Newfoundland and Labrador—Politics and government—1855-1934. |
LCGFT: Biographies.
Classification: LCC FC2173.1.S68 R69 2023 | DDC 971.8/02092—dc23

We acknowledge the support of the Canada Council for the Arts.
We acknowledge the financial support of the Government of Canada through
the Department of Heritage and the Government of Newfoundland and Labrador
through the Department of Tourism, Culture, Arts and Recreation for our
publishing activities.

PRINTED AND BOUND IN CANADA.

Breakwater Books is committed to choosing papers and materials for our
books that help to protect our environment. To this end, this book is printed
on recycled paper that is certified by the Forest Stewardship Council®.

INTRODUCTION

ACKNOWLEDGEMENTS

Putting together a book like this depends on the collaboration of a lot of people. Along the way, I was fortunate to receive valuable pieces of information and feedback from conversations with Glenn Deir, John Fitzgerald, Jim Hiller, Gus Lilly, and Jeff Webb. Melvin Baker directed me to sources and provided much useful information that I might otherwise never have come across.

Help from the staff of The Rooms Provincial Archives, the Newfoundland section of the A. C. Hunter Library (especially John Griffin), and Archives and Special Collections at Memorial University (especially Linda White) was indispensable. A long-shot visit to the Family Research Center in Tucson, Arizona, with the aid of its helpful personnel, turned out to be very informative.

For inside information on the Strong side of the family, I am especially indebted to Carolyn Strong Molson, who also helped to make my brief visit to Little Bay Islands in 2017 most rewarding and memorable.

Most of all, I was fortunate to be able to interview Robert A. Squires and the late Richard J. Squires (grandsons of Sir Richard), who graciously provided family information, documents and photographs available nowhere else that considerably enhanced the entire project, as did their cousin Elaine Wilson. I realize that for them I was on a delicate mission, which makes their generosity and cooperation all the more valued. They gave freely of their time and left me free to report what I found.

Maureen Rowe read an early draft at various stages, and the final product reflects her prudent comments and advice. Tim Rogers and Sue Khaladkar were kind enough to review the manuscript with their usual care and insightfulness.

The professionals at Breakwater Books worked with dispatch in preparing the book for publication. I am especially obliged to Claire Wilkshire. Finally, I owe an immense debt of gratitude to editor Sandy Newton for her help in putting the manuscript in shape with unflagging diligence, patience, and expertise.

INTRODUCTION

Anyone with even a casual awareness of Newfoundland history has heard the name Richard Squires: a man first elected prime minister in 1919 and twice forced out of office under a cloud of scandal and disgrace. His accomplishments during his first term—sponsoring memorials in European battlefields honouring Newfoundland's fallen in the Great War, creating Memorial University College, finalizing a deal that brought a pulp and paper industry to the Bay of Islands—have long been overshadowed by his reputation for dipping into public funds and using his position for personal gain.

Richard Anderson Squires came to high office when the game of politics was rife with patronage, favouritism, and corruption. He was both a product and ongoing cause of this sorry situation, which achieved its highest expression during his terms as prime minister. Still, to write him off as a small-time crooked politician—"a common garden-variety thief," as a friend snickered when I mentioned I was writing about him—is to shortchange the man. Despite his striking flaws, he had a memorable character. He was smart, charming, and charismatic. He was a proud Newfoundland patriot who threw his heart and soul into public life. He lived large, fully enjoying the celebrity and trappings that came with political success. He was given a knighthood. He was a resilient politician, able to breeze through scandals and dishonour without embarrassment. And yet his career ended in disgrace following the rowdy riot of 1932, when Newfoundland's legislative building was trashed by an irate crowd.

Raised as a motherless child in Harbour Grace, the young Richard Squires was unremarkable except for his deep passion for books. He developed an interest in politics when his father ran (unsuccessfully) for elected office. He excelled as a student and capped his high school years in St. John's by winning the country's top scholarship. That success paved the way to law school and a legal practice that quickly gained recognition as the most successful in St. John's. By then he had his sights firmly set on a career in politics and the highest elected office in the land.

Squires was anything but subtle in the pursuit of his goal. A fearless and relentless self-promoter, he enjoyed a flamboyant lifestyle: fancy clothes, cigars, a stylish residence, a chauffeured motorcar, and a yacht. He embraced travel and glamour. All this (and more) irritated his detractors, who were only too willing to pile on him at the first suggestion of wrongdoing.

In some ways, he was his own worst enemy. Like his father, he could not manage money. He was a perpetual conniver, up to his neck in gossip and intrigue, with a knack for slip-sliding around accusations of misconduct. Nevertheless, he maintained a loyal cadre of supporters who admired his dogged determination, brilliant election strategizing, and refusal to bow to his accusers.

When Richard Squires had the bit in his teeth, there was no stopping him. He poured his full energy and all his personal wealth into his first campaign for prime minister. The fight consumed him even as he watched his finances dwindle. But he was hubris personified: supremely confident in his ability to govern and to get back in the game in the face of defeat. It was a character trait that served him well, until it didn't.

My interest in researching Richard Anderson Squires was to determine how all this could exist in one man, to determine how a scholarly, accomplished, and gifted individual could repeat his mistakes so spectacularly. My purpose was neither to sugar-coat his actions nor further denigrate them, but to try to understand what lay beneath them. I wanted to know what drove Richard Squires: how his career developed, who were the major players of his time, and how they affected him. I wanted to know about his family, immediate and extended, and how they might have helped or swayed him. And I wanted to know more about the woman who stood by him through all the tumultuous ups and downs: Lady Helena Squires, a dynamo in her own right and the first woman elected to the Newfoundland House of Assembly.

In other words, I wanted to put a human face on the man behind the notorious reputation and infamous deeds. Here is what I found.

CHAPTER ONE

Early Roots and Youthful Days
1880–1898

R ichard Anderson Squires could trace his roots back to the community of Broad Cove on the north shore of Conception Bay, about twenty-six miles as the crow flies from the capital city of St. John's. Its harbour is notched out of the rocky coastline and anchored by a perfect arc of pebbled beach. In the early decades of the nineteenth century, Broad Cove resembled hundreds of other outports along the Newfoundland coast. The people there— all five hundred of them—were fishing families, their rickety wharves, stages, and houses strewn loosely around the shore.

As they had for generations, Broad Cove men spent their summers rowing back and forth to the nearby inshore fishing grounds, hand-lining for northern cod, splitting and salting their catch and spreading it to dry for sale to the merchants of Harbour Grace, fifteen miles away by road. They spent the rest of the year keeping their property and fishing gear in repair, building boats, and generally doing whatever was necessary to make sure their families survived. The women looked after the housekeeping, vegetable gardens, and livestock, helped with drying the fish, and kept the family clothed and fed. There was not much commerce or formal community life. Broad Cove had no shops, no church, and no schoolhouse. The children who went to school walked to Adam's Cove, the next settlement, two miles away.

At mid-century, Gregory and Sarah Squires were living on the north side of Broad Cove with their three sons: William, John, and Alexander (the youngest, born in 1852). The boys grew up pitching in with the fishing and other chores needed to keep the family going. The three of them also went to school, which was unusual for Broad Cove boys. They grew up well-educated for the sons of a fishing family.

Sarah died when Alexander was still a youngster. Gregory married the widow Eliza Moores in 1864 and she brought three children of her own into the family. The Squires household doubled overnight from four to eight, and two more sons of Gregory and Eliza followed close behind. As the boys grew, space in Gregory's fishing boat became more than a little cramped. When William and John were old enough to leave, they moved on to start new lives in Harbour Grace. Around 1870, Alexander, father to Richard, followed.

In Harbour Grace, the three brothers stayed close to each other, close enough to end up marrying three related women. By the time Alexander got there, William had wed Harriet Parsons of Bear's Cove, a little village on the eastern edge of town; he carried on making a living in the fishery. John and Alexander had bigger plans that required leaving the working-class stamp of the outport fisherman behind. John Squires established himself by marrying up—to Amelia Hippesley, daughter of two school-teachers (her mother, Louisa, was also a Parsons from Bear's Cove). White-collar work was his fancy, and he had set himself up as the Harbour Grace photographer. In January 1874, Alexander followed suit, gaining social status when he married Amelia's sister Henrietta, some ten years his senior, who was living with her widowed mother on Water Street.

The marriage presented the chance for an ambitious small-town newcomer to achieve recognition and respectability in Harbour Grace, for like John, Alexander was bent on making a name for himself in business. Harbour Grace, a town of seven thousand people, offered plenty of opportunity. Though not in the same league as St. John's, more than three times its size, Harbour Grace was twice as large as the other major outports of the day—Carbonear, Brigus, Bonavista, Twillingate, and Burin. Edging the shores of a five-mile-long inlet, it was known as Newfoundland's "second city" (or, more optimistically, a "metropolis"). By the late 1800s, Harbour Grace had

Alexander Squires, 1852–1934

a three-hundred-year history firmly tied to the North Atlantic fishery. Most of its men were still fishermen by trade, and summer breezes still carried the whiff of salt fish drying in the sun. Some of the men went away to fish every year on schooners sailing to the coast of Labrador. They set out their potato gardens before leaving in the spring and found the potatoes dug by the time they got back in the fall. It was said that some had never seen potato plants growing.

Harbour Grace had enough businesses to give it a real downtown. A walk along Water Street took you past dozens of stores and offices. Among the grocers and suppliers and the twenty-some public houses were an array of specialty shops: watchmaker, tinsmith, tailor, shoemaker, bookseller, and printer. Included in the professional class were physicians, druggists, accountants, and bookkeepers (and the lone photographer, Mr. J. Squires). A police force of twelve kept the old stone courthouse a centre of activity, providing enough work for one or two barristers. A few wealthy merchant families, like the Ridleys, Rutherfords, and Munns, were the high society. Their firms dominated the waterfront, doing trade in salt cod with markets in the Mediterranean, South America, and the West Indies. They gave Harbour Grace an international flavour, with tall-masted schooners coming and going and the taverns catering to sailors from around the world.

Newfoundland's second city also had churches of significance and schools of good reputation. The first thing sailors saw, coming into the harbour, were the twin spires of the Roman Catholic cathedral, its dome modelled grandly after St. Peter's in Rome. The building was iconic, though Protestant roots also ran deep. Harbour Grace claimed distinction as the first mission for Methodism in the New World (1766) and remained the epicentre of the movement in Newfoundland. The Church of England had a sombre stone church built in 1835 and the Presbyterians a Free Kirk (1855). As far as schooling was concerned, the Harbour Grace Grammar School was among the finest in the country. Spain was a major trading partner for Harbour Grace merchants, and Spanish was taught at the grammar school. The highbrow crowd had their own literary society, and the *Harbor Grace Standard*, established in 1859, put out the weekly news from home and abroad.

For a young man with the drive and ambition of Alexander Squires, Harbour Grace had much to offer. Within a few years of arriving, he had opened a shop on Water Street selling groceries and general provisions. Chafing with impatience and anxious to move ahead, he was also running a trading schooner on voyages up the northeast coast of the island by 1880.

Sadly, things had not gone as happily at home. His new wife, Henrietta, lost her mother a month after their January 1874 wedding and Henrietta herself passed away the following October. Five years went by as Alexander ground away at his business. Then, in January 1879, he remarried. His new wife was Sidney Jane Anderson, only child of the late Richard Anderson, a Protestant Irishman who stood out as one of the more colourful members of the Harbour Grace gentry.

Alexander would have known his new father-in-law by reputation only—Richard Anderson died in 1864—but what a reputation he had. In an era when attorneys required general literacy but no special legal training, Anderson had sufficient schooling to practise law as well as attend to business interests. At court he was brash, a renegade, and no stranger to controversy. The record shows at least one occasion when his insolent language and refusal to keep quiet got him barred from the court and fined for contempt. On another, he flatly refused to garb himself in the robes of a barrister, though protocol required him to do so. Outside court, too, he was a man not to be tangled with. Successful in business, he left Sidney Jane (his main heir) a large estate:

Sidney Anderson Squires, 1847–1880

Fruitland, located about a mile past the Catholic cathedral toward Bear's Cove.

At thirty-two, Sidney Jane Anderson was sliding past the marrying age when she wed Alexander Squires in a ceremony at Fruitland. She brought a sizable dowry to the marriage, further elevating Alexander to the position of respected citizen and country squire. The couple lived in style at Fruitland. Alexander's second marriage looked to be unfolding like his first, however, when his mother-in-law died a year after the wedding. This time, happily, there was an addition to the family along with a funeral. Just two days after her mother's death, on January 18, 1880, Sidney gave birth to a son. She named the boy Richard Anderson Squires.

The mixture of joy and grieving over the next few months could not have been easy for Sidney. Alexander was neck-deep in his business and, come summer, left on one of his voyages to the north. Sidney pined for him, writing from her bed early one morning in July, looking to catch the day's mail:

> I am looking forward to the pleasure of your return. We are very lonely and miss poor Mamma, so that I feel your absence more than I did last summer, or else I have grown fonder of you and can't bear you out of my sight.

A kiss from you now would be better than breakfast . . .
[Anderson is] growing a lovely boy; you will be quite
proud of him when you come . . . Baby sends you dozens
of kisses and his Mama would have no objection to deliver mine personally. Hoping to see you soon.

Sidney never recovered from the birth of her son. She died in
September, six weeks after sending that letter, without seeing
Alexander again. Her property at Fruitland passed to her infant
son. As administrator of her estate, Alexander took charge of his
son's inheritance and, perhaps to meet business obligations,
promptly sold off the livestock (a fine American horse and some
cows and sheep) and a set of farm implements. He also began
generating income from the property, offering for rent two "com-
modious dwellings, suitable for persons in comfortable circumstances," and a third house with two tenements.

As well as overseeing Fruitland, Alexander ploughed ahead
with his trading schooner and his shop, where he had his hands
full trying to make ends meet. He was not a good businessman,
in fact, and he faced a number of lawsuits from creditors. At the
same time, he had trouble collecting his own accounts: December
1882 found him suing more than twenty customers for unpaid
bills. But he soldiered on with the shop and kept up his northern
voyages until 1886, when the business failed. The shop closed,
his schooner, *Flying Mist*, was sold at auction, and he went into
bankruptcy.

Luckily, Alexander still controlled his son's interest in Fruitland, and he now turned his attention to the farm. Within two years
he was back on his feet with another schooner; the year after that,
he opened a new shop on Water Street. The *Harbor Grace Standard*
welcomed him as "one of the new and enterprising businesses of
Harbour Grace." In a flurry of newspaper ads, he announced the
"Lowest prices at Squires' Cheap Grocery Store."

And what of young Richard Anderson Squires—or "Anderson," as everyone called him—growing up an only child in a home
with no mother and a father consumed by business, away for

months at a time? Small and reserved, Anderson was a smart fellow who learned to read at an early age and developed a passion for books. He took drawing and music lessons but mostly kept to himself, devising his own amusements. Apart from his family, it seems he had few childhood friends, preferring the companionship he found in his books.

Anderson grew up with no mother's love or nurturing, but there were surrogate mothers to help Alexander raise his son. His brother William's wife, Harriet, with three boys of her own, was not far away and a frequent visitor to Fruitland. The widow Catherine Burrows, who formerly occupied one of the tenements, moved in to become part of the Squires household. Anderson was fond of "Aunta Burrows" in his younger years but longed to have his father around. "I am very lonely without you. Make haste and come home as soon as you can," wrote the plaintive eight-year-old to Alexander, away on another voyage, and later: "It is very lonely since you left . . . I go to school every day. I am fourth in my class . . . In music I am learning the Cuckoo Waltz and the scale up to E with three flats . . . I am sending you your pipe and Aunta is sending some fish."

At school, Anderson was a quiet outsider but a model student, well behaved and diligent in his work. He attended the elite Harbour Grace Grammar School and made the honour list for general proficiency, good grades in the academic subjects, and his excellent conduct. For a time, he attended the Methodist Academy in Carbonear. His home life took a turn for the better as he was reaching the age of ten, when his father, now thirty-seven, married for a third time, to fifty-five-year-old Sarah Comer. Sarah, the stepdaughter of Richard Anderson, was young Anderson's aunt and no stranger to the Squires household. Alexander's brother John Squires came from Fortune Bay to officiate at the wedding (he had given up photography for life as a Congregationalist minister). Sarah, a cheerful, kind-hearted woman, had been teaching at the little school in Bear's Cove. She now pitched in with raising Anderson, who warmed to his new stepmother.

Young Richard Anderson Squires

Anderson grew up as part of a sizable, if somewhat scrambled, extended family. His two grand-fathers each had two marriages and his father was now on his third. There was a wide assort-ment of half- and step-relatives and a large number of cousins in his uncle John's family—certainly enough family members to give a young boy a sense of belonging to a diverse if loosely connected clan. Anderson was familiar with many of them; his father was generous in welcoming any and all relatives to their home in Harbour Grace. As in later life, the young Squires was connected to a large circle of people, but close to only a few.

Sarah brought to the marriage a section of the Fruitland estate inherited from Richard Anderson (another small portion had gone to her brother). After their mar-riage, Alexander extended his farming enterprise on the expanded estate. In the fall of 1890, back in business on Water Street, he stocked a full range of farm produce at his shop, including milk, butter, eggs, and root vegetables—all at the "Lowest Prices in Town." He began making a practical study of agriculture, experi-menting with new crops and ways to increase his yield. The long, hot summer of 1892 was a remarkable growing season, and the farm had a record year. Watching his father cultivate the land and tend the animals had an impact on young Anderson. He was not the type to roll up his sleeves and dig in the dirt, but he took a keen interest in the process.

As if shopkeeper, coastal trader, and commercial farmer were not enough to occupy him, Alexander next turned his attention to politics. He had wandered in this direction before, in 1885, when voters in Englee and Conche (stopping points on his northern trading route) got up a petition to have him run in the fall election. Alexander threw in his hat as an independent candidate, unaffiliated with any party. He published a thoughtful and well-articulated platform but, faced with a failing business, was forced to withdraw.

He ran again as an independent in 1893 for the district of Harbour Grace, favouring the policies of Sir William Whiteway's Liberal Party, the "party of the workingman." This time he ramped up his campaign with gusto and became a popular speaker on the hustings. Despite his best effort, however, he made a poor showing in the election, coming in second from last in a field of eight and winning only five per cent of the vote.

In 1894, Alexander announced his intention to run again in a by-election for the Bay de Verde district, but he ended up campaigning for the Liberals instead. He threw his support behind Whiteway again the next year, in a Harbour Grace by-election. Alexander's enthusiasm for Whiteway and the Liberal Party was surely not lost on young Anderson, now in his impressionable teen years.

From a young age, Anderson followed his father in the Methodist faith. The family were churchgoers, and Sunday mornings meant a walk or carriage ride to the white clapboard Methodist church on Water Street, just on the downtown side of the Catholic cathedral. There was also no shortage of special services and prayer meetings during the week. A string of visiting preachers brought the Word—the Methodist version of it—to the Harbour Grace faithful. As a devoted elder in the church, Alexander always found room for them at Fruitland.

It's no surprise, then, to find Anderson in his early teens as a Sunday school teacher and member of the Epworth League, a Methodist association for young adults. His attendance at the church and the League gave him his first platform for public speaking. He addressed a Sunday school meeting when he was twelve, holding forth on why parents should play a more active part in the "nursery of the Church," where "souls are modelled for Eternity." He showed an obvious knack for it and soon found himself invited to speak on other topics, such as "The Life of Abraham" and "The Introduction of Methodism into America."

At fifteen, the budding young orator enrolled in the Methodist Superior School on Noad Street, a mile and a half up the harbour from Fruitland, beyond the business district. Here, Harvard-educated schoolmaster John Hillyard taught a curriculum preparing students for the standard exams set by Newfoundland's Council of Higher Education (CHE). Anderson did very well in the junior matriculation exams in June 1895, placing second among all students outside St. John's. He made the honour list in the senior exams in 1896, which ended his schooling in Harbour Grace.

Despite his stellar performance in his final two years, Anderson did have a weakness in Latin. Hillyard gave him some private tutoring during his last summer home. Otherwise, Anderson enjoyed the life of an idle teen: his diary portrays a boy loafing around, sleeping in, and staying up late. He still loved his books, but he was now more sociable, strolling uptown on weekend evenings, getting together with the other young people. He was especially friendly with the Trapnell sisters, Susie and Lizzie, daughters of the keeper of the Harbour Grace jail, spending a good many evenings at their home. Some days he borrowed a boat for a lazy row around the harbour.

Anderson also had a special mentor in family friend Alfred H. Seymour, sheriff (and later magistrate) at the courthouse. A Sunday school superintendent, active temperance worker, and former private secretary to Prime Minister Whiteway, Sheriff Seymour loved trout fishing and introduced Anderson to a special spot ("Seymour's Gullies") up the railway track. It is not hard to imagine the talk turning, as they sat around the campfire at the end of the day, from trouting to politics and the law, Methodism, temperance, and perhaps the legendary escapades of Anderson's grandfather, Richard Anderson.

Rowing around the harbour, trouting with Sheriff Seymour, mingling with other teens, the young Anderson saw the summer of 1896 slip gently by. With the warm days drawing to a close, he boasted in his diary about escorting Miss Lizzie Davis on an afternoon carriage drive to Freshwater and Carbonear. It was a pleasant finale to growing up in Harbour Grace. When September came, he packed his trunk and boarded the train with his father, heading to a new adventure in higher education in St. John's.

On their arrival in the city, Squires father and son engaged one of the horse-drawn cabs from the line at the Fort William train station. They drove through the bustle of downtown to the foot of Long's Hill and stopped at Methodist College, Newfoundland's foremost institute of advanced learning. A cluster of three buildings housed the college, the principal's residence, and a three-storey dormitory ("the Home"), providing lodging for some forty out-of-town students. Trunk in tow, Anderson and Alexander walked up the front steps of the Home to find Rev. Mark Fenwick, the congenial administrator, who assigned Anderson to a shared bed-room on the third floor.

Rebuilt in brick after the Great Fire of 1892 that had destroyed much of downtown St. John's, Methodist College was a thoroughly modern institution when Anderson arrived in the fall of 1896. It boasted bright new classrooms, a lecture hall with a full pipe organ, a top-notch laboratory, and special rooms for music and art. Under the eye of long-time principal Robert E. Holloway, the college offered a post-secondary program for young men and women equivalent to first-year university (Newfoundland had no university at the time). The college would be home to Anderson for the next three years.

Principal Robert Holloway was an exceptional scholar and teacher who lent much intellectual oxygen to the air around him. Small-framed and frail, fighting the effects of lingering tuberculosis, he nonetheless possessed enormous spirit, his deep-set eyes reflecting the depth of an agile mind. His own schooling in England had given him a solid grounding in both the arts and sciences, and he had a knack for conveying information to his students and the general public in language they could understand. People flocked to the college for his public lectures and demonstrations—on the latest developments in electricity, for example, or the workings of the telephone. After the discovery of x-rays in 1895, Holloway built an x-ray machine and, as a favour to a physician friend, used it to examine the deformed hand of a five-month-old infant. This was said to be the first use of x-rays for medical diagnosis in North America.

Holloway's wide-ranging interests extended to geology, botany, astronomy, and that perfect Victorian juncture of science and art: photography. He was also ahead of his time in advocating equal educational opportunity for boys and girls. There should be no such thing as "boys' subjects" and "girls' subjects," he believed. Rather, all students should be encouraged to apply themselves to whatever subjects fit their natural ability. About half the students at the college were girls when Anderson enrolled, including Holloway's own daughter Elsie. Holloway urged them to "keep up the intellectual credit of the sex and boldly go in for the same work as their male competitors." He was very pleased whenever they outdid the boys in class.

Richard Anderson Squires stepped into this enlightened fortress of learning with some trepidation, although he was not totally among strangers. His old schoolmaster John Hillyard from Harbour Grace began teaching at the college the same year. And Anderson's cousin, Beaton Squires, his Uncle John's son, was a fellow out-of-town student from Fortune Bay.

Academic work at the college was demanding, but Anderson proved up to the challenge (though he continued to struggle with Latin). Toward the end of his first year, in May 1897, Holloway wrote to Alexander Squires:

> I cannot allow the present term to finish without expressing my satisfaction with Anderson and his work. He has

made great advances in his education, and I feel confident that he will do us all credit in the coming examinations. His ability is certainly above the average, and his industry and attention are equally satisfactory. His exceedingly elementary knowledge of Latin is unfortunate but he will make good progress in that next year. I hope he will put in an hour or two a day on Latin during the holidays.

Encouraged by his success, Anderson grew to enjoy college life and became a dedicated collegian, wearing the college's red and blue cap with pride. But what is college without a bit of mischief from time to time? Anderson recorded in his journal the time Fenwick charged him ten cents for a chair he'd broken while horsing around with his roommate and the evening Mrs. Fenwick caught him on the girls' floor without permission. Unlike her husband, she overlooked it, since it was his first offence. "Not first offence but first time caught," Anderson noted slyly. Visitation between the sexes improved after the girls presented a petition to have the boarders finish their study before supper, which would give everyone more time together in the evenings. It was not exactly in line with Victorian protocol, but the easygoing Reverend Fenwick agreed, and social life at the Home took a turn for the better.

Anderson's time at Methodist College was easier on him than it was on his father. Alexander Squires was not a good money manager, and running a business was once again proving hard on his purse. In fact, he had barely scraped together the $165 for Anderson's first-year tuition. His brother John was better off, even on the pay of a clergyman, and Alexander borrowed his son's second-year fees from him, backed by a mortgage on Fruitland. It was money well spent, for academically Anderson was going from success to success. In 1897, at the end of his first year, he wrote the CHE senior exams again, flying through with first-class honours and placing third in the country.

In his second year, Anderson really buckled down to his

studies. He took special tutoring in Latin and paid extra for a private room with quiet study space. His father's striving for achievement was showing up in young Anderson. So was his interest in politics. He became engrossed in the 1897 general election that fall, keeping a list of the candidates and a tally of the vote in the back of his diary. On polling day, he went down to the St. John's East voting station to get the returns first-hand. The Liberals took that electoral district, but overall the Whiteway party was defeated by the Conservatives, led by James Winter. It was no doubt a disappointment to a keen young Liberal like Anderson Squires.

Countering that emotion, he was delighted when his friend Susie Trapnell came in from Harbour Grace to teach at the Methodist orphanage. They began seeing each other on Sunday evenings after prayer meetings at Gower Street church. A romance seemed in the offing, but it would not happen at the expense of his studies. His dedication to the task paid off in the top-level London matriculation exams in 1898, in which Anderson won the Jubilee scholarship for the highest marks in Newfoundland. The coup was a first for Methodist College—a "brilliant success," said Holloway, declaring a half-holiday for the whole school. The senior students loaded into carriages to celebrate with an afternoon picnic at Pearce's Farm in the Goulds. The man of the hour was Anderson Squires.

The scholarship awarded Anderson $200 a year for three years of university study. On Holloway's advice, he postponed using it for a year, staying on at the college as a special science student. He took advanced courses, including practical chemistry, and assisted Holloway with demonstration experiments in the lab. There was an unforeseen benefit to this delay. That year, a petite, somewhat frumpy but single-minded merchant's daughter from Little Bay Islands—Helena Strong—took up residence at the college. The Jubilee award winner caught her eye. Her daughter Rosemary later described their crossing of paths this way:

Picnic at Pearce's Farm in honour of Anderson Squires, 1898. Anderson is in the first row, far left.

Mother realized my father's potential almost immediately—she also observed that he had few social skills, having grown up as an only child who spent most of his time reading and studying. Mother had a twin brother and related easily with men. She was soon able to attract the interest of my father, who was very much an academic. They had to meet secretly; it was against school rules, so he would send her notes with a detailed map indicating where they should meet and at what time.

In Rosemary's telling of it, the strong-willed outport merchant's daughter fell for the bookish shopkeeper's son and took on the task of putting a bit of polish on him. One suspects it was more than this—that Helena saw Anderson Squires as the ticket to a better life, to higher levels of society and financial success. They both came from families that were above the crowd in Harbour Grace and Little Bay Islands and they wanted that to carry on in the wider world ahead of them. It was a dream they shared from the start, one that endured in a liaison lasting a lifetime.

Helena was the outgoing, sociable side of this partnership, and that suited Anderson well. He admired her social ease, friendliness, and strength of character. He valued time to himself and was happy enough to have someone to offset his more reclusive side. In Anderson, Helena Strong saw an intellect worthy of respect and the promise of greater things to come.

CHAPTER TWO

———————

Law and Marriage
1898–1908

The young woman who came crashing into the life of Anderson Squires in the fall of 1898 had her own story to tell. Her hometown of Little Bay Islands was a prosperous fishing village in Notre Dame Bay, on Newfoundland's northeast coast, and her father, James Strong, was among the most prosperous of merchants there. The Strong presence in the community went back to Helena's grandfather William, who had relocated from Twillingate in the 1850s with his wife Elizabeth and two sons, James and Joseph. In Little Bay Islands they found a quiet, scenic harbour that offered a secure anchorage, ringed by steep wooded hills and protected by the hump of Macks Island, plunked squarely in the harbour entrance.

By the time the Strongs arrived, the community was already home to thirty families: about two hundred people, all Methodists. William Strong claimed a section of shoreline in the southwest corner of the harbour with a stretch of gently sloping land running half a mile back from the beach. He put up a simple two-storey house a few hundred feet from the water and built fishing premises—a wharf and stage, plus flakes and sheds. His sons grew up in the fishery but, like Gregory and Sarah Squires of Broad

Cove, William and Elizabeth Strong never allowed fishing to get in the way of schooling. They sent James, the older boy, to the Methodist Academy in St. John's, the forerunner of Methodist College. He came back to settle in Little Bay Islands with as much book learning as anyone in the place, though he preferred to spend his time working with his hands, at the fishery and whatever odd jobs he could find.

In the winter of 1868, James and his brother Joseph did what many outport men did to tide them over until the new fishing season: they went sealing. Rough and dangerous work, but in a good year a man could make as much as $200 in a month or six weeks. James and Joseph pooled their earnings, brought in a supply of goods from St. John's, and set themselves up in business as "J. & J. Strong." When Joseph bowed out in 1878, the name changed to "James Strong."

By that time, James was married to Annie Mursell of Little Bay Islands. A decent, upright man with a benign but authoritative air, he kept building the business. In 1885 he joined Richard Mursell, his wife's brother, and A. C. Hynes, to form the Little Bay Islands Packing Company. As time went on the name changed again (to Strong and Mursell) and he added canned lobster to an existing trade in salt cod, salmon, and seal pelts. He built extra wharves and filled the beach with sheds, storerooms, workshops, and two-tiered flakes for drying the fish. Still there was no containing his expansion—when he ran out of space along the shore, he put up two sheds on a flat, low-tide ridge of rock in the middle of the harbour. By 1890, James Strong was far and away the leading merchant of Little Bay Islands. "I always enjoyed doing a large business," he told a friend in later years.

On October 29, 1878, James Strong's marriage to Annie Mursell produced a set of twins: William Allen and Helena Emiline (or Lena, as family would call her all her life). She was apparently so tiny at birth that the midwife took one look and muttered, "That'll never amount to much." Her twin William, always called Will, was a big, brawny boy. Eventually his adult height of six feet would dwarf Lena's of five foot two, but she stood up to him with a mind of her own, determined not to live in his shadow—or anyone else's. Their mother died when Will and Lena were seven, leaving the twins and a younger brother, age three. James Strong soon remarried Lydia Rooney of St. John's. The union would add four more sons and a daughter, Bessie, to the family.

The nineteenth-century system of education in rural Newfoundland was rudimentary at best, with teachers poorly qualified and poorly paid, but a few communities stood out for rising well above the standard. One was Harbour Grace, another was Little Bay Islands. For its size, it had excellent amenities—a doctor, a bank, a library, and well-stocked shops—and it was able to attract capable teachers from England. There was a literary society and a touch of the cosmopolitan to the community, with steamers coming and going, taking James Strong's salt cod to overseas markets. Robert Holloway passed through with his camera in the summer of 1899 and was hosted at lunch by Lydia Strong. He was much taken by the setting, capturing it on film as "one of the prettiest in our island of pretty harbours."

Unlike Anderson Squires, with his solitary childhood in Harbour Grace, Lena Strong grew up in a community where everyone knew each other and in the company of a twin brother who rarely left her side. And she had the status that came with being the daughter of a very big fish in a small pond. As youngsters, she and Will enjoyed carefree days running in and out of the big two-and-a-half-storey house across the road from their father's fishing sheds and wandering up to the back field where wild raspberries intermingled with the "tame" ones imported from England. Their world changed, however, with the arrival of Lydia Rooney. The new stepmother was a St. John's lady and curiously quirky—she never wanted her picture taken, for example, and was in the habit of scratching her face off any photos in which she did appear. For Lena, Lydia was an unwelcome addition to the family, and sparks flew between them. Lena stayed close to her father

James Strong family, 1898. Front row: Hubert, James, Bessie, Norman. Back row: Lena, Will, James, Lydia Rooney, Lydia's sister Polly.

and Will, finished school, and went off to Methodist College in St. John's. The fact that she was sent there perhaps speaks as much to her disruption in the family as to her scholastic ability.

Along with that shift, however, came the encounter with Anderson Squires and then the whirlwind courtship in the secret hideaways of Methodist College. The timing was fortuitous, coinciding with Anderson's extra year assisting Holloway. By the end of it, Lena's newfound beau had decided to apply his Jubilee scholarship to the study of law.

First he needed another year of undergraduate study not available in Newfoundland. But before heading to Halifax's Dalhousie University, Anderson took a few months to lay a foundation in St. John's for his future law career. He knew that once he'd earned his degree, he would still need a two-year clerkship with a senior member of the bar before writing the bar exams to practise in Newfoundland. He set out to get an early start on his apprenticeship by clerking with the firm of Browning and Conroy in the summer of 1899. He may have been steered there by his father, who had run against Donald M. Browning in the 1893 election. Browning, representing the Liberals, fared little better than Alexander Squires in that encounter, but he later entered the House of Assembly as a member for the district of Twillingate.

Toward the end of 1899, Browning gave up his legislative seat and his law practice to become Registrar of the Supreme Court. When Anderson returned to St. John's after his makeup year at Dalhousie, he was thus obliged to find another sponsor for his clerkship. His second choice was a good one, a man steeped in both the practice of law and the art of politics: Edward P. Morris.

Born with a sharp wit and a gift of the gab, Morris had risen from a working-class family on Lime Street in St. John's (his father was a cooper) to the senior ranks of the Newfoundland legal profession. He was also well up the political ladder, serving as a Liberal member of the House of Assembly for St. John's West since 1885 and as attorney general for Prime Minister Whiteway. Anderson joined his firm as a summer student in March 1900, just before the Liberals came to power under a new leader, Robert Bond. Morris, not the fondest of Bond's associates but the most senior Catholic politician of the time, became justice minister and the number two man in the new administration. There could hardly have been anyone more suitable as mentor to an aspiring political neophyte like Anderson Squires.

Meanwhile, what about Lena? After Anderson left for Halifax, she stayed for a second year at Methodist College, where her academic record was respectable but unexceptional. She avoided the sciences, choosing instead the literary courses like composition, English grammar, and scripture history, though she did take geometry, algebra, and arithmetic, as well as book-keeping. In 1900, as Anderson returned to Dalhousie for his first year of law, she enrolled at Mount Allison Ladies' College, a combination liberal arts academy and finishing school in Sackville, New Brunswick.

Sackville was a town of 1,500 at the time, large enough to warrant a stop on the trans-Canada railway line but offering nothing comparable to the colourful mélange of life in St. John's with a population of 40,000. It could, however, lay claim to having the first women's college in Canada, turning out cultured and educated graduates for half a century. Lena joined a student body of one hundred–plus, studying fine art, music (especially choral work), household science, the art of social conversation, and the other skills needed by a young lady intent on taking her place in polite society.

The young women at the Ladies' College were cloistered in a four-storey residence next door to a small gymnasium where they took their exercise, which included lawn drills designed to encourage proper deportment. Supervision was strict. Young men at the Mount Allison College and Academy campus next door were forbidden in the ladies' academy, though they all shared space in the White House, a lecture and music hall resembling a grandly overstated Greek temple. The female students were allowed out for shopping once a month, but only in the company of a teacher. They were expected to attend church twice on Sunday, parading along in their long flowing dresses. The college allowed visitors on Saturday evenings, in supervised public gatherings. Visits in private were permitted with family members only, which attracted a surprising number of "cousins" from the male side of the campus.

While concentrating on the arts and home economics and learning to refine her social graces, Lena also took teacher training. She graduated in 1902 with a Mistress of Liberal Arts diploma. She then went home to Little Bay Islands, all the while keeping in contact with Anderson as he worked through his Bachelor of Laws degree, doing well enough after all his struggles with Latin to graduate with distinction in the upper level of his class.

Once he was permanently back in St. John's, Anderson settled in as a student-at-law with Morris' law firm on Kimberly Row and took lodging at 9½ Freshwater Road, a short walk from the office. The sharp young lawyer was someone you would notice if you passed him on his way down Long's Hill—his well-cut suit and wire-rimmed glasses gave him a serious, bookish look. He still had a career to build in St. John's, but in Harbour Grace his reputation was already made. "There can be little doubt a brilliant future lies before the talented young native," said the *Harbor Grace Standard*.

It was at this point, at the beginning of his law career, that he began using the name Richard A.—rather than R. Anderson—Squires. That was how he was known at Dalhousie, and it had a more natural ring to it for someone with their eye set on public life. In any event, he left his youthful name behind—though in the Squires and Strong families (and in Harbour Grace) he would always be called Anderson. We, too, will acquiesce to his change for the remainder of these pages.

In 1902, Richard Squires's father turned fifty. Tiring of the ups and downs of entrepreneurship, Alexander had closed up shop two years before to concentrate on farming at Fruitland, which he still held in trust for his son. He had been less than successful navigating the world of business and had little to show for all his labour. In the coming years, in the slipstream of his son's achievements, he would spend his time comfortably enough as a leading citizen of Harbour Grace and elder of the Methodist Church. In 1902, he was a member of the Road Board and the Methodist School Board and was later appointed welfare officer for the district.

Richard A. Squires finished his clerkship, passed the exams, and was admitted to the bar in January 1904, joining the thirty-odd members of the Newfoundland Law Society. He became a partner in Morris's firm and set about building his own clientele. Playing up his hometown connections, he began running his legal card in the *Harbor Grace Standard* (a practice he would continue for years). As time went on, he was no stranger to the court in Harbour Grace. Financially ambitious, he also began to supplement his income by selling insurance as an agent for Imperial Life.

Squires on graduation from
Dalhousie Law School, 1902

The long-distance courtship with Lena continued while she passed the winter of 1904 teaching school in Botwood. She then returned to Little Bay Islands for another year, presumably having established some reconciliation with her stepmother. Then, on June 15, 1905, Richard climbed aboard the train for central Newfoundland and Little Bay Islands. Two days later, he and Lena were married in the Methodist hillside church, packed with Lena's family and friends, which was pretty much the entire community. Two of Lena's cousins, Joseph and Minnie Strong, were the official witnesses. Richard brought his bride back to St. John's and they set up house at 239 Gower Street, a stone's throw from his law office, Gower Street Methodist Church, and Methodist College.

In Harbour Grace, Richard Squires was well known; in St. John's, not so much. As an outharbour man, law degree notwithstanding, Richard knew he would have to work to gain credibility with the St. John's establishment, much as his father once did in Harbour Grace. And, like his father, he went at it with a vengeance, at a pace that made heads spin. For a start, he became a regular attendee and speaker at the Methodist College Literary Institute (MCLI), one of the oldest debating societies in North America. Institute members gathered in the lecture hall on Wednesday evenings for debates on current affairs, both local and international. Some of the questions tackled were "Does trial by jury meet the requirements of the age?"; "Have trade unions benefitted Newfoundland?"; and "Was England justified in entering into an alliance with Japan?" An ardent member and effective debater, Richard relished the verbal jousting of the debates that helped him further polish his public speaking skills.

Then came membership in one organization after the other: the firemen's union, the Longshoremen's Protective Union, Gower Street Methodist Church, the Loyal Orange Association, the Masonic Lodge, the Sons of England, the prohibitionist International Order of Good Templars, and the St. John's Curling Club, to name a few. A practised speaker with a good grasp of governance, Squires usually found himself elected to office in the organizations he joined. He was polished, articulate, and full of energy, but lacked the bonhomie of a man like Morris. He was not at ease with everyday banter and not a man you could get close to. He made many acquaintances but few friends.

Bit by bit, though, his profile rose, and his cases began to catch the public eye. One example was his defence of Walter Hart of Harvey Road, peddler of hop beer, who was charged in the summer of 1907 with selling liquor without a licence. The Constabulary seized some of Hart's popular brew on August 4 and had it tested by Dr. Brehm, the medical health officer, on August 21. He found it had five per cent alcohol, well above the two per cent allowed by law. It looked like a slam dunk for the prosecution—but not so fast, said Richard Squires. When the case went to trial, he got Brehm to admit that the delay in testing could have increased the alcohol in the beer by August 21. Then he had two witnesses testify that they had consumed largequantities of Hart's beer on August 4 without being intoxicated "even to the slightest degree." The court decided that the law could not be applied unless the beer was tested immediately upon seizure and dismissed the case. The decision went over well in the beer parlours of St. John's.

Lena was also out to win acceptance in St. John's, to overcome any stigma of being from the bay. She took on a lot of church and community work, especially as a singer and reciter. She had special success in coaching young people at George Street Methodist Church in music and elocution. And, like her husband, she was driven to climb the social ladder. These early years for both of them were an ongoing quest for social acceptability.

As Richard's income grew, and perhaps with the help of Lena's dowry, he got into funding mortgages (a common practice of law firms at the time). Some were in his name, some in Lena's. Together they began buying rental properties, sometimes flipping them for a quick profit. They also started a family. Daughter Sidney Elaine arrived in March 1906 and James Alexander was born in September the following year. It was a busy life, with frequent trips back and forth to Harbour Grace for Richard to see clients and keep in touch with his father as he worked the farm.

During this period, Alexander was delving more and more into the study and promotion of agriculture. In 1907 he served as the first vice-president of the Harbour Grace Agricultural Society, organizing exhibitions of farm produce and working to bring regulation to the industry. Lena and the children went to live with him at Fruitland during the summer and fall of 1909. Lena gave birth to a second son, Robert Holloway, in Harbour Grace that October.

By this time, Richard A. Squires, solicitor, insurance agent, real estate investor, community volunteer, and family man, was well on his way toward new challenges and a new career in the world of politics.

CHAPTER THREE

Look Out, Politics
1908–1913

In the early years of the new century, as Richard A. Squires was working his way through law school, Newfoundland was digging its way out of a decade of economic and political chaos. Major highlights and low points began with the Great Fire of 1892, which laid waste to downtown St. John's. The conflagration destroyed over two-thirds of the city and left more than eleven thousand people homeless. The election of 1893, the one contested unsuccessfully by Alexander Squires in Harbour Grace, kept William Whiteway and the Liberals in office, but most of the government members were then unseated after the fact on charges of corrupt practices during the campaign. A stopgap Conservative government led by A. F. Goodridge lasted less than a year, ending with the collapse of Newfoundland's two commercial banks. The reinstated Liberals carried on as the country teetered on the edge of bankruptcy and then was righted by the determined efforts of Colonial Secretary Robert Bond, who secured financing abroad for a last-minute bailout of the colony.

Bond rode a high wave as the saviour of Newfoundland through another interlude of Conservative rule that began with the 1897 election, the one watched so closely by young

Anderson Squires at Methodist College. In 1898, facing another financial crunch, the Conservatives contracted with Robert G. Reid, builder of the trans-Newfoundland railway, to take over the public services of the country—the telegraph, the postal service, the coastal steamer service, and the railway (plus millions of acres of prime timber and agricultural land) for a price of $1.3 million. Bond called it an outrageous giveaway and brought down the government in a vote of non-confidence. Richard Squires's future mentor Edward Morris joined him in a Liberal coalition to ensure the government's defeat. Morris was tight with the Reids and had stepped away from Bond and the Liberals to support the public services contract, but he became the lynchpin for Bond's coup. In 1900, a reunited Liberal Party under Bond swept into office with a landslide victory at the polls. Morris became minister of justice.

This was the political context in 1902 when Richard Squires joined the Morris law office. Prime Minister Bond was a hero—a man of principle and unbeatable, or so it was said. After a tumultuous decade, the mood of the country was upbeat as a new era of prosperity beckoned. St. John's turned the page with a rebuilt downtown, new housing, and modern services taking shape. An electric street trolley, installed by the Reids, ferried people back and forth from the city's east end to its west end in bell-clanging, plush-seated cars. Landmark stone buildings appeared—a new train station, a courthouse, and post office— and the first moving pictures came to the Nickel Theatre.

Bond was the eleventh man to serve as prime minister under Newfoundland's system of responsible government, instituted in 1855. To summarize: its legislature, modelled after the parliament of Great Britain, consisted of an elected House of Assembly and an appointed Legislative Council, the upper house of "sober second thought." Represented in St. John's by the governor, Britain still held final authority over the affairs of the colony, including appointments to the Legislative Council. Elections, generally a two-party affair, were held every four years, contested by the Liberals, tagged as the party of the working man, and a second party (usually called Conservative) that represented the interests of business. At that time, eighteen electoral districts sent a total of thirty-six members to the House. The parties ran slates of candidates, all men, as were the voters who elected them. The leader of the party that won a majority in the House became prime minister and was invited by the governor to form an administration. The prime minister in turn recommended men to serve in the executive council (cabinet) to run the departments of government. Members of the executive council were normally, but not necessarily, elected members of the House.

In 1904, the year Richard Squires made partner in the Morris firm (and Morris received a knighthood), a general election confirmed Bond in office for another four years. Morris continued as minister of justice. With his eye already on politics, Richard looked ahead to the next election. Naturally, he was a Liberal. Openly ambitious and a bit of an upstart, he was altogether too aggressive to suit the straitlaced and reserved Robert Bond, but not to worry, Edward Morris would be his ticket to the game.

Indeed, Bond's fortunes eventually waned and by the third year of his second mandate, he was not wearing well on the electorate. He had gotten himself involved in an unwinnable trade war with the United States that ended up hurting the Newfoundland fishery and some of its merchants—one of whom, Michael Cashin, was a member of his own party. Cashin was a burly, well-off fish merchant from Cape Broyle and the government member for Ferryland district. He abandoned Bond in 1905 to sit with the Opposition. The prime minister had also fumbled when it came to bringing new development to the colony. He struck an agreement with British interests to develop a pulp and paper mill at Grand Falls, a massive project by world standards, but offered major concessions to get it underway. "Another giveaway!" cried the Opposition, who likened the deal to the detested Reid contract of 1898. Morris, an ambitious schemer in his own right with his eye fixed on the prime minister's office, began plotting to displace

Bond. He resigned as minister of justice in 1907 and followed Michael Cashin to the Opposition side of the House.

The Conservatives, at this point loosely organized and anxious to find a leader, wanted Morris to join them. But Morris saw no advantage in that, choosing instead to launch his own party—the People's Party, he called it—to stand against the government. With buckets of Reid money behind him, he assembled a group of disaffected Conservatives, former Liberals (including Michael Cashin), and political newcomers such as the brash and flamboyant John Chalker Crosbie. Included in this group was his law partner and protégé Richard A. Squires, once a Liberal and now an opportunist.

All of this shifting about from party to party may seem strange viewed though today's lens, but apart from Bond (and his predecessor William Whiteway), politicians' allegiance to political parties was fluid in that era, held in place not so much by policy or ideology as by the opportunity for personal gain and advancement. Shifting from party to party, or hatching a new one, was not that hard to do.

When the time for the 1908 fall election rolled around, Richard Squires was set to go. He jumped in for the People's Party in the three-member district of Trinity, which encompassed most of the settlements around Trinity Bay. It was a field of six contenders—three Liberals and three for Morris's People's Party. Two of his opponents, George Gushue and A. W. Miller, were Liberal incumbents for the district. A third, Robert Watson representing the People's Party, had been elected as a Conservative twice before.

For all his hobnobbing in St. John's and his connections in Harbour Grace, Richard still faced the challenge of being a new face in Trinity Bay. Touted by his party as one of the "rising young men" of the colony, he mounted an assertive, hard-hitting campaign, lashing out at Gushue, a man of good reputation many years his senior and Bond's minister of public works. One morning in October, when the six candidates were all in Hants Harbour, the two of them lit into each other on the road in front of a crowd of voters. According to the Liberal-influenced *Evening Telegram*, Gushue deflected all of Squires's ridicule and had the crowd cheering for him before the verbal set-to was over.

Bond was content to fight the election in his own district of Twillingate, relying on his record of fiscal responsibility and a scandal-free government. It was Morris who injected life into the campaign. Financed by the Reid corporation, he campaigned with gusto, stumping and glad-handing his way through all eighteen electoral districts with the promise of better days to come. Endowed with an overactive promissory gland, he pushed a platform of no less than thirty pledges—everything from lowering taxes to providing higher widows' allowances and old age pensions, improving the coastal boat service, and building new schools and hospitals. The clincher (and payback to the Reids) was his commitment to boost employment (and prop up a financially troubled railway) with the construction of new branch lines to dozens of coastal communities.

In the face of this onslaught, Bond showed considerable staying power. When the results were in, the Liberals and the People's Party had elected eighteen candidates each. The result was unprecedented—a tie election.

It was a tie that hung by a thread.

In Trinity Bay, Richard Squires had lost—but just barely, only five votes behind People's Party candidate Robert Watson. A recount was pointless—Squires winning over Watson would merely substitute one Morris candidate for another. Harbour Grace, however, was a different matter. Here the ex-sheriff and Richard's old fishing buddy, Magistrate Alfred Seymour, had resigned his position in a snit with the Justice Department just before the election and stood as a candidate for the People's Party. Liberal Eli Dawe had edged him out by one vote. A reversal here would give Morris the government. Seymour asked for a recount. The result gave Dawe a majority of three. Game unchanged.

The question of who should form the government with a tie

vote thus landed on the desk of Governor William MacGregor, a dour Scotsman who had developed a fondness for Morris and his genial ways. Morris gained the upper hand in the wrangling with the governor that followed—his affable, down-to-earth approach to the crisis bested Bond's cerebral, legalistic meanderings.

MacGregor asked Morris if he could form a government. Oh yes, he replied cheerfully. He couldn't, of course, since no elected members had seen fit to change sides (despite some innovative attempts at persuasion). Morris couldn't possibly govern with a tied legislature, any more than Bond could, but that wasn't the point. Once placed in power by MacGregor, Morris had the all-important advantage in the runoff election to follow: the ability to dispense money for patronage and government works.

The election date was set for May 8, 1909. Richard Squires ran again in Trinity Bay. He had spent the intervening months gearing up for the campaign, sending out copies of the *Evening Chronicle*, Morris's propaganda paper, to every voter in the district. And in case anyone wondered where the papers came from, he included a photo of himself for good measure. Truth be known, he overdid it. This was brash, American-style campaigning unheard of in Newfoundland—and expensive (to the tune of about $3,500, well over $100,000 in today's currency). But Richard didn't skimp when it came to self-promotion, especially at election time.

Again he stirred up attention with brazen accusations against Gushue—one Liberal called him a "whipper-snapper" and "gasbag"—and he was turned out of a campaign meeting in Green's Harbour just two days before the vote. This time, though, his intense efforts paid off. He topped the polls in Trinity, and Squires, Watson, and newcomer E. G. Grant swept the district for the People's Party. At the age of thirty, Richard Anderson Squires had a seat in the House of Assembly. Alfred Seymour joined him, this time winning a clear majority in Harbour Grace. Sir Edward P. Morris and the People's Party formed a new government to replace Robert Bond and the Liberals.

And what a different style of government it was. Unlike Bond, who favoured well-behaved, upstanding men for his cabinet, Morris chose some hard-hitting self-seekers not at all above using a cabinet position to enrich themselves. Michael Cashin was a prime example of the type. The new minister of finance and customs was rough and outspoken. (He would be described by his son Peter as a hard father with "a violent and uncontrollable temper." His father had beaten him more than once, even when he was in his twenties, and Peter left Newfoundland in 1910 to avoid more whippings.) John Chalker Crosbie was another minister without portfolio and founder of what would become a Newfoundland dynasty, Crosbie was also not a fellow to be trifled with—a coarse, moon-faced man who pulled no punches. One afternoon during the 1909 campaign, he stood by on the wharf in Western Bay as one of his men kicked Robert Bond into the harbour. Donald Morison, a restless man who had left the judiciary to return to the more lucrative life of a politician, was named minister of justice and attorney general. Then there was Morris himself—devious, obligated to the Reids, and now freed from the constraints of the prudent style of government practised by Bond.

The People's Party came to power when the country of Newfoundland was doing well. People were full of optimism with the economy in an upswing. The fishery was gaining strength; the pulp and paper mill in Grand Falls and the iron ore mines on Bell Island were humming. Like Whiteway and Bond before him, Morris talked up new industrial development to lessen Newfoundland's dependence on its long-standing raison d'être: the fishery. He encouraged advancement in farming by promoting agricultural societies like the one started by Alexander Squires and associates in Harbour Grace. In forestry, he opened the door to foreign investment in undeveloped timberlands. He also jacked up spending on public services. But his grand plan, as promised in 1908 and 1909, was to push railway branch lines through to key coastal communities: Bonavista, Heart's Content, Grates

Cove, Trepassey, Fortune Bay, and Bonne Bay. Work on the lines started as soon as the votes were counted in 1909. It was a windfall for the Reids and would soon become a huge drain on the public treasury, but in the beginning Morris could take credit for creating thousands of construction jobs and bask in the glow of approval that went with that.

As a rookie backbencher, Richard Squires was not prominent during his first session in the House. He attended to his constituents, presented petitions on their behalf (mostly for road improvements), and supported educational reform and the cause of temperance. Despite his touted speaking skills, his maiden speech in the House on February 17, 1910, was plodding and long-winded, extolling the value of the new railway lines for Trinity Bay. He briefly crossed swords in debate with Robert Bond, now Opposition leader, who opposed the branch lines.

Still the consummate self-promoter, Richard had copies of his speech distributed throughout his district. Some voters were unimpressed. The people in Shoal Harbour in particular were miffed, since they had to give up their homesteads to make way for the new Bonavista branch line. Voters in Elliston grumbled about the line passing them by. Their new MHA told them that he could do nothing about it and laid the blame on his colleague Robert Watson, who had a place in the cabinet. Also disgruntled were the people of British Harbour, to whom Richard had promised a telegraph office during the campaign. "If I do not keep this promise," he told them, "I will never return to ask for your votes again." (Three years later, with no telegraph office in sight, a writer from British Harbour in the Evening Telegram expressed the hope that he would at least keep that part of his promise.)

Though a disappointment to some voters, Richard worked hard to address the needs of his constituency. That usually meant getting them government money for roads and wharves. He was prompt in attending to the countless details confronting all MHAs: addressing complaints about welfare officers, appointing telegraphers and members of government boards, helping men in search of work in St. John's, and looking for money to get them through a tight spot. In March 1911, sealers from Elliston travelled in to join the seal hunt and swamped his office, asking him to cover their board and lodging until they could find berths on a vessel. "They think I am a sort of bank," he confided to a friend, "not realizing that every dollar I pay out comes from my private income, the money I earn with the sweat of my brow from daylight to dark. I fancy they must have the idea it is some sort of poor relief."

Working hard as an MHA and balancing that with a flourishing law practice, Richard Squires caught the eye of William Coaker. At the time, Coaker was farming on a remote island in Notre Dame Bay and serving as leader of the fledging Fishermen's Protective Union (FPU). A difficult man in many people's opinion, he was also a reader and thinker who, in his off-hours, had worked up a blueprint for a fishermen's union that could stand up to the merchant class, the "bloodsuckers of St. John's," as he called them. Driven by a pent-up fury at the plight of the fishermen, Coaker singlehandedly canvassed the coastal communities of Newfoundland, building the FPU's membership into a force to be reckoned with. Journalist P. K. Devine was blown away after meeting him in 1903, seeing "political energy enough to run the whole country" and "indignation enough against the treatment of the masses by both the merchants and government to return thirty-six men to the House of Assembly."

In October 1909, with the Union gathering steam, Coaker wrote Squires to see if he would act as its solicitor and make himself available to individual members for legal advice. Richard replied that he was "fully convinced that a Union amongst fishermen would, if properly organized and directed, be of incalculable advantage to the fishermen" and offered his services free of charge. He was also ready to assist members individually for a yearly retainer once he knew what kind of services they would need. None of this came to pass, but with both men on their way to political careers, they were by no means done with each other.

At the end of 1910, impatient to move out on his own, Richard Squires left the Morris law office, settling up with $7,000 for his share of the practice. By early in the new year, he was established on the top floor of the Bank of Montreal building on Water Street, a block from the courthouse. Richard soon found that election to public office was good for business. Fully engaged and sharp as a whip, he had a way of making clients feel they were the sole focus of his attention and that he had only their interests at heart. But any lawyer connected with the party in power expected to have legal work come his way, and Richard received his share of public prosecutions. His community network was expanding as well, and he was becoming an "old boy" in many of the organizations he served. Shortly after the 1909 election, he was appointed a governor of the Newfoundland Savings Bank. In the Orange Lodge, he rose to the position of Provincial Grand Master (and would host the Grand Lodges of British North America at their convention in St. John's in 1912).

Although his law practice thrived, the number of attention-getting cases—the kind that Richard could use to make a bigger name for himself—were few and far between. Sensational criminal trials in St. John's were rare—the city had not seen a murder in years. One bizarre case that did put him in the limelight came along in 1912: his defence of Charlotte Butler, of 18 Colonial Street, St. John's. She was arrested for stealing and harbouring stolen goods by two constables who showed up at her door and found the place crammed with articles of clothing and other personal items, neatly packaged and labelled, including sixteen pairs of women's and children's boots tucked away in her oven. At her court appearance, represented by Richard A. Squires, Mrs. Butler was remanded while the Constabulary looked for the owners of the goods and prepared charges. The case drew a lot of attention, and the courtroom was packed when it finally came to trial. Despite the large amount of property involved, the police could establish only two charges of theft: an apron from a Mrs. Pitcher, a tenant of the accused, and a doormat from a

Mr. Bradshaw. Bradshaw's case was withdrawn when, questioned under oath, he was unsure whether the doormat was his. Having got the charges down to one stolen apron, Richard made the case for a light sentence, but the judge was unsympathetic. Mrs. Butler went to jail for three months.

Shortly after he set up his own law office, Richard and Lena moved their family residence uptown to 44 Rennies Mill Road. Their new home was not a mansion, but it was certainly a step up from Gower Street, in a swankier part of St. John's, backing onto Bannerman Park. Once settled, Richard and Lena became the picture of a modern young couple accumulating the trappings of success. The automobile, one of the novelties of the time, was beyond their reach, but Richard was one of the first in St. John's to have a motorcycle (as was his father in Harbour Grace). In 1911, with motorized travel just beginning, Richard joined a group of enthusiasts forming Newfoundland's first motor association. Dedicated to encouraging the use of motorcars and cycles, it pushed for road improvements and, pending the introduction of highway regulations, the policing of inconsiderate driving. Richard made good use of the motorcycle in travelling back and forth to Harbour Grace. He also took a few late-summer swings through his district—an official from the government Board of Works clinging on tightly on the rear seat—scouting out roadwork deserving of patronage.

Richard had Lena behind him as he progressed through his dual careers, but, nonconformist that she was, she by no means restricted herself to the role of dutiful spouse. Going against the tenor of the times, which had a wife and mother firmly planted in the home, she chose to expand on her Mount Allison studies by attending Emerson College in Boston, the largest school of oratory in America. Teaching "oratory as an art resting upon absolute laws of nature" and giving "a thorough training in all the principles upon which this art is based," training at Emerson enabled students to become teachers of elocution and oratory, as well as public readers. Lena wanted to improve her skills by studying with the best.

After their daughter Elaine's birth in 1906, she applied to Emerson for the 1907–08 school year. She had to withdraw when James came along in 1907 and was delayed again by Robert's birth two years later. By 1911, however, even with another son (Richard Jr.) newly arrived, Lena decided she had waited long enough. She left St. John's by steamer in September with nurse-maid Hannah Parrott and four-month-old Richard. Once settled in Boston, she began evening classes at Emerson. Lena finished two semesters, then took some time in New York before returning home in June.

Her training in Boston helped polish Lena's diction and added a pleasing cadence to her speech. Daughter Rosemary later recalled that she spoke with beautiful "clarity and rhythm":

> I remember Mother giving directions to one of our maids who was less receptive to direction than most. Mother paused, looked at Minnie and said, "Minnie, I don't believe you understood a word I said!" Minnie replied: "I don't know that I understands what ye says, but I luvs to hear ye talk."

Lena also had an air about her that commanded attention and respect. She embodied the idea of lifelong learning as she pursued further studies over the years, striving to become a first-class chatelaine. She would take a summer course at Harvard and domestic science at a cooking school in Boston founded by the legendary Fannie Farmer, who introduced standardized recipe measures to the culinary world. Kitchen gardening, farming, and horticulture were likewise absorbed, and she later delved into interior decorating in New York.

Lena's avant-garde lifestyle and liberated ways might have made her a natural advocate in the crusade for women's right to vote, but there were complications. As she was planning her first foray to Emerson College in 1906, the suffrage movement was gathering steam in St. John's. Led by Armine Gosling, a forty-five-year-old Canadian schoolteacher, it was not the kind of boisterous marching and placard-waving association that defined the movement in England and America. Among Gosling's cohorts, though, were a few with a more radical bent, harbouring an outrage against the repression of women in a man's world.

In the fall of 1909, a few of the more vocal of Gosling's movement spoke out on women's issues at a men's debating club (likely the MCLI). The members banned them from future meetings for their "caustic" views. In response, the women opened their own meeting place—the Ladies Reading Room—taking bright and cheery quarters on Water Street and stocking them with the latest newspapers and magazines from England and America. Within weeks they had more than a hundred members. Women in feathered hats and puffed-out dresses would drift in to chat and read the news from abroad. They began serving tea on Saturdays, and Gosling started a current events club for lectures and debates on social issues, including the status of women.

Lena Squires, enlightened and sociable as she was, was drawn to the quiet ambiance of the Reading Room and its sometimes not-so-quiet current events club. She was one of its featured speakers, in fact, lecturing on the works of the Bengali poet Rabindranath Tagore, winner of the 1913 Nobel Prize for Literature. Her patronage of the Reading Room, however, did not extend to empathy for the suffrage movement. Indeed, she actively opposed it. She saw no need for any change in her own status, a married woman who had the freedom and means to come and go as she pleased. And as for women's right to vote, Richard was firmly against that, in keeping with his social clique, and she stood firmly behind him.

The final year of his first term as an MHA brought Richard a few life changes. In July 1913, his stepmother Sarah, approaching eighty years of age, died after a swift decline into "senile decay." Remembered for a life of "quiet, cheerful, earnest performance of duty and unselfish services," she was laid to rest in the Methodist cemetery in Harbour Grace. That summer,

Richard advanced another step up the social ladder: he commissioned construction of a forty-foot sailing yacht, fitted up with a twelve-horsepower engine and sleeping accommodations for six. The extravagance set him back $1,400, about the price of a new motorcar, and he was bent on showing it off. He hired a captain as soon as the boat was ready in August, and with Lena and all four children—Elaine, James, Robert, and Richard Jr.—spent the golden days of late summer cruising around Trinity Bay.

The next election was due in the fall of the year. Richard ditched the motorcycle in favour of the yacht for this campaign, touring the district in style with his running mates R. W. Fowlow and Brian Dunfield. As the October 30 election day drew near, Liberal propaganda in the *Evening Telegram* blasted "the bumptious Mr. Squires" as one of the "grabbers" of the Morris party because of the amount of legal work directed his way from the government. If re-elected, he would be lining his pockets further as minister of justice, they said.

The political landscape of this campaign was clearly different from Richard Squires's earlier efforts, and in more ways than one. William Coaker, driven by a combination of raw energy and popular appeal, had worked to fashion the FPU into an organized body of twenty thousand fishermen, sealers, and loggers, with a Union party ready to break into politics. It was a fired-up party of commitment, and its candidates came charging out of the north in an alliance with Robert Bond's Liberals. When the votes were counted, the FPU had elected eight candidates. Along with the Liberals' seven, they had reduced the People's Party majority from sixteen to six.

Both the Trinity district and "the bumptious Mr. Squires" fell to this Liberal-Union coalition. Richard had mounted another vigorous campaign, but this time the results for him weren't even close. The People's Party was still in power, however, and Morris was still prime minister, which meant that the day was not done for Richard Squires, not by a long shot.

CHAPTER FOUR

Justice Minister and War
1914–1917

William Coaker came to the House of Assembly with his troop of Unionists as a brash outsider, the indignation spilling out of him at the merchant elites of St. John's. His presence dominated the 1914 session. "It is too bad of me to be taking up so much of the time of the House," he told them, "but I have a wonderful lot to say." That he did, relentlessly pushing his party's program of reform: a minimum wage, free and compulsory education, night school for adults, outport hospitals, and more, all aimed at improving the lot of the working man.

His long list of demands did produce a wonderful lot of talk but yielded little in the way of results in an Assembly controlled by the Morris majority. Proposals to regulate working conditions in the logging camps and at the seal hunt did make it through the House, but they failed to survive the government-dominated Legislative Council. Some of the FPU MHAs, lives spent in a fishing boat, were uncomfortably out of place in the House of Assembly—or in St. John's, for that matter. The newly arrived governor, Sir Walter E. Davidson, was quite taken by Coaker's success in bringing the FPU into politics. He invited Coaker and his outport members to dinner at Government House and was

William Coaker, 1871–1938

dismayed when half of them declined because they had no clothes suitable for a formal dinner and no confidence that they had the table manners required. Davidson instead had them in for lunch (to "sup" rather than to "dine," as he put it in his diary).

As for Richard Squires, his second electoral defeat was but a temporary glitch in his political advancement. His pushiness and undisguised ambition, not to mention the showiness with the new yacht, may have annoyed voters and helped him lose the election, but he was in it for the long haul. The defeat in Trinity Bay squelched hopes of a cabinet post—or rather, postponed it. His time came after the March 1914 session of the House ended. Morris appointed him then to the Legislative Council, the upper chamber, and at the cabinet table Richard got what he had angled for: minister of justice and attorney general.

According to John Evans, editor of the *Newfoundland Quarterly*, Richard Squires was the youngest man to attain that position in Newfoundland, which in "the natural course of events will be a stepping-stone to the Premiership." Richard was, said Evans, "one of the most brilliant and successful of the younger generation of legal practitioners in the Colony and his prodigious industry and powers of application have greatly aided him in pushing his way into the front ranks of the profession." With the mainstay of revenue for the *Quarterly* coming from page after page of government notices and proclamations, Evans was unlikely to be anything less than laudatory about decisions made by Morris. Coaker, on the other hand, who was on the record as wanting to see the non-elected upper house abolished, felt no inclination to be supportive. He called the appointments of

Richard Squires and Sidney Blandford, another defeated Morris candidate, "outrageous" and piled on the adjectives. Squires and Blandford were "shamefaced," "political undesirables," "monkey-like political poltroons," and various other unmentionables. Morris escaped the noise by ducking off to England on business.

In mid-March, Coaker and former farmhand Charlie Bryant, now his personal assistant and travelling companion, were witness to one of the worst sealing disasters in Newfoundland's history. They had joined the hunt as observers, taking passage on the Job Brothers' SS *Nascopie* to see first-hand the working conditions experienced by the sealers. They joined in the slaughter at the front, enjoying the camaraderie of the men on board when they rested from the hunt. Heavy snow, a big sea swell, and winds howling from the north kept all hands on the ship the evening of March 31 and all the next day. The men and boys were snug in the hold, amusing themselves with singing, recitations, and accordion music. The day after, their mood was shattered by news about the sealers of the SS *Newfoundland* left out on the ice to perish in the storm.

The *Nascopie* men with sons and brothers on the *Newfoundland* were grief-stricken as they learned the details of the tragedy in bits and pieces. Hunting on the floes, the sealers had walked from the *Newfoundland* to the SS *Stephano*, captained by Abram Kean, who gave them a midday meal, then put them back over the side, with the wind picking up, to make their way back to their own ship. He steamed away, leaving the men out of sight of both ships when the snowstorm hit. Each captain apparently thought the men were aboard with the other, which neither could confirm because, as a cost-cutting measure, the owners of the *Newfoundland* had taken out its wireless set. On hearing the full extent of the disaster—132 sealers abandoned on the ice, 77 frozen to death—Coaker telegraphed Job's, asking them to recall the fleet out of respect for the dead. Their answer was that they would not interfere with the prospect of taking more seals. "Heartless in the extreme," Coaker wrote in his log. On board the *Nascopie*, the men gathered for an emotional three-hour memorial service. When the ship finally returned to St. John's, people on the dock recoiled at the sight of the contorted, frozen bodies being offloaded like so much cargo.

Coaker said the disaster might have been averted with a properly regulated hunt. He wasn't alone in laying the blame squarely on Abram Kean for leaving the men on the ice in the face of uncertain weather. Coaker savaged him in the pages of the *Mail and Advocate*, the FPU's newspaper. Attorney General Squires ordered a coroner's inquest, which absolved Kean of any wrongdoing.

A commission of inquiry by three Supreme Court judges followed. Coaker, fuming that it was taking too long, said he had no confidence in St. John's judges and refused to appear. Two of the commissioners found only that Kean had committed "a grave error of judgment," and the third said that he had displayed "commendable care" for the safety of the sealers. Kean filed a defamation suit against Coaker. Coaker unloaded on Squires for mishandling the investigation.

Apart from the Kean controversy, Richard Squires ran the office of justice minister smoothly and efficiently, very much hands-on. He was a no-nonsense workhorse, ploughing through reams of correspondence from people looking for work, money, and free legal advice. Though he was no longer their MHA, voters in Trinity Bay still turned to him for assistance. Elisha Button wrote in from New Melbourne looking to have him invest in his fish business. It seems like an attractive opportunity, replied Richard, and he would like to help, but he was being used as a "financial life-buoy" by a number of his friends in St. John's and was having trouble getting his loans repaid. Aaron Smith and Sons, brick makers on Random Island, asked if he could do something about the state of their roads, which were nearly impassable. Richard wrote that he could do nothing for them, at the same time getting in a dig about his election defeat. He was not a good loser:

I regret exceedingly that the roads in which I took such an interest during my term in office have been so disregarded during the last two or three years. From what happened last election I feel that one would be justified in coming to the conclusion that the less interest one takes in public affairs the more chance one has for re-election for the District. I have now no more Political connection with the District of Trinity than I had the day before I was elected for it in 1909. I served the District well and at a great sacrifice to myself personally during the four-and-a-half years representation of it, and the thanks which I received from the people, particularly from the people in your section of the District, was a rejection by an over-whelming majority when I sought re-election on my record for the four years in which I had represented them. I regret very much that there is no way by which I can help you.

Whether in good or ill humour, Richard fielded all inquiries and solicitations coming to his office, priding himself on dealing with them briskly and honestly. "I know I am always getting into trouble by telling people the facts instead of propagating the old bluff of 'Yes, I will do my best for you,'" he told a Harbour Grace man looking for a government job. "There are a whole lot of people in Newfoundland who are so used to being jollied along in connection with Government matters that they don't understand a man when he says in plain English that the matter has not been considered, will not be considered for some time, and when considered will be a matter of selection out of probably a hundred applicants . . . I feel that your chance is very slight."

As a member of the Legislative Council, Richard showed an intelligent grasp of the issues and was well-spoken in debate. But straightforward as he was in his correspondence, publicly he strayed into the way of the politician: hedge, hedge, hedge. Like Morris, the lawyer in him could argue either side of an issue and the politician in him leaned toward the side that would benefit him most with the voters. It coloured him as a waffler. Look, for example, at the question of prohibition, which came before the legislature in 1915. The issue had the electorate divided along religious lines. It was strongly supported by Protestants, less by the Irish Catholics, who seemed to place a higher value on public drinking houses. Coaker, a teetotaller, was squarely behind prohibition, in line with his Protestant constituency in the north. Richard Squires, on the other hand, was elusive. He was not against drinking on principle, he said in the legislature, and hesitated to infringe on personal liberty by taking away the right of consumption, but he thought prohibition was necessary to curb the social evils brought on by the intemperate use of intoxicating liquors. A plebiscite on prohibition saw it favoured by an over-whelming majority of voters (still men only) and it became law in 1917.

Meanwhile, matters of much greater consequence had taken place—Newfoundland had gone to war. On August 4, 1914, with St. John's looking forward to the next day's Regatta, word flew through the city of a stark message received at Government House: "War has broken out with Germany." The next morning, warm sunshine greeted the people straggling down to Quidi Vidi Lake, but their mood was anything but festive. Later in the day, though, Governor Davidson's arrival prompted an outburst of patriotic cheers and the spirited singing of "God Save the King" and "Rule, Britannia."

Everyone understood that Newfoundland, Britain's oldest colony, was now at war. The question was: how would the country contribute to the war effort? Davidson had the answer to that. A plain-spoken administrator in his mid-fifties, highly regarded in the colonial service and possessed of a drive to get things done, he saw himself as the right man in the right place at the right time. Big, robust, and full of life—he took his daily exercise by walking to the top of Signal Hill—Walter Davidson was accustomed to taking charge. Though he had no military experience, he decided right away that the work of directing a war effort was too important to be left to the colonials. We need to raise a thousand naval reservists and five hundred soldiers, he told Morris and the cabinet, and we need them by the end of October.

That was a tall order for a country with no military force apart from a contingent of the Royal Naval Reserve, most of whose six hundred members were tied up in the summer fishery. Fortunately, there was a ready source of willing recruits in the paramilitary boys' brigades that were associated with

Governor Walter E. Davidson,
1859–1923

the churches—the Church Lads' Brigade (CLB) of the Church of England, the Catholic Cadet Corps, and the Methodist Guards. Within a week, Morris had pledges of their support. He then passed the baton to Davidson, who took over responsibility for Newfoundland's role in the war.

It was an extraordinary abdication of duty by Morris and the cabinet—the only elected government in the British Empire to hand off its military command to an unelected official. Davidson took up the reins with characteristic fervour. He put together the Newfoundland Patriotic Association—fifty hand-picked community leaders charged with selecting, training, and equipping Newfoundlanders to go to war. Then he organized a pumped-up rally of three thousand patriots at the CLB Armoury featuring stirring speeches by government officials ("Mr. Squires spoke brilliantly," Davidson's diary notes). The gathering gave him the support he needed to begin building an army, all the time marvelling at how readily the government had backed away from the task at hand. "It is a curious position that a collection of citizens nominated by me should be entrusted with so much power, the political leaders holding no office as members of any of the

Executive Committees," he wrote in his diary.

In the days that followed, volunteers lined up at the Armoury to answer the call to service. By mid-September, the Newfoundland Regiment was but a few men shy of the promised five hundred and the first recruits were under canvas in a cluster of bell tents on the shores of Quidi Vidi Lake, where townspeople gathered to watch them go through their arms drill, foot drill, and skirmishes. Their military uniforms were modest: white shirts, one set of hastily sewn fatigues, and puttees of navy-blue serge—the khaki worn by British soldiers was not available. Neither was their headgear—Australian-style slough hats—nor had their rifles arrived before they were to set sail for Britain, though they did receive a supply of ill-fitting greatcoats from Canada.

Come October, the troops prepared to move out. They marched down to the waterfront through streets crowded with thousands of family members and friends out to see them off. Every building was bedecked in red, white, and blue bunting. The men were in fine fettle—they all expected to be home by Christmas—as they quick-marched along behind the band of the Catholic Cadet Corps. By now their fatigues were well lived in, though concealed by the oversize greatcoats flapping around their blue puttees. With barely a month of basic training, they were hardly an elite force, but a more cheerful and determined bunch would be hard to find. The sight of the troop ship, the SS *Florizel*, steaming out through the Narrows with the men on deck waving their last goodbyes brought home the reality of war to St. John's.

Richard and Lena Squires were, of course, firmly behind the cause. At the time president of the Girl Guides at Methodist College, Lena was sidelined by illness over the summer and had to travel to New York for surgery. Home and recovered, she made herself available to perform songs and recitations at fundraisers for the war effort. She was a founding member of the Women's Patriotic Association, established by Lady Davidson, who converted the drawing room of Government House into a communal knitting centre. Women regularly gathered there to knit and sew, turning out socks, shirts, mitts, and scarves by the thousands for the Regiment's soldiers overseas.

As a cabinet minister, Richard became an ex officio member of the Newfoundland Patriotic Association. Unlike some—Morris and Cashin, for example—he was not a roll-up-your-sleeves contributor to its work. "He never served a day . . . on any Committee, Sub-committee, or other appendage to that organization," said one of his critics. "Mr. Squires contented himself with speech mak-

Rockwell Kent, 1882–1971

ing and that is his record from the beginning of Newfoundland's war enterprise up to its close." This description of him as all talk and no action may be severe, but Richard Squires was more given to the former than the latter. He made speech after speech after speech, to any and all who invited him. And he did not disappoint. Speaking to the Loyal Orange Association ladies' auxiliary in February 1915, he "held the audience spell-bound . . . with one of those patriotic addresses for which he is famous," said the *Evening Telegram*, bringing the members "to the highest pitch of excitement and loyalty."

In a bizarre sidebar to wartime events, Richard found himself, as attorney general, drawn into the case of Rockwell Kent, an American artist educated in Germany, recently settled in Brigus. Kent had fixed up a cottage for himself and his family on the edge of town, out near the harbour entrance, where he built a little studio and kept it strictly off-limits to visitors. Kent was a born radical and mischief-maker. As tongues wagged about goings-on at his cottage, he went out of his way to antagonize. People pegged him as a German sympathizer, perhaps even a spy. Kent's response was to post a sign on his studio door proclaiming it to be a "CHART ROOM, WIRELESS STATION, BOMB SHOP" and to walk around the community singing German folk songs.

The people of Brigus were not amused. Before long, Detective John Byrne, lone member of the Newfoundland Constabulary's criminal investigation department, showed up from St. John's. Stocky and moustachioed, his derby hat cocked to one side, the detective sauntered out to Kent's door, where he was greeted cordially but denied entrance to the studio. Byrne ordered Kent to St. John's to report to Inspector General John Sullivan, the chief of police, who tried to bully Kent into behaving himself. Police harassment, said the artist, and went to the American consul, who complained to Prime Minister Morris. Morris turned to Squires to look into the matter. There's nothing to look into, Richard reported after talking to one of his contacts in Brigus. The fracas is purely of a personal nature, and Kent presents no threat to the security of the country. His report went on:

> Now that the residents of Brigus find that he has been identified by the American Consul, I am quite sure that they will be as courteous to him as the local entanglements in which he may involve himself will permit. The mere fact that he is vouched for by the American Consul is an absolute guarantee that he will receive every courtesy at the hands of the Inspector General of Constabulary and the police force.

This turned out to be wishful thinking on Richard's part, as Kent carried on with his provocative ways. On a carriage ride to Harbour Grace, he passed a small internment camp set up for prisoners of war and asked the driver pull over. Kent stood up in the carriage and gave a short address in German to a handful of German nationals, now considered prisoners, working in the yard. The men dropped their picks and shovels and cheered.

"My God, man," his driver said, "You will have us both arrested. What did you say to them?"

"Well, I didn't say very much," said Kent. "I merely said that the Kaiser is winning, you will soon be out."

Kent became such an irritation to the locals that over the following winter there were mutterings about lynching. In the summer of 1915 on a sky-blue morning in July, Kent wrote in his memoir, he was out by the door chopping wood when along came the local constable and another man in plain clothes (presumably Detective Byrne). They exchanged pleasantries and the plain-clothes man cleared his throat.

"Mr. Kent," he said, "You and your entire family are ordered to leave Newfoundland at once."

"Whose are the orders?" Kent asked.

"The inspector general's."

Kent asked to see his papers and chatted pleasantly about the weather as he went over them, the constable looking on.

"Well," the man said finally, "I guess we'll go. Goodbye."

Kent went inside shortly after. "Kathleen," he said to his wife, "I'm getting fed up with Newfoundland, aren't you?"

"You know I am," she replied.

In little more than a week they were gone.

As the war continued, recruitment by the Patriotic Association bolstered the strength of the Newfoundland Regiment, which was training in Scotland under British officers. Men began to drift into St. John's from the outports to join up. Among them was nineteen-year-old Norman Wheatley Strong of Little Bay Islands, Lena's half-brother, who had been working as a clerk in his father's business. Tall and slender, Norman enlisted in February 1915 and was called into service in mid-May. He stayed with Richard and Lena on Rennies Mill Road while going through basic training and sailed overseas a few months later with a company of two hundred and forty soldiers, many of them from the northeast coast.

Norman's company reached Europe on the troopship HMS *Calgarian* via the Azores and Gibraltar. A three-week tropical cruise, scoffed the men in Scotland, who had endured rough wintry crossings of the North Atlantic. The latest contingent brought the Regiment to full fighting strength of fifteen hundred men. The most senior soldiers, training hard all winter, were now in peak condition and straining for battle. Promoted to lance-corporal in November, Norman finished training in March 1916 and moved on to France, where the British were preparing a massive campaign along the River Somme. It would include an assault in the gently rolling hills by the German-occupied village of Beaumont-Hamel.

A cruelly miscalculated exercise executed by inexperienced, ill-prepared commanders, the Battle of the Somme began on the morning of July 1, 1916, after a week of heavy bombardment by the British forces intended to soften up the enemy lines. The intense artillery fire was ineffective against the Germans, who were dug in as deep as sixty feet underground in a complex network of tunnels. They also had advance intelligence of the July 1 ground attack. When the shelling suddenly stopped at 7:30 a.m., the Germans rushed out to man the thousand-plus machine guns set up for their defence.

The British troops soon came out of their trenches, expertly trained in hand-to-hand combat with rifles and bayonets, each man carrying an extra sixty pounds of gear. They were fully prepared for a mopping-up operation of a mostly destroyed enemy line. The Germans were outnumbered seven to one, and the sight of so many soldiers pouring onto the field unnerved them. But their anxiety quickly turned to disbelief as the advance unfolded, for the soldiers were under orders to walk—not run, but walk—to the enemy lines.

The Germans did not need to aim their machine guns. They just loaded, fired, and reloaded, sweeping bullets into the rows of soldiers advancing slowly toward them over open ground. Attached to a British army division, the men of the Newfoundland Regiment joined the fray in their turn. They climbed out of the trenches, formed up, tucked in their chins, and trudged forward into the hail of gunfire.

The carnage of that day was beyond belief: 57,000 British troops slaughtered along the Somme, 742 of the 810 men of the Newfoundland Regiment killed or wounded on the fields of Beaumont-Hamel.

In St. John's, wartime casualty lists appeared in the *Evening Telegram*. But that summer in the outports around Newfoundland, a man of the cloth knocking at the door meant one thing and one thing only. Mothers knew the news he brought, as soon as they saw him walking up to the house. In Little Bay Islands, the telegraph operator handed Rev. Thomas Pitcher a message from Regiment headquarters on July 26: "Regret to inform you No. 1522, L Corp Norman W. Strong, son of Mrs. Lydia Strong, Little Bay Islands, has been reported killed in action July first. Kindly inform relatives."

For Lena Squires, the news was a terrible blow—the second death to affect her that year, after the loss of her six-month-old daughter, Madeline, in May. Richard wrote an acquaintance that Lena had "felt the loss of the little girl very keenly" and had left for a vacation on the mainland to help get over her grief. For Lena, the last member of her family to see Norman alive, the war touched her in a way she couldn't forget. She called her fourth son, born the following June, Norman Wheatley Squires.

But like many others forced to put aside their own personal tragedies, Richard and Lena carried on with their busy lives. On the business side, Richard's law practice, looked upon as the most successful in the city, took on the work of winding up the estates of soldiers killed in active service. The Opposition objected, charging that, as attorney general, Richard Squires had written the enabling legislation to benefit his own law office. True or not, there was a lot of business to be done, and he took in J. Alex Winter as a partner at the beginning of 1916, moving the practice's office to a ritzy suite in the Bank of Nova Scotia building. Not one to miss an opportunity to promote the firm, he published announcements of the new partnership and the new location in the *Evening Telegram* for the next six months.

Along with his work for the law office, mortgage and real estate investments, and the insurance agency, Richard was also still active in a slew of community groups, often in an executive position. At various times he served as president of Dudley Lodge of the Sons of England, president of the Methodist College Literary Institute, worshipful master of St. John's Masonic Lodge No. 579, and an executive member of the International Order of Good Templars. In the Loyal Orange Association, he was grand master of Leeming Lodge, then of the Orange Grand Lodge of Newfoundland (serving from 1913 to 1917). He was also involved in the Newfoundland Council of the Boy Scouts Association and sat on the board of governors of Methodist College.

The Squires family were members of Gower Street Methodist Church and also attended Wesley, where Richard spoke frequently at the men's bible class. He reached across religious boundaries, as well, as a benefactor of the Salvation Army. In speaking on legislation to recognize the Army as a religious institution in Newfoundland, he told the Legislative Council about meeting its founder, William Booth, in Boston. Then an aged and infirm man, Booth had nevertheless inspired Richard with his powerful presence. Richard had also toured around New York City observing the Army at work with the poor, praising it as the most practical example of Christianity for the uplift of humanity that he had ever witnessed.

Reaching further still from Methodism, he nurtured a relationship with the Roman Catholic Church as a confidant of Archbishop Edward Patrick Roche, who was himself an influential voice in public affairs and the powerful leader of the Catholic flock. Richard was seen at summer picnics at Mount Cashel orphanage and midnight mass at the Basilica at Christmastime. Not many Protestants networked to that extent, but not many had the guts and political aspirations of Richard Squires.

Richard and Lena loved to travel, and they travelled a lot in these years. It's doubtful if any members of the privileged class in St. John's could keep up with the Squires's excursions abroad.

Leading up to the war years, the couple made routine trips to the United States, usually in the hard-weather month of January, staying at posh hotels like the Touraine in Boston and the Waldorf-Astoria in New York. They went to the theatre and the opera, caught up on social trends and the latest fashions. In New York, Richard had his suits tailored on Fifth Avenue and his spectacles attended to by an upscale optician. Lena did a lot of shopping, and neither of them was shy about sitting for a photograph. Over the years, they each amassed a portfolio of suitable-for-framing studio photographs and glamour shots that would do any celebrity proud.

Helena Squires, ca. 1920

In 1916, the Squires's dispensed with the yacht in favour of a new motorcar, more practical for getting around and another visible expression of their rising status. They made good use of it for summer excursions to Harbour Grace in the ensuing years, staying at Fruitland with Richard's father, who was still a relief officer and gentleman farmer. Lena spent many weeks there in the summertime, with the children and their long-time nursemaid, Hannah Parrott. Richard kept a pony and cart for Hannah to take the children out on picnic lunches. When the house at Fruitland began to fall below Lena's standards (eventually she refused to have any of their friends in), Richard got after his father to spruce the place up.

When in Harbour Grace, Richard took a trip every now and then to visit relatives in Broad Cove, where the Squires name was still common. One of them later recalled how popular he was at the time, handing out tiny Newfoundland five-cent pieces to the boys and girls. As well as spending time with Richard's father in Harbour Grace, the children—Elaine, Jim, Robert (Bobby) and

Squires children, ca. 1913: Elaine, James, Robert, Richard Jr.

Richard Jr. (Dicky)—enjoyed many summer days with their cousins in Little Bay Islands.

With their parents' whirlwind travels and Richard's hectic work schedule, the children spent a lot of time in Hannah's care. The Squires law office was not far away, but going home for lunch in St. John's was out of the question for Richard—he saw it as a waste of time and a distraction from work. He did take his evening meal at home, but after the children had gone to bed. "I would be crazy if I had to turn up at particular hours for my meals and had to sit down with four youngsters and look after them during the course of a meal," he told his father. "I would not do a day's work in a week." He did make an exception for family dinners on Sunday, so the children were able to share a meal with him at least once a week.

Workaholic that he was, Richard had little time left for casual reading in these years, which had previously been a favourite pastime. That didn't stop him from putting together a large personal library, however, with special editions and collected works by popular authors such as Thomas Hardy, Mark Twain, and Robert Louis Stevenson, plus beautifully bound works of Charles Dickens and Jane Austen. "I am a book-lover," he once confessed, "not only in the sense of the contents of a book, but there is a joy in the touch and appearance of a well-bound, well-printed book." In his travels, Richard frequented the stores of antiquarian booksellers to build his collection, which also included a set of Plutarch's *Lives*, a multi-volume compilation of *The World's Great Classics*, and an assortment of Bibles of all shapes and sizes.

Richard's public persona earned him celebrity status in St. John's. He went around in a chauffeur-driven car, with a derby hat and ever-present cigar. Like many gentlemen in the capital, he aspired to having a country home near the city. With that in mind, in 1916 Lena bought a small block of land nestled on the south side of Waterford Bridge Road, near Waterford Lane. That fall, Richard was in touch with Rudolph Cochius, a Dutch landscape architect engaged in the development of Bowring Park, about designing a summer estate. Cochius drew up a master plan, adding a tennis court and vegetable garden at Lena's request.

While clearly not ignoring life's creature comforts, Richard kept his political radar well tuned and his sights set squarely on the office of prime minister. He worked away at recruiting and maintaining a core group of supporters and recognized the clout of a newspaper—the medium of mass communication—as essential to turning ambition into success. Morris, and Whiteway before him, each had a newspaper that got their message out, but none of the dailies in St. John's were particularly enamoured of Richard Squires and his high-flying ways. He saw a need to create a press of his own.

In 1916, that door opened. The financially troubled *St. John's Daily Star* had been launched the year before by Harris Mosdell, a schoolteacher-turned-journalist with a Bachelor of Medicine and a former editor of Coaker's Union paper. Richard and Lena seized the opportunity to buy the paper, each of them putting in money to keep it afloat.

Around this time, Richard received a cash "donation" (presumably for his political war chest) of $5,000 from the Reid corporation, a significant amount considering that the annual salary for a cabinet minister of the day was about $4,000. To some observers, such a "contribution" to a politician, coming as it did while Squires was justice minister and serving on a committee to arbitrate a dispute between the Reids and the government, smacked of influence peddling. At best, accepting the funds showed a serious lapse of judgment on Richard's part. Word got around and it sullied his reputation. Coaker in particular minced no words, calling it "an out-and-out bribe." He made much of it in his haranguing of the government and Water Street merchants during House debates and in the pages of the Union paper.

To put Richard's action in perspective: under Edward Morris, government members were having no trouble finding ways to partake of the spoils of office, especially during the economic boom brought on by the war years. John C. Crosbie and Michael Cashin (some called him "Cash-In") both gained lucrative government contracts, and Morris-connected lawyers such as Michael P. Gibbs (a former mayor of St. John's) and St. John's East favourite William J. Higgins found their services much in demand. They were all at the receiving end of Coaker's diatribes, too. He called them out for their brazen self-enrichment at the expense of the working class and for profiteering in wartime, when the price of basic commodities had skyrocketed. Eventually, Coaker forced Morris to strike a commission on the high cost of living. Its work shone a light on some of the wild and reckless abuses of merchants in the marketplace and gave rise to an excess profits tax on businesses in 1917.

And there were other changes afoot on the political scene in 1916. First came a merger of the Liberal and Union parties. Robert Bond, the grand old man of the Liberals, who had been thoroughly put off by Coaker's partnership in the 1913 election, left politics shortly after. He had continued to hold sway with

James M. Kent, his successor as Liberal leader, however, and was firmly opposed to any talk of a coalition with Coaker and the FPU. But in 1916, Morris appointed Kent to the Supreme Court, which cleared the way for William F. Lloyd, a mentor of Coaker and solicitor for the FPU, to take over as party leader. Lloyd was an upstanding British gentleman, a former educator and newspaper editor, whose strength as a politician was a talent for compro-

William F. Lloyd, 1864–1937

mise and appeasement. Within a week, Lloyd had struck an agreement to join forces with Coaker. The new Liberal-Union Party was anything but an equal partnership, however, for Lloyd was no match for the wound-up dynamo running the Union show. He was leader of the new party in name, but it was Coaker who called the shots in the alliance.

Edward Morris went to England for the summer of 1916, where he gadded about London and crossed the Channel to visit the battlefields of Europe. Approaching sixty, he was growing weary of politics—he had, after all, been at it for more than thirty years, eight of them as prime minister. The prospect of a life of retirement in Britain held a definite appeal. He came back to St. John's in the fall but returned to London early in 1917 to represent Newfoundland at the Imperial War Conference. That kept him out of the country until May.

During these months, concern was growing in Newfoundland over the recruitment of soldiers. The Newfoundland Regiment, now officially designated "Royal" for its outstanding service in the war, was having trouble keeping its ranks full, and recruiting numbers had fallen short for two years in a row. There were few eligible men left in St. John's and it was a challenge to attract men in the outports, where fishermen were getting record prices for their catch. Recruiting officers sent around by the Newfoundland Patriotic Association, still an unelected committee of St. John's elites, were met with a shrug. Governor Davidson, not a popular man in the outports, put down their apathy as natural to a community which had lived apart for a hundred years without any substantial immigration or infusion of new blood or thoughts. While inbreeding might have explained it, at least for an upper-crust, class-conscious governor, the situation was nonetheless serious. By 1917, it was looking more and more as if conscription would be the only way to keep the strength of the Regiment intact.

There was an election due in the fall of 1917. Morris could see his popularity waning toward the end of his second term and knew that going to the people on the issue of conscription was risky at best, suicidal at worst. Sensing Morris's weakness, Coaker and Lloyd were calling loudly for an election, but in July Morris once again showed his skill as master manipulator and deal maker. He brought the Liberals and Unionists into an alliance with the People's Party, a special wartime coalition called the "National Government." The stated objective was to put politics aside in the interests of a solid administration while the country was at war. No 1917 election would be needed, they declared.

This move took the pressure off Morris and moved the conscription issue further down the road. The National Government finally assumed responsibility for the war effort, taking the reins from Davidson and the Patriotic Association. A new Department of Militia was created, headed by John R. Bennett. In September 1917, Morris slipped off again to England.

Morris's self-centred manoeuvring began to fray the relationship with his protégé Richard Squires, clearly nipping at his prime ministerial heels. He would not have been pleased when the *Daily Star*, now Richard's public mouthpiece, criticized the new coalition and even called for Morris's resignation. In putting together a cabinet for the National Government, Morris was apparently ready to dump Squires, who was moved to colonial secretary only after another minister retired. William Lloyd became attorney general and acting premier, and Coaker, now edging close to the seat of power, came in as minister without portfolio.

Rumours had begun circulating as early as June 1917 of a pending abdication by Morris. The talk was that he might be taking a governorship in the West Indies or be named High Commissioner for Newfoundland in London. Morris, Coaker, and Lloyd denied the stories, but it seems clear that the National Government came together with the understanding that Morris would be gone by the end of the year and would hand the premiership to Lloyd.

Walter Davidson finished his time as governor in the fall of 1917 and was replaced by Sir Charles Alexander Harris. Unusually for a governor, Harris came with a personal connection to Newfoundland: he'd spent his childhood in St. John's, where his father had been headmaster of the Church of England Academy (later Bishop Feild College). In the Legislative Council, Richard Squires welcomed him with typical flowery eloquence, waxing on about how "one who spent his early days in this Colony becomes imbued with a very love of our soil and rocks and hills and seas and sunsets, and no matter where he travels he will never erase from his vision the memory of our Island Home or from his heart the love which our rugged country inspires." The new governor, he said "has come to us not as a stranger performing an honourable official duty towards his King and Empire, but rather as one whose heart beats in unison with Newfoundland, its sorrows, its struggles, its victories and its ideals."

As 1917 drew to a close, Harris had a hasty introduction to the twists and turns of Newfoundland politics. Edward Morris, after publicly promising that he would be back to run the country, announced that he was staying in England. The news hit St. John's like a bombshell. The New Year's levees at Government House, the Church of England's Bishop's Court, and the Roman Catholic

Palace (Richard Squires was at all three) were abuzz with the chatter. A few days into January, word came of Morris's appointment to the House of Lords as the first Baron Morris of St. John's and Waterford. Not bad at all for a lad from Lime Street, now well on his way to spending his retirement years in the boardrooms and clubrooms of London. But his reward left his country in a flutter.

The jumble of confusion and resentment toward Morris provoked a skirmish over who would fill the office of prime minister in Morris's creation, the National Government. As colonial secretary and Morris protégé, Richard thought it should be him. But Morris snubbed him. He had already agreed to have the premiership go to Lloyd and this was the recommendation he sent to Government House.

The MHAs of the People's Party tried to resist the appointment of Lloyd, a Liberal. There was a short flurry of backroom dealing when a majority of party members, led by Michael Gibbs, threw their support behind Squires. But Richard had no backing from the Liberals (whom he'd deserted to support Morris), and certainly none from Coaker. The flurry was in vain; this train had already left the station.

Lloyd took over as prime minister. Gibbs and Squires resigned from cabinet, likely under pressure, but kept their seats in the Legislative Council. Failing to achieve the pinnacle of political office, Richard had no choice but to back off and bide his time.

Not to worry, another opportunity would come his way.

CHAPTER FIVE

Prime Minister in Waiting
1918–1919

In January 1918, after giving up his cabinet seat in the wake of Morris's resignation, Richard Squires turned back to the practice of law. He had some catching up to do. Five years as minister of justice had been both a win and a loss for his firm. It had brought in government business, but his cabinet position had barred him from acting as defence counsel in criminal proceedings. Also, he had declined to take on any government litigation cases apart from some work as Crown prosecutor. Now free of cabinet constraints, he wasn't long drumming up business and was back in Supreme Court within weeks defending a large corporate client with deep pockets—the Great Lakes Transportation Company—in a lawsuit arising from the shipment of fish to the European war zone. The *Evening Telegram* noted that before his appointment as justice minister, Richard Squires had the largest law practice in St. John's. Business had since been "drifting from his firm," it reported, but his re-entry into the arena as a practising barrister "will mean a great impetus in the business connections of the law firm of Squires and Winter."

That may be how it appeared, but in fact Richard was far more interested in political advancement than in growing his law

Harris Mosdell, 1883–1944

practice, a fact not lost on Harry A. Winter, hired to assist with litigation and court work. Winter had been in practice with his brother Alex before Richard took in the latter as a partner, and he had just spent two years as editor of the *Evening Telegram*. He had some misgivings about joining the Squires firm, which were justified when he got into the office and saw that the law took a distant back seat to Richard's political aspirations. He left after a year.

Richard still needed a "great impetus" of business to maintain the lifestyle of a high roller and keep the money-losing *St. John's Daily Star* afloat. The newspaper was turning into a financial sinkhole. James Strong had helped out by buying shares in the business, but it still only limped along. The *Star* had its share of advertising (none now from the government, however), but circulation was low and the printing plant often lay idle. And there were problems with staff turnover. Editor Mosdell resigned in September 1917 to take a position with a Toronto paper, though early 1918 saw him turn around and make his way back to the *Star*.

Mosdell was an effective editor but not a good operations manager. For that, the business depended on Richard—who was no better. He seemed always preoccupied with matters of law and especially politics. While he possessed considerable charm and powers of persuasion, it was becoming clear that Richard Squires was not cut out to run a business, nor to give proper guidance to the people running it for him. Management was definitely not his forte.

Julia Taylor was a diligent young accountant at the *Star*. During the time Mosdell was in Toronto, she was at her wits' end, doing the work of two people, trying to manage the collection of accounts and payment demands from suppliers. "Dear Mr. Squires," she wrote in early February 1918, "I have been thinking over the matter of leaving the *Star* and have been down to your office several times but you are always busy." She was making eight dollars a week and had an offer from the Grenfell Institute for forty dollars a month eventually rising to sixty. She knew that Mosdell was on his way back and said she preferred to stay "if you will give me ten dollars a week starting today . . . also a guarantee that I will not have the same bother with money that I have had the past three weeks, as I wouldn't stay under these conditions for fifteen dollars a week." Richard asked her to come down to his law office that afternoon, where he told her he would not stand in her way of going with Grenfell if she thought she could do better. In fact, if she was giving him the correct figures, it would be to her advantage to leave, since there was no way that the *Star* could match that kind of wage. On the other hand, he said, switching on the thousand-watt charm, she was a very valuable employee and the paper would be very sorry to see her go. Miss Taylor stayed—and at the same salary.

The troubled *Star* carried on into the spring of 1918. Back at the editor's desk, Mosdell cranked out much heated rhetoric against the National Government and attacked the Reid Newfoundland Company for delivering slipshod rail service. The Reids had profited on building the branch lines for Morris, but the operations side of the business was a perennial money-loser, and the company had allowed the infrastructure of the rail system to deteriorate badly. The railbeds were in terrible shape and accidents were commonplace. Richard also spoke about the sorry situation in the Legislative Council. In 1919, he related what had happened to Helena on a trip across the island. She was reading in the train's drawing room after supper when the porter came in and doused the light. "Why are you putting the light out?" she asked. "Well, we do not know what time we may topple over, and it is not safe to leave the lamps lit," was the reply. It was barely possible, Richard went on, to go from St. John's to Port aux

Basques without the train tipping over. In fact, travelling any-where in Newfoundland by rail was a slow, rough, and dangerous ride. That year, he said, a train going from St. John's to Placentia left the track three times on one trip alone.

Badmouthing the railway did not sit well with a government that was cozy with the Reids. Nor, of course, did criticism of the government itself. In April 1918, Lloyd's cabinet used the provisions of the Newfoundland War Measures Act in a heavy-handed move against the weekly *Plaindealer*, shutting down the newspaper for its attacks on the government. Edward Earles, doorkeeper of the House of Assembly and one of Richard's moles at the Colonial Building, told him of overhearing a conversation in the men's room between John C. Crosbie, the minister of shipping, and William J. Higgins, Speaker of the House. Crosbie was saying now that they had closed the *Plaindealer*, they would keep a close watch on the *Star* and look for a chance to shut it down, too.

Sure enough, on May 29 an order-in-council instructed the Constabulary to "enter and take charge of the office of the *St. John's Daily Star* with all its contents, consisting of machinery, presses, typesetting machines, types, paper, and all other things of every description." Also, it was to seize and destroy the issues of May 23 and 28. A police squadron marched down to the *Star* offices on the corner of Gower and Adelaide Streets, cleared the building and sealed it, leaving two officers on guard. Richard rushed over to the courthouse to seek an injunction, arguing that the government had gone beyond its authority in shuttering the entire business of the *Star*, including even its job printing plant.

It was, indeed, a harsh move smacking of retribution. Privately, Governor Harris, who had signed the order-in-council with the understanding that the paper would be treated reason-ably, was appalled at the tactics of the police and demanded that they release the building. It won't happen, said Michael Cashin, acting prime minister while Lloyd was out of the country. He told Harris he should stand down while the matter was before the court. Richard soon obtained an interim injunction, however, and within days the paper was running (or at least limping along) again.

The political agenda in the spring of 1918 was dominated by the question of defining Newfoundland's role in the war, especially with regard to the need for more troops. Two years of recruitment shortfalls had reduced the Newfoundland Regiment to the brink of disbandment. Despite (or perhaps because of) Governor Davidson's aggressive recruiting outside St. John's, men were not coming in to join up. Outport fishermen were not at all eager to go off and fight a "foreign" war. Coaker, who from the beginning had opposed Davidson's helming of the war effort and had refused to have anything to do with the Patriotic Association, began recruiting on his own. He personally brought in a complement of sixty-eight men, but that was not nearly enough to make up the shortfall. Whenever talk of conscription came up, Coaker was on the record with the same position: he would never endorse it without having it first put to a referendum.

In May 1918, with the Regiment in desperate straits, the National Government brought a conscription bill before the House. If passed, it would call into service all single men between the ages of nineteen and thirty-nine. There would be no referendum, just conscription. Coaker found himself in an impossible position: take a patriotic stand along with other MHAs and uphold the country's obligation to the Empire, or keep his word to his followers and oppose conscription? The conflict tore him apart. "I never want to live those days over again," he later recalled. "Every hour during day and night was to me torture and I could not eat or sleep." In the end, he stood behind the bill, though he downplayed it in a letter to the Union membership, saying that if voluntary recruitment were to revive there might be no need for conscription at all.

His reservations counted for little, however. He had gone back on his word and there was pushback from the FPU, which by this time had turned into a mini–corporate conglomerate. Now much more than simply a union of workers, it had retailing, wholesaling, shipping, exporting, and publishing divisions, all headquartered in Port Union, a town built under Coaker on the Bonavista branch rail line (where the FPU also had shipbuilding and hydroelectric companies). The whole enterprise was financed by the sale of dividend-paying shares and debentures to the Union membership. Coaker himself, once a fervent reformer and now a corporate executive, lived in a well-appointed home in Port Union, dressed in tailored three-piece suits and stylish fedora hats, and rubbed shoulders with the likes of John C. Crosbie and the Reids, the very elites that he had so passionately scorned. His caving in on conscription tarnished his reputation as the incorruptible spokesman for the fishermen and hampered the growth of his Union enterprise.

In St. John's, the conscription bill passed the House and went to the Legislative Council, where Richard bobbed and weaved on the issue, all the time using it as fodder to undermine Lloyd's administration. He was opposed to conscription on principle, he said, and it was with "deep sorrow" that he now saw the necessity of introducing it to save Newfoundland's honour and the honour of the Empire. He also slammed Coaker for his "infamy and treachery" in voting for the bill while telling the Union it wasn't so bad—it might not be needed at all.

The Military Service Act passed the legislature and in September 1918 the first conscripted draft of fifteen hundred men left Newfoundland for England. The Armistice ending the war was signed on November 11, 1918, before any of the conscripts saw active service.

In St. John's, however, the sniping between Coaker and Squires wore on. Coaker had been hard at it in the *Evening Advocate* in January 1918, accusing Squires of mishandling money in his days as colonial secretary and using misbegotten funds to pay staff in his own law office. Richard denied it and sued Coaker for libel. At the jury trial in June, he testified that on his appointment in 1917, he had undertaken a reorganization of the colonial secretary's office and merely hired Jean Miller and Louise Saunders from his law office to help with the transition. Fair enough, said the jury, clearing him of the charge and awarding $250 in damages.

As the Military Service Act was making its way through the House, Newfoundland was hit with a second wave of the "Spanish flu," a deadly disease characterized by high fever, loud, hoarse coughing, and a desperate gasping for air. It killed as many as fifty million people worldwide and more than two thousand in Newfoundland, where it touched the family of Richard Squires. In the first days of 1919, Richard and Lena left St. John's for their customary winter getaway on the mainland. Alexander Squires, visiting over Christmas, took Elaine, now twelve, and Jim, age eleven, back home with him to Harbour Grace to spend a few days. While they were there, his housekeeper took sick. Worried that it could be the dreaded flu, Alexander sent the two children back to St. John's. But for Jim, it was too late.

Richard relayed the sad news in a letter to his half-uncle Henry Squires:

> My wife and I were in New York in January. Our little boy Jim took ill with influenza while we were away. My wife rushed back and got home a few days before the child died. I myself could not get back so soon, with the result that on January 18th, my birthday, while I was at North Sydney I was greeted with a message saying that he was dead.

Once again Lena grieved deeply over the death of a child. As with the death of Baby Madeline, we hear nothing from Richard about his own feelings, or indeed whether he had any. His father certainly did—he was extremely upset and blamed himself for Jim's passing, taking weeks to come to grips with the loss. "I meant to have written you time after time but I felt so grieved over losing James," were the words he finally expressed to Richard in a letter of February 10.

Richard's reply was light on consoling his father and sharing his grief. Technical, logical, and detached, his words seem very much like the opinion of a solicitor, with not a hint about how his son's death might have affected him.

> Nobody knows where Jim contracted the Influenza. He was well enough to be out on Sunday and Monday and it was not thought that his slight indisposition amounted to any more than the natural shake-up of the journey over. However, it is not a matter of any importance whatever as to whether he contracted it before he went to Harbor Grace, whether he contracted it at Harbor Grace, on the train over, or at Sunday School. The result is the same, and it is not a bit of good to be worrying about the consideration of circumstances which cannot in any way affect results.

Alexander was hardly over the death of James on Monday morning, February 24, when more bad news came his way. He was at work at the welfare office when a man rushed in and shouted, "Your house is on fire!" Flames were roaring through the old building by the time Alexander got there. Although the house was technically Richard's, Alexander still controlled it as executor of his wife's will. He carried no insurance and lost everything. Arrangements were made to move into a boarding house until Richard rented the MacKinson property next door for him. He would later buy it for Alexander as a permanent place of residence.

Spring of 1919 brought a welcome change of fortune. A challenge to airmen to be the first to fly across the Atlantic had been issued in England, and the North American take-off point— being farthest to the east and closest to Britain—was Newfoundland. Handley-Page, a large British manufacturing concern, entered the competition and approached Alexander Squires about building an airstrip at Fruitland. Richard negotiated a lease agreement and the company shipped in the Atlantic, a huge, fourteen-ton biplane broken down into a hundred crates for travel. The plane was reassembled right on the field, with the pilot, Mark Kerr, standing by to make aviation history. He was still gearing up on the afternoon of June 14 when John Alcock and Arthur Brown took off from St. John's. They made it safely across and became the first to make the historic journey. Richard Squires, always up for history-making, managed to get a few of his own letters in the once-in-a lifetime mail packet that accompanied Alcock and Brown.

With the war over, 1919 was a whirlwind year for politics in Newfoundland and for Richard Squires. The National Government, conceived through the messy alliance engineered by Edward Morris, was now without a raison d'être—but transitioning out of it proved as awkward as transitioning in. William Lloyd, well-tailored and well-intentioned, was less than effective as prime minister, his government weighed down by patronage, the whiff of corruption, and a dysfunctional cabinet. Coaker was devoting most of his time to Union business, and Crosbie and Cashin were making hay on their government contracts. The electorate was uninspired by it all.

Lloyd made himself scarce over the winter of 1918–19, representing Newfoundland at postwar meetings in Europe. When he came back, he tried to prolong his tenure by calling a snap election for May. In response, a public meeting filled the Casino Theatre, denouncing an election with no voters' list ready and no Opposition party in place. Senior Liberals turned (again) to Robert Bond for leadership, but Bond had sworn off politics. "I must now leave that work to younger and more robust men," he told them. (More revealing was his private comment a few months earlier: "I have had a surfeit of Newfoundland politics lately, and I turn from the dirty business with contempt and loathing.")

It was not only public resistance that quashed the idea of a May election. Coaker threw a fright into Cashin by announcing that he would run candidates in districts previously uncontested by the Union, a clear shot at trying to win control of the government. That set off alarm bells for Water Street merchants, already feeling competition from the Union Trading Company. It also rattled the Catholic hierarchy, who wanted less, not more, of a Protestant strongman like Coaker. The St. John's MHAs made it clear to Prime Minister Lloyd that there was no way they were going to support a spring election.

Where all this was heading was anybody's guess. Richard, of course, kept close tabs on it, watching and waiting. "Things are so uncertain in Government circles at the present time that nobody knows what developments may arise from week to week," he wrote to one of his followers in April. "The Government itself appears to have gone to pieces."

The final disintegration happened in a peculiar sequence of events in the House of Assembly. On the afternoon of May 20, Finance Minister Michael Cashin, who had just brought down a budget with a record-setting three-million-dollar surplus, rose to speak. He praised the financial record of the National Government (crediting himself for his gifted management) and went on to declare that as far as he could see, its mandate was now fulfilled. He then took the Assembly by surprise with a motion of non-confidence—in his own government! Prime Minister Lloyd, already knowing that a break between Cashin and Coaker was imminent, had handed his resignation to the governor just an hour before, and so informed the House.

Several members attempted to speak to Cashin's motion, but the Speaker would not allow debate without a seconder. After minutes of embarrassed silence, Lloyd got up and seconded the motion of non-confidence in his government himself! It was a surreal moment, as the *Daily News* reported:

> The House broke into laughter, and it was no wonder; for it was witnessing a scene that had no parallel in the political history of any country, and could not occur elsewhere . . . It was ludicrous to the extreme, but the climax came when the motion . . . passed unanimously.

In effect, the government had voted itself out of existence. Cashin's pre-emptive move was in fact a stroke of genius.

With it, he isolated Coaker from the governing coalition, which was his intent, leaving himself as the sole contender to lead the government. After the vote, Governor Harris invited Lloyd to dinner, who let it be known that he had wanted no part of a scheme to fracture the government for political purposes and rather than see that happen, he chose to have it fall. Lloyd advised Harris to call for Cashin to form a new administration.

Richard Squires, always in tune with political intrigue, claimed to know exactly what was going on. "For many weeks, arrangements have been progressing, under which the Government would divide up in the interests of the Government on the one hand and Mr. Coaker on the other," he wrote to a friend on the day of the non-confidence vote. And, he added, sounding already in campaign mode:

> The Government realized that it was quite impossible for them to hope for success as a united party. This idea of dissolution has consequently been staged and is being put through at this moment . . . The parties in charge of affairs feel that they have been so successful in the many bluffs that have been worked off and have found the people of Newfoundland so easy and tame in connection with political matters, that they think the people are willing to be robbed, swindled and bluffed by anybody and under any circumstances and to any amount, and they think they can now stage a split and get away with it and the Government.

Of course, Michael Cashin did get away with the government, as leader of a hastily formed party he called Liberal-Progressive. In a few days, he took a new cabinet over to Government House for a swearing in. The ministers included brewery owner John R. Bennett (colonial secretary), John C. Crosbie (minister of shipping), businessman Albert E. Hickman (minister of militia), veteran MHA William J. Woodford (minister of public works), and A. B. Morine, a noisy and contentious political warhorse (minister of justice and attorney general). Unionist John Stone deserted Coaker to become Cashin's minister of marine and fisheries, a move that Coaker never forgave. William Lloyd slid out of politics with relatively clean hands and, through Cashin's patronage, right into the plum position of Registrar of the Supreme Court.

Now outside the fold again, Coaker was free to rant and rave against Cashin's government both in the *Evening Advocate* and from the Opposition side of the House. He ran into some severe pushback from Morine. Perhaps the smartest and craftiest—and least popular—politician in Newfoundland at the time, Morine, a transplanted Canadian, had a varied career weaving through three decades of public life in his adopted country. Sharp and outspoken, he had become such an embarrassment when he worked for the Reids that they sent him on a six-year exile to Toronto in 1906, in effect paying him to stay away from Newfoundland. On returning he took up with Coaker, who paved his way into the legislature as the member for Bonavista. But then the two of them fell out, as Morine, a born renegade, usually did with those who joined forces with him. Now embedded with the Cashin government, he faced Coaker across the floor of the House of Assembly, where Coaker still sought to dominate proceedings.

One afternoon in late May, Coaker was especially vocal, berating his former allies Stone, Hickman, and Morine as traitors to the FPU. Morine sat quietly, taking notes. When the House resumed for the evening session, he stood and took aim directly at the Union leader. Coaker had been planning a coup, he charged— a coup that was foiled by Cashin's motion of non-confidence. He then launched into a tirade as only he could, wave after wave, accusing Coaker of taking money from the fishermen and using it for his own ends, of running the Union as a one-man show, of plotting to take over the country. Coaker squirmed and Morine twisted the knife. Now, he said, as justice minister and the representative for Bonavista, the district with the largest number of shareholders in Coaker's enterprises, he just might launch an inquiry into the business of the Union to see that the people's money was being properly used.

That hit a nerve.

Coaker jumped up, shouting and cursing. He picked up his inkwell to throw at Morine but fumbled and spilled the ink all over himself. He threatened to throw his desk at him, then to go over and choke him. He called for Cashin and the Speaker to silence him. They just sat back amused, enjoying the show. Morine kept it up. "You sit down now and take your medicine," he told Coaker. It was all great sport for the people watching from the gallery. At one point, Morine told Coaker he would not be circumscribed by him. Coaker shouted back that he didn't want to circumcise him, a slip of the tongue that sent the gallery into gales of laughter. The whole session was more like a rowdy political rally, the crowd above applauding and cheering the speakers on the floor. Adjournment finally came at one o'clock in the morning.

The House prorogued on June 4. Cashin called an election for November 3. And with the new political order established, Richard Squires considered his options. Coaker and the FPU were still strong in the northern districts, from Trinity Bay to St. Barbe, and on the north shore of Conception Bay. Cashin, with the blessing of Archbishop Roche, could count on the Catholic vote in Conception Bay South, St. John's, and the southern Avalon. A small band of leaderless Liberals still clung to the hope that Bond would change his mind and come back. Richard looked at his position: he had a network of contacts nurtured over fifteen years, including the influential Loyal Orange Association, where he had ascended to the lofty position of grand master of the Grand Black Chapter of British America. But he was without the backing of any political party, so his followers were unlikely to coalesce into a solid political base. Bond's endorsement was out of the question ("that creature Squires," he called him in private correspondence), which meant that the pro-Bond Liberal clique would have no truck with him. He was left to manoeuvre behind the scenes, to scavenge what support he could from disaffected Liberals and the former ranks of the People's Party, while polishing his image as a credible alternative in the pages of the *St. John's Daily Star*.

Richard still saw the *Star* as the key to his success and was willing to suffer its financial strain. On a paid circulation of seven thousand, the paper continued to lose money, and problems persisted in the way it was run. "The *Star* is distributed to stores 1–2 hours behind the other papers, and sometimes not at all," he grumbled in a memo to Mosdell. The post office was also late in getting the paper to the outports, which Richard blamed on interference from his enemies inside the government. But he pushed on; he had to maintain the paper at all costs—costs that were mounting all the time.

Calls for cash kept coming from the *Star*'s accountant, Julia Taylor. At the end of April 1919, she asked Richard for money to cover accounts payable, trying to couch the request with a positive spin. "Things are certainly looking brighter and by the end of June we hope to be running on our own," she wrote. But June came and another $250 was needed to cover wages. "Have quite a bit of money still due but can't seem to get much this morning."

Richard's response revealed frustration. "You people seem to be in a worse position financially than when the papers had little advertising and very little circulation," he groused. "Do you think that the *Telegram*, the *News*, the *Herald* and the *Advocate* have a private bank account to fall back upon two or three times a week?" But grouse about it was all he did. Any reasonable judgment about his finances was obscured by his obsession with getting elected.

"Please note that this week alone we have paid out over $250 due to expenses of various kinds incurred on behalf of prospective morning paper," Mosdell wrote to him in June. Yes, with the election approaching, Richard had decided to double down and start a second daily, the *Morning Post*, sister paper to the *Star*. Of course, in addition to whatever additional exposure he thought this would bring, the financial strain just grew worse.

"We are in an awful box this morning," Miss Taylor moaned in mid-July, looking for $800. By now, the *Star* was on shaky ground with its newsprint supplier, the Anglo-Newfoundland Development (AND) Company in Grand Falls. The daily had even been forced to suspend circulation in the outports for a time for want of paper. Richard blamed the Reids for intentionally slowing delivery of newsprint from the Grand Falls mill.

Before July was over, he found an investor to ease the financial pressure, however. He persuaded James Sellers of St. John's, importer of Ceylon, India, and China teas, to put $3,000 into the *Star* and $2,000 into the Post. Sellers was reluctant at first, saying it went against his policy of investing only in businesses that he knew something about. "This newspaper idea is one quite foreign to me, and it is because you are identified with it, and upon your own personal representation, and because I think you will make a success of it that I have departed from the faith of my forefathers," he told Richard. Poor Mr. Sellers. He should have followed in the steps of his forebears.

At the end of the month, Richard transferred the assets of the *St. John's Daily Star* to the *Daily Star*, a new company with the same officers and employees, doing the same business from the same location. He then put the old company into voluntary liquidation. This effectively stymied the court action the government had brought against the paper under the War Measures Act, still ongoing, and gained some relief from creditors. His two papers pushed ahead, with more Squires money, into the fall. Incredibly, Richard was even thinking of expanding the business by that time, writing to Sir Edgar Bowring, Newfoundland's High Commissioner in London, for help in finding linotype operators in England.

His money problems mounted as the date of the election neared, and his scanty funds were diverted to cover expenses for the Squires campaign. It was too much altogether for the long-suffering Julia Taylor, who wrote him on October 31:

Seeing that you are not prepared to assist us today, and as I am unable to raise $200 during dinnertime, I am now going home to lunch and am going to stay there until some more satisfactory arrangements are made. Tomorrow is wages day, and although we have been doing our very best to raise money, yet you must understand that with all the extra people we have been paying and all the money going out for which there is absolutely no return as yet, we cannot come near making both ends meet.

I regret having to bother you when you are so busy, but I certainly cannot take the responsibility of the financial end up here when I have absolutely no control of expenditure. While we are very busy, I am not afraid of work, but cannot stand the unpleasantness of having the Bank and other people continually chasing after me for money, with no satisfactory arrangements for meeting same.

We don't know how, but they managed to avert that crisis, and the two papers stayed in business. Richard Squires, fiscal caution thrown to the wind, was betting all on the crucial election, and going into it with a mountain of debt.

CHAPTER SIX

Prime Minister
1919–1920

In January 1920, two months after his election as prime minister, Richard Squires summarized his rise to power this way: "I retired from the National Administration after Morris retired and undertook the organization of Opposition forces. On retirement of Bond, the Liberal leader, I was asked to undertake leadership of the Liberal Party with a large number of former Conservatives dissatisfied with the National Government."

Not exactly. This neat, streamlined version of what had happened places Richard at the centre of the action and deftly overlooks some pertinent details. Merely a matter of selective memory on his part? A conscious effort at revising history in his favour? A bit of both? Whatever the reasons, look into how events actually unfolded and a somewhat different story takes shape.

When Michael Cashin sidelined Coaker and the Liberal-Union Party to take office in May 1919, Richard set out to pick up whatever support he could from those opposed to Cashin—no matter their previous party allegiance. He used the *Star* and eventually the *Post* to position himself as a prospective leader of government, despite the fact that when the election date was set, he had no party to lead. It was also clear to him that once he declared his interest, the surest way to defeat Cashin was to join forces with Coaker.

This fact was not lost on Coaker, either. By July there were signs of a truce between the two, or at least an easing of hostilities. In August, the *Twillingate Sun* reported:

> The *Star* and the *Advocate* have now joined forces, and with the *Star* goes Mr. R. A. Squires who with Mr. Coaker will lead the Opposition . . . The thing that must be very amusing to most people is to see the brothers of gutter journalism locked in a long-lost-brother embrace. Since the 1913 election there has been nothing too bad for the *Advocate* to say of Hon. R. A. Squires while ever since its creation the one aim of the *Star* has been to kill Coaker. And now they clasp each other's manly hands, tell the hoodwinked voters of Newfoundland that it was all a mistake, and—live happy ever afterwards!

Coaker, however, would not confirm an alliance nor talk business with Squires until he had a party affiliation. Richard's challenge was to bring together some disgruntled Cashinites and orphaned Liberals into a coherent political group, but getting Liberals on board was not going to happen until Robert Bond was off the field. And though Bond had refused to join in the spring election, his followers still awaited his final word on opposing Cashin in November.

In August, the Prince of Wales made an official visit to Newfoundland. Bond came into St. John's from his Whitbourne estate for some formalities on August 12. Squires called on him that evening and offered his support should Bond decide to lead the Liberals in an election campaign. If you do, he said, Coaker will not oppose you in the Union districts north of Trinity. Bond, still smarting from Coaker's about-face on the same promise in 1913, was not interested in any such undertaking. Furthermore, he told Squires, he "would not consider the formation of a third political party—because it would simply mean assuring to Coaker the balance of power, and the dictatorship of the government of the Colony." Bond planned to spend the rest of his days in retirement, he said, but added evasively that he would not hesitate to re-enter the political arena if convinced that he could render good service to his country.

On August 21, Richard called together a few dozen followers in the upstairs meeting room of the *Daily Star*. Bond is not coming back, he told them, and proposed that they organize a party to run against Cashin. All agreed and they went ahead with a leadership election. Richard, the only one in the running, was elected. An acceptance speech all prepared, he talked about the "great burden" of undertaking the leadership, knowing that he and his family would be subjected to the bitterest personal attacks and abuse in attempting to "cleanse the public life of Newfoundland of corruption and graft." The new alliance needed a name and Richard suggested Liberal Reform, a party dedicating itself to making Newfoundland a fair and honourable place to live. "*THE GRAFTERS MUST GO!*" shouted next day's headline in the *Star*, announcing the formation of the new party.

The *Daily News*, no admirer of Squires, had a different take, writing that his leadership of the Liberal Reform Party was received in St. John's with "an understanding smile." What observers of the political scene would have understood was that, much as Richard wanted to be seen as the successor to Bond, he had no backing from Bond supporters, who had said as much by boycotting the meeting at the *Star*. "Mr. Squires lacks two great essentials in leadership: the ability to do the right thing at the right time in the right way, and public confidence," said the *News*. "The unanimous verdict yesterday with regard to the new political formation was that it had absolutely no chance in the election."

Two days after forming his party, Squires reached out to Coaker. "The Liberal Reform Party is satisfied that immediate political action means an overwhelming victory at the Polls in November next," he told him. "Every day's delay gives the enemy an opportunity for intrigue and the purchase of waverers." In the interests of creating "the most aggressive opposition possible" to "cleanse the public life of this Colony from the scandal and shame which is now resting upon it," he sent Dr. Alex Campbell, one of his closest confidants, to discuss with Coaker "the most efficient means by which all those who are earnestly opposed to the present Government of graft may bring about its defeat."

Squires may have been all set to move into action, but Coaker was still not convinced that Bond meant to stay out of it. In fact, within a few days of hearing from Squires, Coaker heard that Bond might yet decide to come out of retirement. Coaker preferred not to go to the country hand in hand with Squires if there was any other way. Bond would be infinitely preferable as a political partner. Or, if not Bond, then William R. Warren, a level-headed contemporary of Richard's, once a law partner of Morris and one-time Speaker of the House, who was showing rekindled political ambitions.

It took a few more weeks for Bond and Warren to remove themselves from the picture. When they did, Coaker settled on Squires, though his endorsement of the coalition was less than enthusiastic. "There was no other man in sight," was the only reason he could give readers of the Union newspaper.

Squires and Coaker sat down to plan a strategy. They agreed to divide up the districts to their best advantage and not run candidates against each other. Should the coalition form a government, Squires would become prime minister and control five positions on the executive council. Coaker would be acting prime minister in Squires's absence and fill four council seats. He would also have authority over the fishery.

As the saying goes, politics makes for strange bedfellows—and they could hardly have been stranger than Coaker and Squires. Their public acrimony aside, they came from very different backgrounds and held different ambitions. Despite his blundering on the conscription issue, Coaker retained a strong constituency in the FPU. He stood for a better deal for the working class, especially the fishermen of Newfoundland. Richard put himself forward as a champion of clean and honest government, though it is not too cynical to suggest that he might say whatever he thought was needed to get himself elected. Coaker was driven by a cause; Squires by personal ambition. He desperately wanted to be prime minister and Coaker definitely did not—he was too taken up with Union affairs. What Coaker wanted was the power to bring reform to the fishery (and Richard was happy to let him have it). Coaker was a self-made leader of men, a builder, and of late a success in business. Richard Squires was a clever city lawyer and charismatic speaker, but his track record with the *Star* and *Post* demonstrated a serious deficit in leadership ability and an alarming disregard for sound financial management.

As further agreed between the two, the Liberal Reform Party ran candidates hand-picked by Coaker in the districts where the FPU was strong, and Richard ran his people everywhere else. Some of the Squires faction were sitting members of the House, but he also had a raft of newcomers. Two of them would loom large during his first term as prime minister: his friend and ally Dr. Alex Campbell, who stood for election in St. John's West, and John T. Meaney, a former fisherman and telegrapher turned reporter with the *Star*, who contested the district of Harbour Main. Meaney was a clever operator, clever enough to secure a promise from Richard of a senior post (if he formed the government), regardless of whether Meaney himself was elected.

As far as policy was concerned, Richard Squires was long on generalities and short on specifics. In a thirty-two-page manifesto, he promised to reorganize, reform, and improve practically the whole of government. The few specific commitments included a pledge to build a war memorial in St. John's, as well as a teacher training school and a model farm for the encouragement of agriculture. He also vowed to deal with the Reids to ensure an efficient and economical rail service. The Reid company, in fact, became a convenient punching bag for all sides in the campaign, playing to the widespread frustration with its mismanagement of the railway. Coaker's focus was naturally on the fishery and especially on the price of Newfoundland salt fish exports, which had plummeted after the end of the war. Boldly, he promised that the government would guarantee a minimum price for fish, to the benefit of both the fishermen and the exporters.

Michael Cashin, seeing the threat of the Coaker-Squires coalition, regrouped the remnants of the National Government—including business heavyweights Albert E. Hickman and John C. Crosbie—into the Liberal-Progressive Party. An unimaginative name, but it had strength in the Catholic districts around St. John's, though Crosbie's bold-faced bluster was no help in that. One Saturday night in October, for example, Crosbie pushed his way into the office of the Royal Stores to see if employee Jerome Penney, grand master of the Orange Society, would help lend credibility to their campaign by nominating one of the Liberal-Progressive candidates. Penney told him he wasn't about to help a party that was cozying up to the Catholic Church, and taunted Crosbie, a Methodist, about his own support for it. That set Crosbie on a rant about Squires humbling himself to the Archbishop. He, Crosbie, would never stoop to such a thing, he said; in fact, as far as he was concerned, the Archbishop—and the Pope—could "kiss my ass." Good political fodder, that, and of course the *Post* and the *Star* both jumped on the story. Mosdell wired Crosbie's comment right away to James MacDonnell, the Squires candidate in the Catholic district of St. George's.

As the campaign heated up, the usual pokes and jabs were exchanged. Those aimed at the Liberal Reform Party usually focussed on Squires rather than Coaker. "Squires can't be trusted" was the catchphrase of the Liberal-Progressives. The infamous $5,000 cash payment from the Reids in 1916, which Richard never denied receiving, came up over and over. It was a juicy topic that Coaker had loved to bang away at before suddenly going silent on it as the new coalition came together. Word that Richard had tried to smooth it over by getting a letter denying the payment from the firm's vice-president, Harry D. Reid, made it look all the more suspicious.

Water Street was still painting Coaker as something akin to the devil incarnate, but the FPU leader had nonetheless managed to keep himself free from scandal during his years in elected office. The best that the business crowd could do was to condemn his leanings toward labour reform, warning that if elected Coaker would control Squires and impose his Union policies on the entire country. The Russian Revolution was only two years old at the time and the Bolshevik takeover of the Russian government was still fresh in the minds of the North American business class. Beware the Bolshevik Coaker, the merchants said: he is looking to do the same in Newfoundland.

From the other side of the fence, Richard hammered home the slogan "The Grafters Must Go!" albeit with little in the way of specifics to back it up. It was no secret that government members had been lining their pockets, but so had he. And in the days before conflict of interest was banned in politics, there was nothing new about that modus operandi. So Richard made a lot of noise about Cashin using his position to write a scrip for a buddy for a supply of liquor during the prohibition era, when only a doctor could do it.

While Richard was doing his best to make that a scandal, the *Telegram* broke the news that Mosdell, a non-practising physician, had been doing the same thing all along for such "patients" as John Meaney, the Squires candidate in Harbour Main. The paper also printed some gossip that Richard's campaign was hosting regular meetings of a Methodist College fundraising team "abundantly supplied with liquid refreshments of undiluted strength," that rounds of drinks were "the order of the evening, and that speeches, more fluent than eloquent, marked the proceedings." True or not, the picture of prominent Methodists mixing church affairs with party politics in a well-oiled spree in Richard's living room was less than flattering. Also embarrassing was a bit of bad press from his alma mater suggesting that he had taken advantage of his connection with a college fundraising campaign to build up the Liberal Reform Party. "We are convinced," fellow fundraisers wrote in the *Telegram*, "that the [Squires fundraising] team was used as a political lever to boost R. A. Squires as everything else that he touches is used for the same purpose."

When the slugfest was over and the voting done, Governor Harris sent his official summary to London: "No real matter of policy seems to have been at issue in the campaign. The whole election degenerated into a series of side issues and personal abuse; and I have found that it is a general impression that the scurrility and improprieties of the press have reached a lower depth on this occasion than in any previous election."

Behind all the rhetoric and muckraking, and aside from a bit of cronyism, Richard had actually assembled a credible field of candidates. With Coaker's help, he secured nine Liberal candidates from the 1913 election and two who had switched to the Liberal side from the People's Party, including William R. Warren. The Coaker-Squires alliance lost four former Liberals to Cashin but brought in twenty-one new faces. All told, they successfully positioned the alliance as the new broom to sweep politics clean, and the election was Cashin's to lose.

As the results trickled in after the November 3 vote, Richard personally topped the poll in the three-member district of St. John's West, thought to be a Catholic stronghold, suggesting that all those midnight masses might be paying off. Coaker led in Bonavista, where Morine, his reputation finally catching up with him, trailed six other candidates. John Stone, who had deserted Coaker for Cashin, suffered defeat in Trinity Bay. But John Meaney lost in Harbour Main and Dr. Alex Campbell failed as co-runner with Squires in St. John's West. In all, Liberal Reform, written off so casually by the *Daily News* two months earlier, took thirteen seats. Coaker delivered another eleven, all with large majorities. Cashin remained unbeatable in Ferryland, but the Liberal-Progressives landed only twelve of the thirty-six seats and lost the government.

For some, such a victory would have been a time for celebration and reconciliation, but Richard had a certain pettiness about him. Even after winning, he couldn't overlook a little pocket of opposition he heard about in Trinity Bay. "Would you kindly let me have a list of the names of those at New Harbour and neighbourhood who were political opponents of mine," he wrote to one of his followers the week after the election. "I would also like to know of other active political enemies in your section of the District." Anyone who had not been with him, or was out to get him, was going to pay.

Cashin took a few weeks to wind up his administration before Richard and his cabinet presented themselves at Government House for swearing in on the morning of November 17. The appointments included William Warren as minister of justice and attorney general, destined to be a busy portfolio. Coaker took marine and fisheries, destined to be even busier, at least in the short term. H. J. Brownrigg, a manufacturer's agent who also had run with Richard in St. John's West, became the new minister of finance and customs. Richard himself took the post of colonial secretary, a position roughly equivalent to minister of external affairs, giving him a second salary and much occasion for travel. Dr. Arthur Barnes, a noted educator and one-time Liberal MHA, headed up a new Department of Education, and failed candidate Dr. Alex Campbell came in as minister of agriculture and mines via an appointment to the Legislative Council.

It was not unusual to bring a non-elected member of the upper house into the cabinet (Richard himself had become justice minister under Morris by the same gambit). But the appointment of Campbell did not play well and created the first rift in the Squires regime. James MacDonnell, an opinionated educator and lawyer who had swept the district of St. George's, thought he deserved a cabinet post ahead of an unelected man from St. John's. Richard offered to put him in charge of agriculture and mines but without the cabinet seat reserved for Campbell. That was not good enough for the people of St. George's, said MacDonnell, and crossed the House to sit with the Opposition.

Under British parliamentary protocol, followed in Newfoundland, any MHA appointed to cabinet was required to resign his seat and be reaffirmed by the electorate. This meant going back to the voters in a by-election, normally a pro forma procedure during which the Opposition allowed the person to run unopposed. But this was now politics under Richard Squires, where normal did not necessarily apply. The January by-election for Squires and Brownrigg in St. John's West developed into another brutal skirmish when Cashin decided to run candidates against them, setting up a replay of the rancour and bitterness of the fall. Bring it on, said Richard. He and Brownrigg swept the district a second time.

Meanwhile, as Richard had been battling his way to the prime minister's office, Lena had involved herself in a campaign of a different sort. Following the influenza epidemic of the previous winter, the fall of 1919 saw much interest in St. John's in the welfare of newborn infants. Doctor-attended births were still uncommon at the time, especially among poorer families, and the mortality rate for newborns (and mothers) was disturbingly high. A movement arose to raise money for a maternity hospital, to be run by the Salvation Army. Richard Squires, long an advocate for the Army and its work, pledged the support of the prime minister's office at a kick-off dinner on November 29, but it was Lena—knowing only too well about the loss of infants and the toll of the pandemic—who stepped into a leading role as vice-president of the campaign.

The cause was dear to her and launched her lifelong commitment to proper health care for infants. As the hospital campaign geared up, she also lent her support to a smaller project organized by the Women's Patriotic Association. They felt something needed to be done right away, before the hospital was completed, and set up a temporary maternity ward in a house on LeMarchant Road. This little "hospital" could care for only five sick babies at a time, with a nurse also assigned to counsel new mothers on the value of suitable food, clothing, and nutrition. The clinic would eventually move to Waterford Bridge Road near Road De Luxe, taking quarters in a house donated by Sir Edgar Bowring. Lena's social conscience, coming from the heart, was a stark contrast to the cutthroat world of politics inhabited by her husband.

As the calendar ticked over to 1920, just two months into his term, Richard faced his first scandal as prime minister. Albert E. Hickman, Cashin's candidate in Bay de Verde, had lost the election by only five votes. He now launched a court petition to have the results overturned, citing voting irregularities. In retribution, Richard decided that for every petition against one of his members he would file two against the Opposition. In went claims against Liberal-Progressives William J. Woodford and Dr. W. E. Jones, who had taken the two-member district of Harbour Main.

The Woodford petition was engineered by John Meaney, who had been defeated in the election but remained Richard's eyes and ears in Harbour Main. It backfired badly. The petition accused Woodford of passing out public money during the campaign. Meaney arranged to have it drawn up by lawyer and former politician Michael P. Gibbs and for Holyrood resident Richard Kelly to come in and sign it. Kelly later claimed to know nothing about what he was actually signing, thinking it had something to do with Meaney getting another crack at the seat. For his signature, Meaney promised Kelly a job as line foreman with the government telegraph service, compliments of Richard Squires. Gibbs filed the petition the first week in January.

William Woodford, a plasterer by trade, was a thirty-year veteran of politics as an on-again, off-again MHA (and most recently minister of public works under Cashin). Now getting on in years, he was in poor health and short of money. He was also a long-time acquaintance of Gibbs (who had been a member of the Legislative Council in the Morris years). In February, the two men ran into each other on Duckworth Street in St. John's.

"Woodford," said Gibbs, "I am going to represent the government in this election petition. I am sorry I have to take the case up, being an old friend of yours. I hate like all hell to proceed

William J. Woodford, 1858–1944

against you. However, if there is any way out of the difficulty, would it not be better to try to make some arrangement and have the petition called off?"

Woodford said he was very glad to know that Michael Gibbs was going to be acting in the case and that, as a friend, he expected he would be a little easier on him than a stranger. He admitted that he could not understand what was to be gained in going ahead with it. If filing petitions was what elections were coming to, then as far as he could see, every Member of the House would be unseated, as all of them were doling out money for public works during campaigns. Still, he was prepared to take the consequences.

Gibbs asked again if it would be better to try to make some arrangement: "If you wish, I will see Mr. Squires and we will have an understanding, we will have some conversation over the matter and see if it is not possible to settle up this thing."

When they talked again a few weeks later, Gibbs told Woodford that the Harbour Main petitions would be withdrawn if Woodford could arrange to have Hickman back off his petition in Bay de Verde. Woodford was doubtful, but went to see John Crosbie, who said he would speak to Hickman—which he did, but Hickman refused to budge. Gibbs then suggested that Woodford meet with Squires to see if they could work out something else.

So Gibbs and Woodford went to the prime minister's office (located on the lower level of the courthouse on Water Street) on March 17, St. Patrick's Day. They talked over the situation and Woodford agreed to resign his seat in return for an appointment as superintendent of the poor asylum, a post worth $2,500 a year. In the meantime, Gibbs would arrange to have the election petition against him withdrawn, and Woodford would get a three-month advance on his salary so he could go to the mainland for a medical checkup. So far, so good. Woodford went up to Government House with his resignation and Gibbs went to see the judge about withdrawing the petition.

Then came an unexpected bump in the road: before deciding on a withdrawal, the court asked for affidavits from the parties involved.

Word got back to Woodford, now left high and dry by the delay—out of the House but with no advance on his new salary. He spoke to Gibbs again, bringing up the matter of the affidavits. No need for concern, said Gibbs. He was in touch with the court and there was nothing to worry about: "Oh, you will not be called upon to make an affidavit. The judges gave me to understand that they are making new rules and regulations to govern cases in the future, but they will not apply to our case."

"Well," replied Woodford, "if I am called upon to make an affidavit, Mr. Gibbs, there is nothing left for us to do only to tell the truth of the situation, of all the particulars."

And he proceeded to do just that. Through his own lawyer, Woodford made an affidavit on March 23, outlining the whole St. Patrick's Day agreement with Squires and Gibbs. Two days later the story came out in the *Evening Telegram*—and it was a shocker: the sworn testimony of a veteran MHA with all the details of how Squires had bought him off to resign his seat. The Opposition press was all over it. Michael Cashin was all over it, and the public was all over it. Here was Richard Squires, just finished blaring about graft and corruption, disingenuous enough to be up to his neck in it not six months into his term. A crowd of fifteen hundred people came out in the pelting rain on April 19 to a protest meeting at the Star Hall, at which they dispatched a delegation to Governor Harris, requesting that he not allow the House to reopen with R. A. Squires as prime minister.

Richard denied the allegations, Harris opened the House, and the Opposition immediately put forward a resolution that they not proceed with business until Squires had cleared himself of Woodford's charges. The prime minister has committed a criminal act, they said, and is unfit to lead the country. The majority on the government side easily defeated the resolution. Justice Minister Warren put the question to legal authorities in London, who advised that even if the charges were true, they were not criminal under Newfoundland law.

Still, none of it passed the smell test, and public reaction was so strong that Harris felt obliged to act. He appointed a three-member Royal Commission to look into the affair. His hope was to get members of the judiciary to serve on it, but no one was available. In consultation with Squires (believe it or not!), he appointed former Liberal MHA James D. Ryan, president of the Legislative Council, and Robert K. Bishop, also a Legislative Council member and once a cabinet minister with Squires in the Morris government. The third member was businessman Robert G. Rendell. He had no apparent political connections, but the impartiality of the first two was suspect from the start.

The commission held hearings during July and August 1920, entertaining the readership of the newspapers that rushed to print the proceedings. Woodford, Gibbs, and Squires all appeared, along with other minor players in the affair. Woodford's testimony about his conversations with Gibbs and Squires was detailed and colourful, but his recall of the exact time and date of events was not always accurate. Gibbs and Squires, both experienced prosecutors, pounced on his inconsistencies to knock holes in his story. Richard propelled himself through his testimony with a long-winded statement filling thirty pages of transcript, speaking so rapidly at times that the stenographer had trouble keeping up. In his tumble of words, he portrayed Woodford as agitated and unwell, not able to stay still when they met, wringing his hands and mopping his brow, a man with a defective memory who was not in complete control of his senses. Richard put forward his own version of what was said and what had been promised. There was, he said, no offer of money and no offer of a government job.

The commissioners presented their report early in the new year. Overruling Woodford's testimony, they concluded "the charges made by the said Wm. Woodford have not been substantiated." And that was how the drama ended. Michael Cashin dismissed the whole proceeding as a farce, and he was not alone. But Richard Squires had dodged a bullet, the first of many in a notorious prime ministerial career.

CHAPTER SEVEN

"Good, Clean Government"
1920–1921

Coming to power toward the end of a run of economic prosperity brought on by the war, Richard Squires faced an unenviable challenge: how to govern a country steadily rolling into hard times. The booming war years had been fuelled by $20 million of government borrowing. Now a glut of fish in the European market drove down the price, threatening the foundation of Newfoundland's cod-dependent economy. At the same time, veterans in their thousands were back from overseas looking for work. The 1919 budget surplus touted by Michael Cashin turned out to be a fiction based on projected revenue that failed to materialize.

Richard leaned into the economic headwinds still grappling with the financial woes of the *Daily Star*. He had shut down the *Morning Post* at the end of 1919 (its job was done once the election was won), but the *Star* continued on its unsteady path with disgruntled staff, chronically short of money and trying to cope with the added costs of the election campaign. Fallout from the financial fiasco hit Mosdell, who had co-signed a bank loan for a $1,000 campaign contribution. In April 1920, he was being pressed by the bank for repayment. "What can we do?" he asked Squires. "Needless to say, I haven't a thousand cents."

D. R. Thistle, the *Star*'s treasurer, lost his grip on the accounts. Cheques were being issued with no funds available, he told Mosdell, causing considerable embarrassment. Thistle resigned in May, but the paper plodded on, propped up by more money from Richard. By now, he had funded the *Star* and *Post* to the tune of a whopping $124,000, a few million in today's dollars. It was money accumulated from various business investments and fifteen years of "slaving in his practice," as he put it. In addition to his law earnings, he and Lena had been trading in real estate through the war years and owned a dozen or so rental houses. They also had $25,000 invested in mortgages. Come the summer of 1920, however, the newspaper business had drained him, and he still had a high rolling lifestyle to maintain—expensive tastes, servants at home, a chauffeured Willys-Overland seven-passenger sedan. His combined salary and perks as prime minister and colonial secretary paid him $10,000 a year, a lot less than a busy law practice, as he pointed out in a 1921 speech to the House:

> Richard Squires can earn infinitely more as a legal prac-
> titioner than Richard Squires as prime minister can. Ask
> every legal man in the city if this is not so. The fact is that
> Richard Squires is willing to work for his country for less
> than he can get in private life because he loves his country
> and loves to work for her.

Spoken like a true patriot, but the fact is that in 1920 Richard Squires was becoming seriously tapped out. Not only that, his own bookkeeping was a mess: money from his personal account, the law office, the election campaign, and the *Star* all commingled with no clear separation of accounts.

At the end of July 1920, Richard's law partner, Alex Winter, quit the practice. This left Louise Saunders, student-at-law and Richard's secretary, to handle all the legal work. Jean Miller, his office manager since 1916, was overwhelmed but doing what she could to keep the accounting straight. Richard had a personal account at the Canadian Bank of Commerce with a zero balance.

The law office account was with the Bank of Nova Scotia, over-drawn by $20,000 with loan payments falling due.

As coincidence would have it, the two mining companies operating on nearby Bell Island—the Dominion Iron and Steel Company and the Nova Scotia Steel and Coal Company—were scheduled to renew their operating contract with the government in 1920, just as Richard was really feeling the pinch. Dominion's accountant on Bell Island was Jean Miller's brother, James J. Miller, a political confrère of Squires and a fellow Mason. At Richard's request, he invited senior representatives of the two companies—D. H. McDougall, president of Nova Scotia Steel, and Hector McInnes, legal counsel for Dominion—to St. John's in May for discussions on the contract renewal. While there, Miller made them aware of the prime minister's financial pickle. McInnes took the hint and had Jean Miller pick up a parcel for Squires at the Bank of Nova Scotia. In it was $5,000 cash. Looking to further replenish his bank accounts, Richard told James (Jim) Miller he would appreciate additional funds from his company, say, another $65,000.

Early in August, Richard and Lena boarded the SS *Digby*, bound for Liverpool and a four-month sojourn in Europe. Richard left Jean Miller with a power of attorney to handle his business affairs: to deal with requests for money from the *Star*. There was also the Bank of Nova Scotia, whose manager, a Mr. Glennie, was not amused to learn that Richard had left the country with no arrangement to pay his overdraft. Glennie summoned Jean Miller to his office and told her if she didn't cover the overdraft, he was going to have Squires stopped in Liverpool and sent back to St. John's. With Richard still at sea and unreachable, Jim and Jean Miller went back to see Glennie at his home on a Sunday morning. They got an ultimatum: Cover the overdraft by tomorrow morn-ing, or I bring Squires back. On Monday, Jim Miller personally paid the $20,000 overdraft, reimbursing himself with a loan from his company. There were more "contributions" to come from the mining companies in the days ahead, some $43,000 in all, deposited by Jean Miller into Richard's account. A new operating agreement for the companies was worked out with the government while Richard was away during the fall.

The money from Bell Island brought some relief to Richard's financial predicament (and to his bank manager). But he needed more, and Jim Miller had done as much as he could. Still in Europe, Richard turned to John Meaney, erstwhile political operative of Harbour Main and now acting liquor controller for Newfoundland.

Meaney's appointment put him in full control—with no supervision—of the importing and sales of liquor for the entire country. Prohibition, enacted in 1917, meant he was in charge of supplying liquor to people who could provide medical scrips—as well as anyone else who, in his judgment, deserved it. Forever short of money himself, Meaney was in an enviable position: he could collect secret commissions from suppliers and dispense liquor to anyone willing to slip him a few dollars. Understandably, his record-keeping was loose (a 1924 audit of his department would show at least $100,000 unaccounted for—although the auditor commented that the actual figure could be twice that much).

Meaney threw Richard a second lifeline. Jean Miller knew she could go to him if funds from her brother ran out. In November, Meaney gave her a $1,000 "contribution." Shady dealer though he was, Meaney felt some reluctance, telling Squires when he came back in December, "Your return gives a feeling of relief from unexplainable anxieties." Richard must have reassured him, for the transfers continued. Some came from Meaney personally, with others from the account of the Department of the Liquor Controller. Richard repaid the sum of $4,000 that had accrued by the time he arrived back in

John T. Meaney, 1891–1984

St. John's but went on taking advances from Meaney and his department for another two years, to a total of more than $22,000.

The maelstrom of problems surrounding him as prime minister would have floored most men, but Richard Squires was remarkable at maintaining his equilibrium. Living and working under high pressure, he remained full of energy, controlled, and cordial. Constituents who got past his private secretary (and most of them did) found him attentive and focussed on their concerns. J. R. Smallwood, perhaps his biggest fan, wrote, "No matter whom he is meeting the Prime Minister devotes himself with all of his attention and all of his gifts to that person, so it is doubtful whether anyone ever left his office except under a feeling of having been highly complimented by the country's keenest mind and biggest personality."

Chaos left Richard unperturbed—in fact, he seemed to thrive on it. His perseverance, drive, and composure impressed even Coaker, who years later told FPU members, "No man in the House of Assembly could have performed the task any better than Sir Richard Squires. His youth and energy were equal to all requirements, and only those who sat in Council through these trying years can appreciate what he had to contend with and overcome."

Serious by nature, Richard even showed an occasional flash of humour in House debates. During one session following the 1919 election Michael Cashin was thundering away, listing off the promises Squires had made compared to what he had actually accomplished in government. "In fact, sir, you haven't done one-tenth of what your manifesto promised, and the only good things you've done are the things that I've suggested myself. You've stolen my ideas, you've picked my brains."

Normally, Richard would just sit quietly in response to criticism from the Opposition, but he saw an opening too good to pass up. "Mr. Speaker," he responded, "in my public career I have been accused of many offences, of many crimes, but this, sir, is the first time I have ever been charged with petty larceny!"

Whatever the situation, he exhibited an innate hubris in extremis, with a knack for finding a positive side, real or imagined, to any problem. This side of him was especially frustrating for Governor Harris. "In my effort to keep in touch with the actual state of the finances I am faced by a special difficulty owing to the way in which the Prime Minister is liable to deceive himself into too optimistic a view of possibilities," the governor sighed to his overseers in London.

Britain experienced Richard Squires first-hand in August 1920. A reporter from the *Daily Mail* found him ensconced with Lena at the Savoy, London's finest hotel, his happy talk at full throttle. "Everything is flourishing in Newfoundland," he declared. "There is no unemployment; industry is so good that the Government accounts for last year showed a surplus of £250,000; and for the past two months the island has basked in glorious sunshine." The prospects for the next fishing season were positive, he went on, but the island had one blemish: "The telephones are rotten. But your telephone service does not seem to be much better. My friend has been struggling with one for most of the morning." He quickly added that Newfoundland was to have a modern service introduced shortly.

Lord Morris, Richard's former mentor and colleague, was welcoming and indicated any hard feelings had been left behind:

> Just a line to bid you and your wife welcome to England
> . . . I hope during your stay here I may have an opportunity of seeing something of both of you and extending some little hospitality to you. I have written to two or three of the Clubs, of which I am a member, to put you up during your stay here, although I do not suppose you will have much time for Club life, and after all the Savoy is the best Club I know in London.

Richard availed himself of an offer to spend a Friday afternoon with Lena at the Ranelagh, Morris's country club in southwest London. They brought along their daughter Elaine, now fifteen and enrolled at a girls' boarding school in Kent, studying for the University of London matriculation exam. During the fall of 1920, Morris was a most gracious host, opening doors for Richard and Lena, and occasionally Elaine, to London society.

While overseas, Richard inspected ongoing work at the battle sites in France and Belgium where Newfoundland soldiers had fallen in the war. The gruesome task of collecting, identifying, and interring their remains had fallen to Thomas Nangle, a Catholic priest from St. John's, padre to the Newfoundland Regiment, who had enlisted just after the 1916 Beaumont-Hamel massacre. Tall and striking, with the build of an athlete, Nangle was a legend among the troops for braving the dangers of the front lines, tending to everyone regardless of their religion, and living with the soldiers in the trenches—lifting their spirits, nursing the wounded, burying the dead. After the war, with the horrific scenes of the battlefield still playing in his head, he jumped at the chance to represent Newfoundland on Britain's Imperial War Graves Commission. At the same time, he was appointed Director of Graves Registration and Enquiries for Newfoundland, in charge of collecting and reburying the remains of Newfoundland soldiers killed in action.

Nangle came to St. John's to report on his progress with the war graves shortly after Richard Squires took office. He made an impression on the prime minister with his intense dedication to the task, going at it with a vengeance, as if seeking redemption for the battlefield atrocities he had witnessed but been powerless to stop. As he described it to Richard, he commandeered a crew at each of the combat sites to help dig up bodies and body parts in varying stages of decomposition that had been hastily buried at the time of the action. The workers wore no masks or protective gear and handled the cadavers with their bare hands. The stench of death was everywhere, and most of the men lasted only a few weeks before quitting. Nangle was not only cataloguing the graves, he told Richard, but securing property for a memorial park at each of five key battle locations. He had already engaged a sculptor, Basil Gotto, to create a series of bronze statues of a stag caribou, symbol of the Newfoundland Regiment, for the sites. Richard gave his approval for the monuments without a second thought.

Nangle's project got an extra boost from Coaker, who toured the battle sites with his assistant, Charlie Bryant, in the first few months of 1920. Nangle took them to Beaumont-Hamel, where Coaker had lost a nephew. "Recommend authorize Nangle purchase field Beaumont Hamel to value of Ten Thousand Dollars . . . Matter Urgent," Coaker had wired Squires. Authorization came back the same day.

Now overseas in Britain at the end of the summer, Richard was anxious for a first-hand look at Nangle's work. He crossed over to France with Lena and Elaine in August, and Nangle escorted them on a tour of what he was calling the "Trail of the Caribou": from Beaumont-Hamel, Gueudecourt, Monchy-le-Preux, and Mesnières-en-Bray in the north of France to Courtrai

Major Thomas Nangle, Helena, Elaine, and Richard Squires on tour in Europe, August 1920. At the rear is Nangle's chauffeur Sgt-Major Bill Brown.

in Belgium. Seeing the tortured, lumpy battlefield of Beaumont-Hamel, already considered a holy ground by Newfoundlanders, deeply moved them. Lena was especially touched to stand in the field where young Norman Wheatley Strong had been struck down. For his part, Richard was astounded by the detail and scope of Nangle's work.

During the fall, Richard also travelled to Scotland and to the import fish markets of Rome, Genoa, and Milan. Four months after leaving Newfoundland, he arrived back in St. John's with Lena on December 6, travelling in style on a special train from Port aux Basques. Stepping onto the station platform "with the buoyancy and vivacity of youth," he greeted a welcoming crowd of cabinet colleagues and supporters with "a warm hand-clasp and a cheering and kindly word for all." He was in the pink and never looked better, they said. Soon after, he sang Nangle's praises to the *Newfoundland Quarterly*:

> Newfoundland cemetery plots are the best attended and the most carefully laid out of any burial places in France or England. Nothing remains undone which may add to the appearance and upkeep of the cemeteries.

One of the first acts of the Squires government was to establish a Department of Education under Dr. Arthur Barnes, its purpose to oversee the schools in Newfoundland run by one or the other of the various churches. Barnes was keen on building a Normal School to train teachers and Richard was keen on making that another memorial to Newfoundland's war dead. Others, veterans especially, were not so sure. They wanted a shrine or cenotaph, a tangible symbol of the sacrifice.

In June 1921, a public meeting elected a committee—headed by Robert G. Rendell, commanding officer of the CLB (and a commissioner on the Woodford inquiry)—to raise money for a war memorial. It accepted donations and sold subscriptions to the public at a dollar per share, raising more than $8,000 in a few weeks before fundraising stalled in the sluggish economy. By the end of 1921, committee members were talking about delaying the project until the times improved.

Thomas Nangle heard about the fundraising challenge while in St. John's for Christmas. He extended his stay and in February went with Richard to a meeting of the fundraising committee. There he announced that he had arranged for a donation of $18,000 from Britain's Imperial War Graves Commission. He was prepared to help them raise more, as long as he had "an absolutely free hand as to the [fundraising] methods employed." How could they refuse?

Richard made it clear that whether the project went ahead or not, the government was going to build the Normal School as a memorial to the war dead. Nangle agreed with the veterans that the school by itself was not a fitting tribute to their fallen comrades. A stirring, striking monument was what they deserved. Nangle went on a fundraising blitz and in three months raised another $48,000. In May 1922, he shared with the committee his ideas for the design and location of the monument on Duckworth Street. They left it to him to work out the details.

The veterans were pleased with the progress on the war memorial but also angry and disillusioned at the fact that thousands of them were still unemployed. They had gone to war on the promise that the government would look after them when they came home. Twelve thousand men had volunteered and about half went into battle. More than 1,500 never returned, and 2,331 came back wounded. Many had lost limbs, had a permanent disability, and experienced post-traumatic stress disorder (called "shell shock" at the time). For their service, the government had awarded them a medal and a gold watch and chain. The disabled received a modest pension, as did the widows and orphans of the fallen. What was not provided was employment. A few lucky men took up their former occupations, but in the postwar slump most veterans were sidelined with no source of income and no prospect of work. It was a huge challenge for Prime Minister Squires (as it was for governments in other places) and one that he could do very little about.

The veterans were not without a collective voice. In the summer of 1918, led by Harold Mitchell, a suave young veteran from a St. John's business family, they had organized the Great War Veterans' Association (GWVA) and begun a persistent and no-nonsense lobby of government. They wanted the disability pensions and widows' allowances to be on par with those paid in Canada. They wanted a guaranteed percentage of government jobs reserved for their members. In 1920, the Squires government, still facing declining revenues, not only refused to raise their pensions but, as a cost-saving measure, actually cut them back.

The optics of this were not good, for the cutbacks came at the same time as increased allowances for cabinet ministers and MHAs. The veterans were incensed when the story, true or not, circulated of a Beaumont-Hamel veteran's widow going to the prime minister looking for a higher allowance only to be met by an uncharacteristic lapse of cordiality, turned away with the comment that "Newfoundland soldiers were paid to fight."

Despite the turmoil with the GWVA and the lingering whiff of corruption from the Woodford affair, Richard made good on his election promises of a Normal School and a war memorial. His commitment to overhaul the Department of Marine and Fisheries was also underway, led by Coaker—whose objectives, however, went well beyond the reorganization of a government department. He wanted nothing less than the reform of the entire salt fish industry. And that initiative was turning into a colossal flop.

From the very first days of the Fishermen's Protective Union, Coaker's goal was to shape and control government policy on the fishery. He spent three years sitting at the cabinet table, first under Morris, then Lloyd, then Cashin—always as a minister without portfolio holding little sway on anything, let alone the fishery— but now his day had arrived. No one could deny that the industry was in need of overhaul. The export of Newfoundland salt fish to Mediterranean countries (mainly Spain, Portugal, Italy, and

Greece), the Caribbean, and Brazil was unregulated and unco-ordinated. Four dozen or so export companies based in St. John's—a who's who of Water Street—acted independently and were highly competitive. They were also undercapitalized and in the habit of shipping their fish on consignment with no fixed contract to sell, a practice that worked against them in the international markets. Their product was a perishable commodity: once in the market, it had to be sold. With consignment selling, the shipper was at the mercy of the buyer, and all too often was forced to sell at a loss. In addition, the rush every fall to be the first to get the fish to market yielded a product of uneven quality (much of it subpar), which in itself assured a lower price.

During the war, Europe had experienced a disruption of its fishery, and the resulting demand for Newfoundland fish reached historic highs. Exports increased more than fifty per cent and the price per quintal (112 pounds) doubled to over $14. For a few years, the exporters flourished. Coaker knew that situation wouldn't last once the war ended, especially when Italy set up a government-run purchasing consortium with tight price controls.

Immediately after the election, he began imposing reforms on an industry on the brink of a downturn. He was minister of marine and fisheries for only a day when he made a late-night visit to Government House with a set of regulations establishing control over fish exports. In essence, he called for exporters to be licensed, for the minister's permission to be required for the sale and pricing of each shipment, and for the exported salt fish to be graded for quality control. Governor Harris endorsed the regulations, and they were published two days later, followed by a series of circulars detailing how they would work in practice.

Despite the beneficial intent of these actions and all his work on behalf of fishermen, William Coaker was not the ideal person to bring sweeping changes to the trade. He was a doer rather than a consensus-builder; he was regarded with suspicion by Water Street, and the FPU itself was a major competitor in the export business. Governor Harris labelled Coaker as not a very diplomatic man, one who could be quite reasonable in person but untrustworthy once he got a pen in his hand. It was in Coaker's favour, however, that the idea of a regulated fishery was not new. John Crosbie, as a member of William Lloyd's cabinet and also a salt fish exporter, had brought the merchants together early in 1919 to hold the price against the Italian consortium—which they did until two of them, W. A. Munn and A. E. Hickman, broke ranks and shipped their fish at a discount. But Coaker's effort was different: Crosbie's cartel was an informal alliance; Coaker's regulations were government-imposed.

The enabling legislation cleared the legislature and became law in July 1920. Coaker gave the merchants every opportunity for input into how the regulations would work, even handing management of the program to a codfish exportation board controlled by the fish companies. At a conference of exporters in September, he was clear on what he expected. He was not in the position of minister of marine and fisheries, working day and night seven days a week, for the love of the job, he told them, nor for the $4,000 it paid him. In fact, he would be better off spending his time on Union business. But for the good of the country the fishery needed reform, and someone had to do it. Too many of them were shipping fish of inferior quality—that had to stop. They all had to improve the quality of their product and give up selling on consignment. And that is what the regulations were all about.

For the program to work, Coaker needed a united front from the merchants. Trouble was, not all of them were in a financial position to fall in line. And the regulations came, unfortunately, with no element of enforcement. So in the fall, with the Italians refusing to buy Newfoundland fish at the regulated price, some of the merchants, under pressure from their bank, shipped their fish on consignment. A. E. Hickman, counselled by Morine, went a step further and sent fish to Italy without a permit from the minister. The penalty was suspension of his export licence for the rest of the year, when he wouldn't need it anyway (so much for enforceability). By December, the entire export regulation program was in jeopardy.

Where was Richard Squires in all of this? Again, half in and half out—his usual stance on matters of controversy. Publicly, he favoured the spirit of the regulations, but held back support for Coaker's efforts to carry them out. He confided to Governor Harris that he was using his influence to ease the administration of the regulations and dissociate himself from some of the details in Coaker's circulars that explained how they worked. With Richard, very few things were straightforward and free of intrigue. Did he want less influence by the exporters and more teeth in the regulations? Apparently not, and he was prepared to undercut Coaker in order to stay in favour with the merchants.

After Hickman's defiance in selling his fish without a permit, the codfish exportation board (seven members, a majority of whom were exporters), in its advisory capacity to Coaker, drove a large stake through the program. It recommended removing the regulations for the sale of Labrador fish and all fish going to Italy. Then, in the first week of January 1921, with Coaker out of the country, Squires and Harris called the exporters together to consult on these proposed changes. Not only did the companies support the recommendations of the board, they asked that the government consider scrapping the program altogether. A strong stand from Richard might have made a difference, but he waffled. He and Harris merely asked that the exporters give the matter second thought. The intention of the companies was clear: get rid of the regulations, period.

And that is what happened. In a few weeks, the cabinet rescinded the regulations for Italy. From Europe, Coaker tried to salvage what he could of the program with the other countries, but to no avail. By April, he was back in St. John's, ready to admit defeat. Rising in the House of Assembly, he announced:

> We are going to remove the regulations . . . I may say that this will be forever. The regulations have not failed of themselves . . . they have failed because of the disloyal

opposition of some sections of the people . . . I prophesy that no man in the future will make any attempt at regulating the fishery export business of this country again unless he has the undivided support of the country. It would be madness to attempt it.

Here, as in so much else, Richard was duplicitous. He played politics like a game: stand aside, don't commit. In this case, if the regulations work, share in the credit. If they don't, take the out you've created for yourself and lay the blame on someone else, which this time was on Coaker and the exporters.

So Richard Squires washed his hands of the fisheries regulations and moved into the second year of his term. Here he faced a different but equally thorny question: what to do about the railway?

CHAPTER EIGHT

On and On It Goes
1921–1922

"Since I came home the railway situation as it developed during my absence has been to me a source of very great anxiety," Richard wrote to Edward Morris in January 1921. "Reid Newfoundland Company operation would appear to be hopeless. I always thought it was hopelessly inefficient, but if the reports which I received from the Government Engineer and others be correct, their management has been absolutely chaotic . . . We must have a railway, and we must have somebody to run it. At the present moment it is a mock railroad with nobody to run it."

This at a time when the Reid Newfoundland Company was the most powerful corporation in Newfoundland. The two thousand people on its payroll made it the second largest employer in the country, surpassed only by the government. Along with the railway, it owned a power utility and the streetcar service and dry dock in St. John's. The company also ran the coastal steamship service for the government and controlled hundreds of thousands of acres of land in the interior of Newfoundland, with the related timber and mineral rights earned by building the trans-island railway.

Robert G. Reid, the hard-driving but gentlemanly company founder, had died in 1908. He passed on his steely determination to William Duff Reid, his oldest son, and his more courteous nature to second son, Harry Duff Reid. Both men, and two other brothers, carried on the business after their father's death, building the new branch lines for Morris and working to attract capital to develop their land holdings. The family business had profited handsomely from building the railway, but operating a lightly built, narrow-gauge rail system spanning a sparsely populated island was another matter—it was a serious financial drain. There was never enough revenue from operations to keep the railway running smoothly. As Richard relayed to Morris, by the start of 1921 the entire network was badly in need of maintenance and repair.

After pushing through the branch lines in 1914, the bull-headed and volatile William D. Reid succumbed to the stresses of business. He departed Newfoundland for New York and Montreal, leaving the president's office and company management in the hands of brother Harry. He came back to St. John's in November 1917, ready to take over again, only to find that Harry had other plans. Increasingly concerned about his brother's stability, Harry had him ousted at a tense directors' meeting before the year was over. William Reid moved to Montreal and proceeded to lob a blizzard of lawsuits against the company. Harry took on the task of bringing the company's runaway finances under control.

Over and above his remarks to Morris, Richard joined a growing chorus of complainers about the Reids. It won him no friendship with the firm. As he told a constituent looking for help in getting work on the railway, "From dealings I have had with Reids, a man recommended by me would have more of a black mark against him, rather than a mark in his favour." But his election manifesto had promised an efficient and economical rail service. Just how he would create one remained to be determined.

In June 1920, the Reids were not yet twenty years into their fifty-year contract to operate the railway but already under strong pressure from the firm's bank. So Harry Reid informed the government that the company could no longer afford to run the service. Let them default, argued some in government, then we'll seize control of the railway and its lands. Governor Harris, too, thought that the prime minister should force a default— even if just for twenty-four hours—to strengthen the case for a government takeover should the company go under. Richard, however, felt that plan would produce an inevitable tangle of litigation. And, as far as he could see, the government was in no position to run it any better than the Reids, or even as well as they did. There was no escaping the fact that whoever owned it, the operation needed a large infusion of capital to keep it going— and letting it fold was not an option. The loss of employment would be devastating, and any further development of the island's interior resources would be stymied. Richard also knew that the Reids were talking to British financiers about a second paper mill at the mouth of the Humber River and that alone would require a reliable rail service to the west coast.

And so an alternative approach was announced: government money was offered for repairs to the rail line, for new rolling stock, and for new freight sheds at St. John's and Port aux Basques. In addition, an agreement was made with the Reids to co-manage the railway and coastal steamer service for a year through a joint six-person commission—three members each from the government and the company—chaired by William Coaker. The Reids accepted responsibility for any loss on operations up to $100,000; the government agreed to cover losses beyond that. Richard announced it in the House in early July.

When he returned from Europe at the end of the year, he was less than satisfied with how the plan was working, and he was right to be concerned. The Reids had quickly reached their loss threshold of $100,000, leaving the government to cover excess losses of more than $1.75 million. When the one-year term of the management commission ended in 1921, the Reids were unable to find a suitable replacement executive. So the brothers took over operations again, buttressed by a further government subsidy of $1.5 million.

Harry Reid finally found a manager with railroad experience—R. C. Morgan, former superintendent of the Canadian Pacific Railway—and brought him to St. John's in September 2021. Within a week of sizing up the operation, Morgan changed his mind, handed in his resignation, and fled back to Canada. Richard was on the mainland in October, where he sought out Morgan and talked him into coming back to Newfoundland, first to work for the government and then as general manager for the Reids. But even with Morgan at the helm, the company quickly burned through the $1.5 million subsidy. By April 1922, there were no funds left to make payroll. The whole operation shut down for two weeks in May while Richard scrambled to find a way to keep it going. The way, of course, was more money from the government.

The railway was only one of the financial headaches facing the Squires administration. By the beginning of 1921, Newfoundland's economy was tanking, part of a wider postwar slump. "The finances of the Colony are giving my Ministers some concern at present," Governor Harris informed London in the understated style of British diplomacy. A few months later that "concern" had turned into "grave anxiety." The government accounts were in sorry shape, and no one could deny John Crosbie's blunt assessment: "Figgers talks." Businesses tightened up, jobs disappeared, and people turned to the government for relief in increasing numbers.

In this period of recurring deficits, government funds had to be replenished by additional borrowing. For 1920–21, expenditures of close to $11 million produced a deficit of $2.5 million. In the next fiscal year, the deficit was $1.8 million, and it would be $1.3 million the year after that. This was before spending on capital projects (the railway plus road-building and woodcutting efforts that gave work to the unemployed), which ate up millions more. The public debt stood at $43 million in 1920, already excessive for a small country like Newfoundland. Endless rounds of borrowing drove it to $60 million by 1923. Even with the extra borrowing, there was never enough money to go around.

Newfoundland was, of course, not alone in facing hard times. Squires and Coaker had both seen this in their travels abroad. "As bad as conditions are in Newfoundland, they are better than found in seven-eighths of the world," Coaker reported after a 1921 visit to Europe. Richard, in a trademark burst of sunny talk, told J. R. Smallwood in a letter that the public "knows nothing of the horrible poverty and degradation which I have seen in other lands. This is a country of private ownership of property, to a very large extent, and a personal resourcefulness and independence which I think is of a higher average in Newfoundland than in any other country with which I am personally acquainted." But such optimism was no help to the people desperately scribbling letters to the prime minister, looking for work or money, or both. Or to the businesses struggling day after day to stay afloat.

The malaise was island-wide. In Little Bay Islands, James Strong had been used to doing $1 million or so a year in business. Now, in the early 1920s, with the fishery in decline and stiff competition from the Union Trading Company, his firm was losing close to $100,000 annually. The situation in St. John's was no better. Small factories and manufacturers cut back on workers or closed up altogether. William White of the White Clothing Manufacturing Company told Richard in 1922 that his salesman had travelled the length of the south coast from Placentia to Port aux Basques without selling one suit of clothes and only $300 worth of pants and overalls.

The desperation of the unemployed came to be expressed in more than just words. In the spring of 1921, jobless men in St. John's, many of them veterans, were aggravated and restless. Their discontent was fuelled by ceaseless rhetoric from the Opposition in the House of Assembly, laying the blame on Prime Minister Squires and his government. On April 12, the sergeant-at-arms tried to remove a noisy agitator from the Assembly's public gallery. At that, a mob swarmed in and shut down proceedings. Richard ignored them, picked up his papers, and left. The following week, a delegation brought a petition to the House, led by a one-armed man carrying a Union Jack. His missing arm, it was explained, was in France.

Frustrations boiled over again in May when a boisterous crowd—egged on by John Crosbie, Michael Cashin, and a generous supply of liquor—again crammed into the gallery. Cashin stood and addressed them, shouting and waving his arms, saying that he would lead a riot to clean up the House by violence, if necessary, even if it meant going to jail. Crosbie and John R. Bennett delivered the same message, with somewhat more restraint, but the overall scene was pandemonium. Governor Harris was appalled at how the government "gave way to the pressure of rowdyism" by allowing the public to address the House "in most irregular fashion."

With summer came jobs for some of the men—hundreds went out into the island's largely unpopulated interior, fighting the black flies to build roads from Deer Lake to Bonne Bay and from Badger to Hall's Bay, two of the bigger make-work projects. Other gangs went to logging camps, cutting timber for the government to sell as pulpwood to the Grand Falls mill or as pit props to the mining companies (with mixed results). In St. John's, work crews spent the summer building a road of turnpike quality, 1,300 feet long and a generous 79 feet wide, linking Topsail Road to Waterford Bridge Road and aptly named the Road De Luxe.

Unemployed men were not the only ones putting pressure on the government for action. Many women, at least those of the Women's Suffrage League, had spent years lobbying for the right to vote, finally winning a commitment from Prime Minister Squires that legislation would go through in the 1921 session of the House. "What I say goes," he had assured them. They also had Walter B. Jennings, the minister of public works, behind them in the cause. In August, with no bill in sight, Jennings accompanied a committee from the League to see Richard at his office in the courthouse. One of the women described the meeting this way: "On being ushered into the Presence, we found the self-constituted arbiter of our destinies seated at the table with his back to us, smoking a cigar. He omitted to rise or to greet us in any way, continuing to enjoy his cigar, and we seated ourselves at the table." When they asked why the bill had not gone ahead, Richard gave no straight answer, leaving the impression instead that he had never had any intention of keeping his word. Here was one group that did not leave the prime minister's office feeling "complimented by the country's keenest mind."

The women went next to see Coaker, who was on record as favouring a suffrage bill. He had observed in London that "Englishmen have already realized that it was a mighty good thing for Britain when Parliament gave women a vote." He could give no guarantee, however, that Richard would do the same in Newfoundland. Richard would tell the press in London in 1922 that his government was "distinctly sympathetic" to the suffrage movement, but it seemed that sympathy was as far as they were prepared to go.

Coaker's influence as second in command to Squires waned after the debacle of the fishery regulations, and he began easing back on his cabinet responsibilities to devote more attention to the Union Trading Company. The fiasco had knocked the wind out of him. He tried several times to resign the fisheries post and, in fact, wanted out of cabinet altogether, telling the Union that he could have more influence over public affairs outside the cabinet than in. Gone were the days of the strident reformer—Coaker was mellowing with age and, according to J. R. Smallwood, his demeanour was becoming "a most pleasant and affable one. He is quite simple and unpretentious and friendly to everyone who meets him, in this or any other country. His tastes are simple." He was, Smallwood said, "one of Nature's gentlemen."

Coaker had also arrived at a time in his life when he wanted to get away from the colder months in Newfoundland. In 1922 he took a winter cruise via New York to the West Indies. Unlike

Dr. Alex Campbell, 1876–1940

Richard and Lena, Coaker was un-impressed by New York. The people he met showed "little of intellectual interest—frivolity and sensational stuff is what they want." In general, he thought the place was "as near to hell as anyone can get this side of Mars." The West Indies proved more salutary, and he loved the balmy weather and tropical lifestyle. New-foundland winters for him would soon be a thing of the past.

As Coaker was looking to ease back, the spirited Alex Campbell was beginning to make his presence felt. A cultured, gregarious man with a nervous edge about him, Campbell was as close to Richard as anyone could get. Originally from Prince Edward Island, he came to Bonne Bay, Newfound-land, as a physician in 1902. He moved his practice to St. John's in 1904, where he also bought a fox farm and raised racehorses for a track at the foot of Springdale Street. Drawn to politics, he had run unsuccessfully as a Liberal Reform candidate in 1919, but sidled into government, still unelected, when on Richard's recommendation the governor appointed him to the Legislative Council and a seat at the cabinet table as minister of agriculture and mines.

Campbell was the only member of cabinet that Richard Squires trusted completely. With Coaker losing interest in govern-ing, Richard replaced him with Campbell as deputy prime minister, to take the reins when he was away (which was often). Like Richard, Campbell showed no respect for even the rudiments of financial accounting, nor for the responsibility involved in the stewardship of public funds. Make-work money to hire timber cutters passed through his department in a steady stream, an extravagance of spending that cast a poor reflection on the entire administration. The books of Campbell's department were as chaotic as Richard's own.

On the positive side, all the relief work on roads, bridges, and wharves produced some benefit for the country—but the same could not be said for Campbell's pet project: a program to provide pit props for the mining industry. The idea was impractical in its conception and outrageously mismanaged in its execution, a textbook case of government spending run wild. In addition to lax supervision, there was too little demand for pit props or pulpwood—inside the country or out—to justify the program at all. And even if there had been sufficient demand, most of the wood cut was stolen by the workers before it reached government hands, and advances to pay for supplies for the workforce were pocketed by the suppliers. The wastage wasn't limited to the pit-props project. Coaker's assistant, Charlie Bryant, and the Union Trading Company landed a contract to prepare pulpwood for the AND Company and made $10,000 from the deal. The government lost $120,000. With the sloppy accounting it was hard to be exact, but the cost to the government of Campbell's pit-prop experiment reached at least $1.2 million.

Campbell also took charge of dispensing favours to friends of the party, making himself the go-to man for government patronage. His aggressive tactics in this area irritated Public Works Minister Jennings, who told Richard:

> I do object to the Minister of Agriculture & Mines taking upon himself the prerogative of the Dept. of Public Works, and not only setting men to work without notifying or consulting this Dept., but also setting a rate of pay one-third higher than the amount for which we have been getting work done . . . some of us in the Public Works Dept. are going to be slapped in the face over it.

Campbell was a busybody by nature and fully into political scheming; he shared Richard's paranoia and disdain for the Opposition and was more than willing to use his position to undermine them. "I may say that while I am in this Department

I will no longer extend courtesies to Opposition Members who exhaust themselves in personal abuse of me immediately after I have done them such courtesies as I have been doing constantly since I came to this Department," he told Richard.

Outside the demands of his elected office, Richard was also trying to manage his law practice, which was suffering from neglect. Once he became prime minister, he went to the law office only rarely, usually after supper and always in a rush. While he was out of the country in the fall of 1920, John Meaney began hanging around the place. The janitor soon grumbled about the use of liquor on the premises. Meaney kept the office well stocked with wine for Jean Miller, who had a personal supply stored in the women's washroom. On Richard's return from overseas, he instructed Meaney to stop sending alcohol to the office. No problem, said Meaney, who sent a case of whiskey up to Richard's house instead. It was returned. Apparently accepting cash from Meaney was not a problem, but liquor was a no-no.

The law office got back on track when Leslie R. Curtis, earlier a student-at-law with Richard, came in as partner at the beginning of 1921. He tried to sort out the office accounting, or the lack of it: he found a mingling of legal fees, political contributions, insurance premiums, rents collected for clients, and more. He also discovered that the insurance business, which Richard handled personally, was more than a year behind in forwarding premiums to the Globe & Rutgers Fire Insurance Company in New York. Jean Miller, stumbling along with no oversight, was picking up advances for Richard from John Meaney and on the verge of quitting. Curtis brought in Donald Fraser, a clerk at the Bank of Nova Scotia, to impose some day-to-day order on the place. The first day he walked into the office, he was appalled to find papers and documents stacked a foot high on Jean Miller's desk, which was also littered with sundry scraps of paper. Fraser tackled the muddle of accounts for 1920 and 1921. Richard promised to come by the office first thing every morning to check on affairs. Jean Miller left at the end of July.

In the midst of chaos on several fronts, the summer of 1921 delivered a pleasant ego boost for Richard when he was awarded the distinction of Knight Commander of the Order of St. Michael and St. George (KCMG). With the honour came the title "Sir Richard" and a significant raise in status, especially in protocol circles. He joined the ranks of such compatriot notables as Sir William Lloyd, Sir Michael Cashin, and Sir John Crosbie, who all had received knighthoods for high public service—Crosbie boasted that he had paid for his with "cash on the barrelhead."

Leslie R. Curtis, 1895–1980

The prime minister's knighthood notwithstanding, the Opposition kept up the pressure on him, refusing to close the House until well into the summer. With Minister of Finance Brownrigg seriously ill, Richard found it impossible to escape St. John's for a London conference of Commonwealth prime ministers. Lena, now travelling as Lady Squires, went to Britain on her own, returning home in August with Elaine for an end-of-term visit. The three Squires sons (Bobby, Dicky, and four-year-old Norman) whiled away the summer in boyish outharbour pursuits at their grandfather Strong's place in Little Bay Islands.

In August, Richard boarded the Sunday express train for Port aux Basques and a quick trip to Washington, where a new tariff regime working its way through Congress was threatening higher duties on Newfoundland cod, herring, and cod liver oil. He appeared before the Finance Committee of the House of Representatives with the argument that the tariffs would only hurt American trade, reminding them that the United States imported ten times as much product from Newfoundland as Newfoundland did from them. According to press reports, he left a favourable impression, but the wheels of government in Washington ground on regardless and the new duties came into effect a year later. It was not as if an unknown prime minister of Newfoundland, however persuasive, could change the course of US tariff policy, but credit did accrue to Sir Richard Squires for giving it a try.

While Richard was in Washington, Coaker was taking up the case for a paper mill on Newfoundland's west coast, now a joint venture of the British engineering firm Armstrong Whitworth and Co. and the Newfoundland Products Corporation, controlled by the Reids. The paper mill was a megaproject in every sense, harnessing the hydroelectric power of the Humber River to drive a huge mill employing thousands of men, and carrying the potential for spinoff developments in mining, smelting, and manufacturing. Coaker sailed to London with Harry Reid for discussions on the development and was sold on it. He came home pitching it to Attorney General Warren and the cabinet. Richard, though paying it lip service, was at best lukewarm on the idea.

Richard left St. John's again in December 1921. He travelled with Louise Saunders (formerly his law student, now seconded as a secretary in the prime minister's office) as far as Port aux Basques to finish up paperwork, then went on to Montreal to attend to business with the Bell Island mining companies, recently merged as the British Empire Steel Corporation (Besco). John Meaney also went along as a henchman and go-between, for there were important decisions

to be made about the government contract put in place in 1920. The newly unified firm was seeking an amendment to the agreement that removed two onerous clauses: one required the company to spend $3 million for capital improvements on Bell Island; the other mandated the construction of a blast furnace on the west coast of Newfoundland. Besco also wanted a reduction in the export duty on iron ore.

Louise Saunders, 1893–1969

Richard thought conceding on these two points would be worth $100,000 in "campaign funds." In Montreal, he dispatched Meaney to talk to D. H. McDougall, vice-president of Besco, about a contribution. It was too much for McDougall, who thought he might be able to get $15,000 or $20,000 approved by his board of directors. At that point Richard chose to let the matter rest, which was a disappointment for Meaney, who was hoping the money could be used to pay back the advances "loaned" to Richard from the liquor controller's office and get himself off the hook.

From Montreal, Richard took Meaney with him to New York to see the Commercial Cable Company, which was expressing interest in becoming part of the Postal and Telegraph Service in Newfoundland. Richard thought his endorsement of that arrangement would be worth a campaign contribution of $15,000 and he sent Meaney to Commercial Cable looking for it. The company turned him down, but Richard had now firmly latched on to the idea of trading government favours for political contributions, and because of the way his funds were intertwined, such "donations" could be a contribution to his party, his newspapers, or himself. The way he saw it, they were all of a piece—it was all political money. To Richard, the *Daily Star* was a political organ, not a business proposition, and he doubted that he could have won the 1919 election without it. Campaign contributions, from whatever source, all went to him personally—not his party. As he put it, he was "leader of the party, campaign manager and treasurer all in one." The money he put into the *Star* was for politics, and political contributions could be used to pay him back or to build a nest egg for the next campaign.

The Besco and Commercial Cable matters kept Richard away from St. John's over the holidays. He spent Christmas with Meaney at the Ritz-Carlton in Montreal, then New Year's at the Waldorf-Astoria in New York. While he was gone, a request came to the government from the Humber developers to guarantee funding of $18 million. Coaker travelled into St. John's from

Port Union trying to hurry a decision, but the cabinet decided to hold off until the prime minister came back. In the meantime, Dr. Campbell kept Richard apprised of affairs at home, with assurances that all was under control. "Don't worry about anything—everything is all right here. No destitution to worry about," he cabled in early January.

There was, in fact, much to worry about. Attorney General Warren was running out of patience with a prime minister traipsing around on the mainland while a decision on an $18 million project awaited at home. On January 10, 1922, Richard received a telegram from Warren while taking his breakfast at the Touraine Hotel in Boston:

> HUMBER PROPOSITION SEEMS TO ME THE MOST IMPORTANT SCHEME FOR FUTURE NFLD STOP THOSE OF PARTY IN ST JOHNS HAVE AGREED TO TERMS AND COAKER WIRES ME TODAY HOUSE OUGHT TO OPEN BY JANUARY TWENTIETH AND TO ADVISE YOU TO THIS EFFECT STOP MY OPINION YOUR ABSENCE THIS JUNCTURE UNJUSTIFIED TROUBLE ALREADY DEVELOPING STOP UNLESS YOU RETURN IMMEDIATELY AND GIVE ATTENTION THIS MOST SERIOUS MATTER I RESIGN MY POSITION JANUARY NINETEENTH.

Three days later Richard wired from Toronto, confirming reservations for his trip home.

Coaker's enthusiasm for a Humber deal had some Newfoundlanders on edge. They were concerned not so much about government funding for the huge development as they were about giving more financing to the Reids as partners in the venture. James Strong, no admirer of Coaker and his Union's commercial intrusion into the fish business, voiced his concern to Richard:

> I do not believe there are twenty men in Newfoundland who have any interest in the country, but who are strongly opposed to anything of the kind being undertaken by the Reids with any government guarantee. . . It looks

as if Coaker has gone off his head on the matter . . . if he should get his way in this Humber deal it will surpass everything he ever did toward the final ruin of Newfoundland.

Richard wrote back: "Mr. Coaker pronounced himself strongly in favour of the proposition," but had later "called upon me and stated he felt this guarantee proposition was not one which the Government should undertake." So, with the prime minister and Governor Harris (and apparently Coaker) opposed, an $18 million guarantee was too much for the cabinet to swallow, and the proposal was shelved.

In April 1922, the railway ran out of money again. Harry Reid shut it down for two weeks, at the same time trumping up a $6 million lawsuit against the government over lack of funding. Richard had started to warm to the idea of the Humber scheme by this point, however. Knowing that its success hinged on a functioning railway, he patched together another financial package to keep the trains running.

Although he was home in July for the birth of a second daughter (Rosemary, the last of his children), Richard was off again to his personal suite at the Montreal Ritz-Carlton before the month was over. From there it was on to New York and then another crossing to England. Lena stayed home with the baby, but Louise Saunders joined him for secretarial service in London. There was a side trip to France in August to take part in a ceremony at the Amiens Cathedral: unveiling a plaque to commemorate Newfoundland soldiers who had fallen in the Battle of the Somme. In England, Richard worked on the finishing touches to a revised Humber deal, significantly reducing Newfoundland's financial exposure in the project.

He was still there in October, when Lena came over to join him at a Newfoundland Club dinner at the wood-panelled, leather-chaired Empire Club honouring outgoing Governor Harris and his replacement Sir William L. Allardyce. Along with 150 guests, Sir Richard and Lady Squires dined on the chef's creation

Squires at Amiens ceremony, August 1922

of *Saumon de Terre Neuve avec Sauce Hollandaise et Concombres*, amid much toasting and speech-making, all under the jovial chairmanship of Lord Morris. The couple then went to Madrid, where Richard negotiated a trade agreement with Spain lowering the duty on Newfoundland fish imports. By the end of November, they were on their way to New York on the Cunard liner *Aquitania*, with Richard's deal for financing the Humber in his pocket.

Trying to pay down the country's stifling debt, William Warren had been doing his own travels on behalf of the government. Over the fall he had undertaken a mission to explore the possible sale of Labrador to Canada. The exact boundary between Labrador and Quebec, in dispute for years, was at the time before the Judicial Committee of the Privy Council in Britain. Even so, knowing that process would take a few years to be resolved, Warren was offering Newfoundland's mainland territory (minus a strip along the coast reserved for fishing) for sale at a price of $50 million. He got nowhere dealing with bureaucrats in Quebec City, Montreal, or Ottawa, reporting to the prime minister:

"Personally I think if we get $25 million we shall be well out of it."
But with the boundary issue up in the air, no one was prepared to
bite, even at half the price.

On returning home to St. John's in December, Richard learned
that Jim Miller was going to Montreal on company business.
The Besco agreement had been amended to suit the company
(with the two troublesome clauses removed) and had passed the
Newfoundland legislature in March. Richard had yet to receive
any sort of kickback, however. He asked Miller to approach the
company for $300,000, to be deposited to a bank account in
New York, where Richard was apparently accumulating some of
his "donations." Miller was reluctant and suggested that John
Meaney accompany him. Certainly, said Richard, who was optimistic enough about the success of the venture to tell Jean Miller
that when he got the money from Besco, she would be looked
after, offering to pay off the $5,000 mortgage on her house.

Miller and Meaney sailed to Halifax to catch the train to
Montreal. In Truro, they encountered Besco vice-president D. H.
McDougall and superintendent H. B. Gillis, also on their way to
Montreal. Meaney met with McDougall in his railcar suite and told
him right out that Richard wanted $300,000 for the concessions
on the contract. McDougall couldn't believe what he was hearing.

"Is Squires crazy?" he asked.

"Yes, crazy for money," said Meaney.

In Montreal, Meaney and Miller booked into the Ritz-
Carlton for three weeks. Meaney went to see McDougall again
about the $300,000, but in vain. The mines on Bell Island were
not doing well, and McDougall had no intention of placing
Meaney's request before the directors. The company, he said,
would be better off keeping the government contract the way it
was.

Richard, in St. John's, was a respectable distance from all this
talk about money. He spent Christmas of 1922 alone. Elaine was
in England, and Lena had not let an infant daughter dampen her
appetite for international travel, taking the children to enjoy the

holidays at a ski resort in St. Moritz, Switzerland. Relaxing on Rennies Mill Road, Richard had time for reflection. He could feel justly proud at the prospect of a major new industry coming to the country, which as an added bonus would bring with it a permanent resolution to the headache that was the railway. He had survived three difficult years in office, and now St. John's was abuzz about the Humber. Across the House, the Opposition party was fumbling, with Cashin widely expected to resign as leader.

And 1923 was an election year.

CHAPTER NINE

Prime Minister Again
(But Not for Long)
1923

The new year began with a bleak outlook for the iron mines on Bell Island. Besco had a large stockpile of ore and a more favourable operating agreement with the government, but international demand, particularly from the steel mills in postwar Germany, was falling. With no warning, the company shut down the mines in January, throwing over two thousand men out of work.

Richard rushed up to Montreal, huddled with Roy Wolvin, the Besco president, and arranged for the free export of ore over the winter, averting an economic (and political) disaster. He did not bring up the matter of the $300,000 but, perhaps to bolster his case for a later try, brazenly told Wolvin that he had not received any of the money Jim Miller had secured from Dominion Iron and Steel in 1920, musing that Miller and his sister Jean must have pocketed the $43,000 for themselves. That comment cost Miller his job with Besco and brought threats of legal action. Still in Montreal at the time, Miller returned to St. John's a mental wreck, distraught over what Richard Squires had done to his reputation.

Miller and his wife turned to John Meaney for help. "If Jim does not immediately take steps to restore his good name and vindicate his character I shall do so in his name," Mrs. Miller told Meaney. "I shall not allow my husband and family name to be disgraced for any man living." Meaney informed Squires that the Millers were prepared to go public, with documents, to tell their version of what really happened with the $43,000. Richard, wary of potential damage just before an election, arranged a meeting at Alex Campbell's house. He told Meaney to straighten it out with the Besco auditors, already on their way to Newfoundland to investigate Miller. How he did it we do not know, but with Meaney's intervention, nothing of the affair leaked out and Richard avoided a public embarrassment. The company audit cleared Miller of any wrongdoing.

That little irritation behind him, Richard was free to concentrate on the election and promotion of the Humber project, his guarantee for electoral success. Without the promise of that new development, he faced going to the polls on the strength of his record—war memorials in Europe and the launch of Memorial College. Despite the recent reduction in Spanish fish tariffs and the quick reopening of the Bell Island mine, his achievements were slim. On the other hand, the Opposition, even in disarray, would have much to make hay with: budget deficits, a ballooning debt, an economy in a nosedive, and the collapse of Coaker's fish export regulations.

Newfoundland elections were normally held in the fall, after the summer fishery had ended, but with the weather still favourable for campaigning. Richard decided he had to strike quickly, to put the Humber proposal front and centre with voters while the deal was still fresh—and before it came to the scrutiny of the legislature.

Financing for the development was coming from the Armstrong Whitworth company in Britain, which held a controlling interest in partnership with the Reids. The British and Newfoundland governments both backed the project with guarantees, and Newfoundland also undertook to provide a reliable transportation system to the west coast. The mill in Corner Brook would be large-scale—twice the size of the AND operation in Grand Falls, employing four thousand men during construction to be followed by permanent jobs for twenty-five hundred, with another twenty-five hundred loggers needed to supply pulpwood to the mill. The impact on Corner Brook, an outport of a few hundred souls settled around Fisher's sawmill, would be huge. Perhaps even greater would be the effect of the related hydroelectric plant on the nearby village of Deer Lake, a railway stop of four houses where the mail and a scattered passenger left the train to travel up the St. Barbe coast.

When it came to elections, Richard Squires was, some people have said (Smallwood definitely did), a brilliant strategist and campaigner. Though he had come to the Humber project in the later stages of negotiation, he took ownership of putting the "Hum on the Humber" and made it the centrepiece of his campaign. It was the one great issue facing Newfoundland, he said, one that rose above politics. He had put the project together and was prepared to see it through if the people wanted it to happen. If they didn't—if they were against industrial development, higher employment, and lower taxes—that was all right, too. All they had to do was vote against him. He was not going to move ahead with approval of the project unless he knew the people of Newfoundland were behind him.

And, of course, they were. Even a group of expatriates living in London, gathered for a pork and cabbage supper with Thomas Nangle, made a point of cabling the prime minister to tell him they were urging Newfoundlanders at home to support him and the Humber project regardless of petty personal politics.

Richard returned from his Montreal trip in February 1923 with the Bell Island mines reopened, presenting himself as a fast-acting, decisive leader who had just saved a principal industry, full of energy and ready to go. Knowing full well that Newfoundland prime ministers lasted two terms at most, he was determined not to miss out on another four years. When it came to all-out self-promotion at election time, Richard Squires was hard to beat. But, as in 1919, to be at peak campaign performance he needed a newspaper.

The *Daily Star* and the *Morning Post* were history. He had liquidated both in 1922, though as the biggest creditor he had salvaged most of the assets for himself. Apart from Coaker's *Evening Advocate*, the other St. John's dailies—the *Evening Telegram* and the *Daily News*—were not at all friendly to him. And so, under the name "Newfoundland Book Publishers," he set up shop with a printing press at the bottom of Prescott Street and lined up financial backers, Alex Campbell among them.

Harris Mosdell, now a member of the Legislative Council, was also on standby. Richard gave him a heads-up before leaving for Montreal in January:

> Dear Mr. Mosdell: I have no idea whether I have any chance of success in connection with this Bell Island matter. The probabilities appear strongly against, but, in any event, I must have a medium through which the public can be informed as to the facts. I would be very much obliged if you could swing out on this newspaper matter with your usual enthusiasm.

On Friday, February 16, 1923, Richard went to Government House to have the House of Assembly dissolved in preparation for a general election, date unspecified. Governor William Allardyce, another career civil servant, reputed to be a tough-minded administrator of quiet efficiency and acquainted with Richard over *Saumon de Terre Neuve* in London, complied.

Richard caught the press completely unawares with this move—except for Mosdell, who was all ready to "swing out" with the first edition of Richard's new tabloid, the *Daily Mail*, on Monday, February 19. The election announcement took up the entire front page. The Assembly has been dissolved, it said, so that Prime Minister Squires can put questions of "major public importance" to the electorate, such as the Anglo-Spanish treaty concluded in the fall, allowing Newfoundland codfish to be imported into Spain with reduced duty. Another question requiring endorsement was the prime minister's work "at great personal sacrifice" for the country—his vigorous and immediate action in the face of the closure of the Bell Island mines. A new Squires government would bring large reductions and readjustment of taxation, reorganization of the railway and the dry dock, and of course the Humber proposition, a matter of the "very greatest magnitude" for the country.

The Opposition was also caught off guard, and fumbling. Michael Cashin, losing his grip on the party, was talking about stepping down. There was another attempt by die-hard Liberals to get Robert Bond back into politics, but even if he had wanted to, his health would not allow it. So on Tuesday, February 20, the Liberal-Progressives elected John R. Bennett their new leader. He was an able businessman and political veteran, but any talent that he might have had for political leadership had been kept well hidden. The party renamed itself "Liberal-Labour-Progressive," to acknowledge its kinship with the labour movement in St. John's.

Richard had the jump on them from the start and poured it on in the *Daily Mail* with large-print headlines announcing his candidates as they came out. Mosdell wrote endless editorials, some stretching to a full page, all taking pot shots at the Opposition, the *Evening Telegram*, and the *Daily News*. Richard was in his element. Completely energized, he was pulling the strings, controlling the narrative, and swamped with offers from potential candidates. By mid-March, fifteen men were asking to run in Port de Grave, which John Crosbie had vacated for Bay de Verde.

Richard had picked Captain Thomas Bonia, just appointed to the cabinet, to run in the three-member district of Placentia and St. Mary's, where people knew him both from his work skippering the Placentia Bay mail boat and for representing them years before in the House of Assembly. Bonia was considering William

J. (Billy) Browne, a scholarly young man with a fledgling law practice, and James (Jimmie) Bindon, a St. John's shopkeeper, as candidates to join him in the race. Both were new to politics, and Bonia had them in to his office on Duckworth Street to get Richard's approval.

They were sitting quietly when the prime minister burst in, charged up and full of bluster in an expensive topcoat and impeccably tailored suit.

"Have you got a cigar, Captain?" were his first words.

"No," said Bonia, flustered, "but I could get you one across the street."

"Get me one!" commanded Squires.

Bonia dispatched a staffer and, once he had his cigar in hand, Richard flipped a chair around, straddled the seat and leaned his arms across the back. Puffing away, blue eyes flashing behind the wire-rimmed glasses, he launched into a spirited half-rant half-lecture on the new paper mill starting up at the mouth of the Humber River and the prosperity it would bring to Newfoundland. Browne and Bindon sat there like two schoolboys, entranced. On finishing, Richard turned again to Bonia: "Is there anything now you want done?"

"Yes," the captain replied. "I want something done for Dr. Hogan in St. Mary's Bay."

"Is he a friend or an enemy?" asked Squires.

"A friend."

"Consider it done. If it is necessary to have him brought out at dawn and have him shot, it will be done."

Bindon and Browne were dumbfounded. After Squires jumped up and left, Bindon leaned over to Browne and whispered, "I believe he is possessed by the devil."

"BONIA, BINDON AND BROWNE FOR DISTRICT OF PLACENTIA" shouted the headline in the *Daily Mail*. "THE THREE BEES—WATCH THEM BUZZ!" By the end of March, the slate for every district but one was filled—and the date of the election had yet to be set.

The exception was the district of Harbour Main. Squires candidates had twice been rejected there, in 1919 and in the by-election that followed, and the acrimony lingered. "I should not be expected to put my hand in my pocket to dig out money for a campaign in a constituency which has treated me twice in this way," he told a party worker. "Within the course of a week or two I presume I shall be selecting candidates from those offering their services for the District of Harbour Main, but to be quite frank with you I am not chasing around looking for candidates for that constituency."

The customary pre-election muckraking soon erupted, this time extending as far as Little Bay Islands and James Strong. Michael Cashin, in an obvious poke at the prime minister, claimed that Strong was not able to pay a $200,000 to $300,000 debt to St. John's merchant Walter S. Monroe, who was running for the Liberal-Labour-Progressives in Bonavista. Richard telegraphed his father-in-law about the charge.

"This is bad for your credit," he said.

"We owe a lot of money but intend paying every man what we owe," Strong replied. "We have stock and fishing property worth more than double our liabilities." Although his business had been losing heavily since 1919, it survived by incorporating as James M. Strong Ltd. in 1923. He and his partner, Richard Mursell, took shares for ten cents on the dollar, losing most of the equity they had built up over the years in order to see their creditors paid.

On April 9, Richard announced the election date: May 3, a short three weeks away. "As you know," he told Captain Bonia, "I believe in maximum pressure for a short period rather than moderate pressure for a long period." Richard himself ran again in St. John's West, with Alex Campbell (newly resigned from the Legislative Council) as a co-candidate. In a gutsy move, Michael Cashin handed Ferryland to his son Peter, now back in New-foundland as a war veteran, and moved to St. John's West to square off against Richard. John Bennett, wearing the title of leader but operating in the shadow of Cashin, was dispatched to the district of Harbour Grace. Coaker, who had resigned from cabinet before the election was called, ran again in Bonavista while campaigning for Squires and the Humber project throughout the northern districts.

As election day approached, pressure built, tempers flared, and political rallies turned rough and raucous. On a Friday night in Bay Roberts, a few hard cases—armed, stoked with liquor, and led by Walter Crosbie, brother of Sir John—disrupted a Liberal Reform meeting, firing off shots inside the hall. There was nothing new about hecklers and professional agitators showing up at political meetings, but armed aggression was something else. Richard was concerned enough to write the superintendent of the Constabulary and the deputy minister of justice about the "terrorist tactics" of the opposing party and requesting a police presence at his remaining rallies.

For the voting public, election times were good times. Public money flowed especially freely throughout the 1923 campaign and in record amounts. As historian S. J. R. Noel put it: "Though a certain amount of government 'pump-priming' was by no means uncommon in past election years, in the spring of 1923 the pump was primed as it had never been primed before." Richard warned his candidates to be careful to respect the Elections Act, and they were. Only one charge of corrupt practice arose, in the district of Bay de Verde. A complaint came from St. John's West that Michael Cashin brought two feeble-minded men from the poorhouse to a polling booth on election day, both of them unable to state their names or where they lived. Cashin said that they were "afflicted by God" and coerced the deputy returning officer into marking their ballots for the Liberal-Labour-Progressives. Richard heard about it but didn't press the matter.

When the votes were tallied, the standings in the House were unchanged: Squires (Liberal Reform) had twenty-three seats, Liberal-Labour-Progressives in Opposition had thirteen. In some ridings, the races were very close, and Richard's own contest was closest of all. Cashin bested him by eleven votes in St. John's West, but Richard squeaked in with four votes more than Alex Campbell in the two-member district. Cashin's son Peter swept the polls in Ferryland, but Opposition leader Bennett lost in Harbour Grace and Crosbie lost in Bay de Verde. The three bees (Bonia, Bindon, and Browne) buzzed out the door in defeat in Placentia-St. Mary's. Coaker again delivered eleven union seats for Squires, including his own in Bonavista.

What did the election results say? Despite the popular appeal of the Humber project, Richard Squires had no higher approval from the electorate than in 1919. In fact, with just over fifty-one per cent of the popular vote, his party had dropped eight per cent in three years. Still, the outcome was an endorsement of his platform, and legislation to enable the Humber project made its way quickly through the first session of the legislature. Richard also acted without delay to reorganize the railway, but at a heavy cost. The government bought it from the Reids for $2 million, along with the dry dock and the coastal boat service, placing the system under the management of an experienced railroader, Herbert J. Russell. The Reid family was left to concentrate on making a return on their land holdings, a large portion of which was tied to timber and water rights for the Humber development.

Richard's successes with putting the "Hum on the Humber" and revitalizing the railway were soon overshadowed, however, as his shady deeds began to catch up with him. This time the trouble started with the appointment of his new cabinet. Before the election, he had promised the agriculture and mines portfolio to Joseph Downey as an enticement to run in the district of St. George's. He also promised a cabinet post to Matthew Hawco if he ran in Harbour Main. Both ran and both were elected. Dr. Campbell, ally and pump-primer-in-chief, was defeated, but insisted on remaining minister of agriculture and mines. Squires and Coaker both tried to talk him out of it, but to no avail. Richard— still as enamoured of Campbell as Campbell was of him—put him back in the cabinet again by the back door through reappointment to the Legislative Council. He did the same for Captain Bonia, who became minister of posts and telegraphs, the position that Hawco wanted. Downey and Hawco, their ambitions scuttled by Richard's betrayal, were up in arms—as were their friends in cabinet, already unsettled over the inordinate amounts of money doled out to voters by Campbell. It was clear that if Campbell were to run into problems, he could expect no support from cabinet members except for Richard himself.

And the problems cropped up soon enough. On June 26, Michael Cashin stood in the House of Assembly to announce that he had in his pocket government cheques that a minister of the Crown had used to pay his personal expenses during the election campaign. William J. Walsh, Opposition member for Placentia-St. Mary's, followed up, naming Campbell as the minister in question and disclosing that the cheques had been used for cab hire. The matter simmered for a week, until Attorney General Warren advised the House that if a member were to make a definite charge he would "do his duty." Walsh repeated his allegation, said that the cheques were for $51 and $21, and named the cab driver. "If that is not a definite charge," he said, "I don't know how to make one." There was no response from Campbell, who was not around to hear the charges; he was at home, suffering a nervous breakdown. Richard stayed mute on the matter but refused to remove Campbell from the cabinet, further alienating the other ministers.

By this time, however, Richard was neck-deep in a scandal of his own: the misappropriation of funds at the Department of the Liquor Controller. Earlier in June, the cabinet had heard enough about fraudulent goings-on with John Meaney and the liquor department to order an investigation by the auditor general. On the night of Saturday, June 16, someone broke into the department and made off with papers from an envelope labelled "R. A. S." and a file marked "Prime Minister." Detective John Byrne, he of the Rockwell Kent affair, now head constable of the police force, interviewed Meaney on Monday. Meaney blamed the file theft on

Harris O'Keefe, one of the prime minister's messengers, who had been hanging around the office, and told Byrne that he believed Squires "was on the back of it," though this he later denied in a letter to Squires. Nonetheless, he was suspended as acting controller and soon terminated from the department. Richard promptly fired Harris O'Keefe.

But it didn't end there. Meaney knew the auditor general's investigation was coming and, no stranger to double-dealing, he did not trust Richard Squires to come clean on the misappropriated funds. To cover himself, he had already prepared duplicates of the Squires records, including the cheques and IOUs presented by Jean Miller that he'd cashed from department funds. The duplicates were what had been stolen—the originals were still in his possession.

The whiff of scandal made for a testy cabinet meeting in early July, in which Richard was adamant that he would not call for Campbell's resignation. In response to one of his comments, a department head told him to "mind his own business." Richard shot back "Don't you talk to me like that." Debate, if it could be called that, came close to a "fistic encounter" according to the *Evening Telegram*.

For Richard, it was downhill from there. John Meaney got word that criminal proceedings could be launched against him. He was already miffed at Squires for three years of reneging on a promise to install him in the permanent position of liquor controller. He had also seen how Richard had turned on Jim Miller just a few months before. Now he was the one on the receiving end of prime ministerial umbrage, and he was not about to sit around waiting for Richard to orchestrate his downfall. Meaney went on the offensive, taking the Squires cheques and IOUs to William Warren, the attorney general. Finding Warren less than sympathetic about getting involved, he approached lawyer W. J. Higgins, now Leader of the Opposition, who took him to see Warren and Coaker, the senior member of cabinet.

Warren, a smallish man, athletic in his younger days but now

William R. Warren, 1879-1927

usually seen through a thick cloud of cigarette smoke, had no choice but to confront Squires. He told him that Higgins was getting ready to lay criminal charges against him on behalf of Meaney, and under the circumstances Warren would have to resign. Richard brought this news to his own lawyer, William R. Howley, who gave him the same advice: Resign. That was his only option, he said. Reluctantly, Richard agreed.

Yet it was in his nature to attempt to wiggle out of it, to make a deal for himself even when he had no wiggle room left. He tried to buy time with Warren and Coaker, to delay stepping down until the end of the year, but Warren was having none of it. So Richard laid out the terms under which he would resign, which he saw as merely passing over the premiership to Warren for a couple of years or so. During that time, he wanted to be looked after financially while acting as legal counsel to the government on the Labrador boundary dispute. He also wanted to represent Newfoundland at an upcoming imperial conference in London and to take charge of the country's participation in the British Empire exhibition the following year. No, said Warren: no, no, and no.

On Saturday, July 21, Richard informed his cabinet that he would resign on Monday and advise the governor to call on former Opposition Leader John Bennett to form an administration. That, for Warren, was the final straw—the man was planning to resign all right, and hand the reins of government over to the Opposition! Who could say what scheming might come after that (or already had)? On Sunday afternoon he delivered a letter to Richard at his home on Rennies Mill Road. "Recent developments have forced me to say to you now that unless your resignation is in the hands of His Excellency by eleven o'clock to-morrow morning (Monday) I shall deliver to him my resignation at noon. I need not repeat to you my reasons for resigning as you already know them."

Monday, July 23, was an eventful day. Rumours of important events unfolding drew a crowd to the grounds of the Colonial Building. At noon, as hundreds milled around, Warren walked over to Government House with his resignation from cabinet. Three other ministers—Dr. Arthur Barnes, W. W. Halfyard, and S. J. Foote—went with him, resignations in hand. Richard Squires was finished as prime minister. He followed shortly after with his own letter, calm as could be:

Dear Sir William Allardyce:

I find that my views upon certain matters of public importance diverge substantially from those held by certain members of my Party, and under these circumstances I feel that it is in the public interests that I should tender my personal resignation of the offices of Prime Minister and Colonial Secretary held by me continuously since November, 1919, and advise Your Excellency to call upon the Hon. W. R. Warren, K.C., His Majesty's Attorney General, to carry on the present Administration or form a new Administration as he may decide.

The air around the Colonial Building hummed with speculation. Warren was with some government members in the Speaker's room when a message came for him to call upon the governor without delay. In the language of diplomacy, Allardyce was "pleased to request that he form a ministry."

Warren was pleased to comply. Just after five o'clock, Richard called a meeting of the Liberal Reform Party in the Legislative Council chambers to bid them farewell, giving no indication of his future plans. Warren met the government members again after the dinner break, and they elected him leader of the party. The crowd outside waited for someone to make an official statement, but it never came and they gradually drifted off.

On Tuesday, Warren announced Richard Squires's resignation in the House and his own intention to form an administration. A generally affable man of good humour, Warren had few enemies, even in politics, though he was unsure how much party support he could count on. He spent his first week as prime minister trying to forge a coalition with Higgins and the Opposition—something like the National Government of the war years—so that the business of the country could carry on partisan-free. This initiative, admirable as it was, failed. That was unfortunate, for public confidence in government (and politicians) had sunk to its lowest level. Everyone knew about Campbell's patronage spree during the election and had heard the whispers about Richard Squires's shenanigans with the liquor controller, though details about that were sketchy. Now they had Squires's unexplained resignation to chew on. With so many questions, there was little enthusiasm for a new prime minister, especially one surrounded by many of the same players.

Warren knew very well that he had his work cut out for him. Coaker and the Unionists were half-hearted in supporting him because he was friendly with the Opposition, as his attempts to form a coalition government had amply demonstrated. They tried to get Harry Winter, Speaker of the House and Warren's law partner, to take the leadership, but he was not at all inclined. Warren pushed on. The new cabinet had no place for Squires allies Campbell and Bonia. They were replaced with Downey in agriculture and mines and Hawco in posts and telegraphs, the portfolios Richard had promised them during the election. Coaker did his part, coming in as minister without portfolio, and the stalwart Dr. Barnes, focussed more on pedagogy than political antics, continued as minister of education.

Prime Minister Warren kept the portfolio of justice minister and attorney general. All eyes were on him to investigate the goings-on of Campbell and Squires, to either bring charges or clear them of wrongdoing. There was much public outcry for an official inquiry, and a formal request from Campbell, who had gone to Prince Edward Island to recover his health. Campbell saw himself as free of wrongdoing and wanted an examination of all relief expenditure, which he said was carried out in conjunction with the district MHAs and went into their hands for distribution. Warren promised a complete and thorough investigation.

Richard remained silent. Lena was in England, preparing to bring Elaine home for the summer break. On the evening of his resignation, he stole away alone, by private rail car, for the solitude of Little Bay Islands. A quiet week with the Strongs far from St. John's invigorated him and he returned feeling "as fit as I did in 1919." He made a quick stop in the city, and then he was on his way again, this time to the mainland. In Montreal he spoke briefly to the press, saying only: "I have no comment to offer regarding the political situation, nothing to confirm or deny or accept or reject." Privately, he reassured an acquaintance that he had "no impairment of health or vigour. Certain members of my Party disagreed with me on certain matters of public interest" but in his mind he was still leader of the party. In fact, he still had his seat in the legislature and the support of a handful of the Liberal Reform members.

And that would be his story in the coming weeks and months. There had been a disagreement, a falling out, a misunderstanding, and he was in retirement from active politics, a robust forty-three-year-old now playing the part of an elder statesman. In Toronto, approached by a reporter as he was leaving the King Edward Hotel, he commented that, in Newfoundland, "We are looking forward to an era of prosperity and of great development in the island." He visited the United States, opining freely on international relations, the state of the British Empire, and anything else the press wanted to hear his thoughts on. Back in St. John's in August, Richard asked again if he might represent the Government of Newfoundland at the upcoming Imperial Economic Conference in London. Not likely, said the executive council, appalled at the nerve of the man. So Richard went anyway. He,

Lena, and Elaine sailed together to England in September—on the same ship taking Warren to the conference—carrying on their lives as if nothing had changed.

Lena, it seems, was made of the same stern stuff (perhaps sterner) as her husband. As his political world collapsed around him, she remained committed to her role as society matron, advancing the cause of child welfare and the health of newborns. In May that year, with her daughter Rosemary turning a year old and the political mess about to unfold, she took a prominent place at a week-long health conference on the care of babies, accompanying Lady Allardyce to its official opening and co-hosting one of the sessions. Her work on the new hospital also proceeded, thanks in part to a timely donation of $10,000 from the prime minister's office, made before Richard's resignation. The Grace Maternity Hospital opened in December 1923, with twenty beds and room for seventy babies—a big step forward for maternity care and infant health in Newfoundland. And she and Richard were assembling land in the Waterford Valley near Bowring Park, coolly developing a large country estate, much larger than the block of land they'd purchased earlier on Waterford Bridge Road. Richard bought eight acres of farmland at the end of May and added to it in November, the beginning of a sprawling property they called "Midstream." It was a working farm comprising a large owner's home, a house for the farmer's family, several outbuildings, and soon-to-be showpiece gardens.

But back to the trip to England, where Richard had no intention of accepting the role of persona non grata—quite the contrary. He and Lena already had their names included on the London social lists for fall events, the first being a luncheon with former British Prime Minister Lloyd George. Where official business was concerned, however, it was a different matter. At the conference, Prime Minister Warren's easygoing speaking style and engaging demeanour made him a centre of attention while Richard was consigned to the sidelines. He spent his time either lobbying Warren or badmouthing his administration. Warren shared his frustration about the situation in a letter to William Halfyard, his colonial secretary:

> Squires is here and is doing everything he can to embarrass me and intimidate me into calling off the investigation, but I am holding my own, and after my interview with him today I have no fear of any trouble. He has been circulating several stories about me, and, in particular, he poses as Leader of the Liberal Party, says that while he resigned his official positions, he [is] still the leader of the Liberal Party, has told this to officials in the Colonial Office (who do not believe him) and he states that you and Barnes deliberately left St. John's so that you would not sit at Council meeting with me at my final meeting before coming to the Conference, because you were so disgusted with the way in which I was mismanaging matters.

Matters had, in fact, already gone beyond Richard's influence. Before leaving Newfoundland, Warren had initiated an official investigation of Squires and Campbell, placing it in the hands of London barrister Thomas Hollis Walker, who had been recommended by the Colonial Office. A man of impeccable credentials, Walker was currently the recorder (chief magistrate) of the city of Derby. He and his wife crossed a stormy North Atlantic to St. John's in December 1923. His inquiry into what the *Evening Telegram* called "the greatest upheaval in the whole of our political history" opened on January 7, 1924.

Much mischief in high places was about to be laid bare for all to see.

CHAPTER TEN

Sir Richard under Fire
1924

The first week of January 1924 brought unseasonably fine weather to St. John's—days mild enough to almost be called balmy. With only a trace of snow on the ground, Richard Squires had no trouble getting back and forth between Rennies Mill Road and his Midstream property in his sleek Studebaker Light Six sedan. The fine weather was big talk around the city—but even bigger than that was the Hollis Walker inquiry, opening at the Colonial Building. Many eyes were watching and waiting for a good comeuppance for Squires, and perhaps a complete and final downfall. Those who had said, all along, that the man could not be trusted now felt they were going to be justified.

There were still some who stood behind him, however. They admired his cleverness, his gumption, his utter dedication to his work. Beyond the drawn-out spats of earlier years, William Coaker reacted to the events of 1923 not with condemnation, but with regret that "so brilliant a leader as Sir R. A. Squires, so young in years, so clever and resourceful, should by the wheels of the gods have to resign the premiership under such circumstances." Later on, Coaker would admit that the trouble with Richard Squires was that he had no conscience. To that can be added—and this more than anything else may be what pulled him through these dark days of his career—he had no shame.

Journalist J. R. Smallwood, one of Richard's staunchest allies, wrote that R. A. Squires was "completely overlooked when the qualities of fear and timidity were being handed around." Looking back later, he opined that the problem with the man was that he didn't know how to handle money. Little doubt on either count.

The Hollis Walker hearings held St. John's spellbound right through the winter of 1924. Witness after witness revealed layers of political scheming and conniving. The gallery of the Legislative Council chambers, where the proceedings took place, were filled to overflowing. Ladies were given preference for admission, and many turned up with their knitting, settling in to watch the high drama unfold. Reporters took down the proceedings, which were printed in the papers every day.

Walker was a wise and experienced arbiter with an air of having seen it all before, at least twice. He was also engaging and entertaining, in contrast to the dull judges who held sway over regular Newfoundland courtrooms. Lawyer William J. Browne likened them to "stuffed figures on the Bench with some mechanical device to allow them to write and turn their heads." Walker, on the other hand, was "lively, quick, witty and always on the point." It was "most amusing to listen to [his] mixture of humour and sarcasm and irony." Ruled by his gavel, the hearings moved briskly along.

Solicitor General Warren led the questioning and cross-examination of witnesses for the government, assisted by Harry Winter and Charles Hunt. Richard was represented by his personal solicitor, William R. Howley, with help from some high-priced talent from the United States—Merton E. Lewis, former attorney general for the State of New York.

The Hollis Walker commission was to inquire into five questions, two of which involved Richard directly. The first of these was whether monies paid to the Department of the Liquor Controller were paid not into the Treasury but to private individuals. The second was whether, during the period when contract negotiations were in progress between the Bell Island mining companies and the government, monies were paid by those companies to Prime Minister Squires. The other three matters looped Alex Campbell into the investigation: was there any wrongdoing a) by the Department of Agriculture and Mines in relation to the pit-prop account and the government's model farm, b) by the Department of Public Charities in expenditure on poor relief, or c) by the Department of Public Works in expenditure on relief?

Warren had drawn up the terms of the inquiry. Initially he had wanted to scrutinize all dealings of the Department of the Liquor Controller. That, however, would have shone a light into too many corners, exposing members of the House who were either receiving Meaney's gift-packs or bribing him to purchase inventory from their own import agencies, or both. Although Warren denied it when accused, there is little doubt that some honourable members had leaned on him to tailor the investigation specifically to Meaney's allegations against Squires. As a result, Walker could not allow the inquiry to stray into the affairs of other politicians.

When he was called to testify, Richard presented a master class in evasion and obfuscation. He could recall all sorts of events unrelated to the matters at hand but fogged over whenever questioning veered in the direction of incriminating evidence. He directly contradicted the sworn testimony of John Meaney and Jean Miller about funds paid to him from the Department of the Liquor Controller. He consistently muddied the waters by going off topic.

Walker was short on patience with his meandering. "No one asked you how it arose," he lectured him at one point. "You do embarrass this enquiry enormously. Will you stop these long speeches?" Warren's questioning about a meeting with Jim Miller brought the following exchange:

Warren: What did you say to him?
Squires: I am telling you what I remember.

Warren: But what did you tell him?

Squires: I can't tell you that because I don't remember.

Warren: I am asking you because I want to see if your evidence agrees with some of the other evidence.

Walker: It would be a delightful change if some of the evidence did agree.

John Meaney was a far more cooperative witness. He was open, articulate, and direct, though with an unsettling touch of arrogance. He stated that he had paid the cash advances to Jean Miller as a temporary accommodation for Richard Squires. She kept assuring him that the money would be repaid and he believed that it would be. By July 1922, however, he decided that the advances had gone too far without repayment and brought it up with the prime minister, who gave "some kind of evasive reply." That was when he brought the payments to a halt.

Jean Miller, when called to testify, was compliant to the point of deference ("Yes, Mr. Warren," "Yes, Mr. Walker"). She stuck to the facts as far as her memory allowed, testifying that she went to Meaney under her employer's instructions. The money she received went to cover bank notes coming due, as well as accounts and wages for the *Daily Star*.

Richard responded to Miller's testimony by claiming that he had never told her to go to Meaney for money and knew nothing about the payments until 1923, except for one amount ($4,000) repaid in December 1920. Miss Miller did all this on her own, he said. In any event, the advances were political contributions. When asked why, when Warren confronted him in July 1923, he had not denied the charges by Meaney, he replied that he viewed the whole matter as "political intrigue," designed to overthrow his administration and force him out of office.

The inquiry turned to the payments from the Bell Island mining companies, and Jim Miller took the stand. He came across as a well-intentioned man, a Squires loyalist but more than a little naïve when it came to the ins and outs of politics. He admitted that he took a chance in advancing the $43,000 to Richard out of mining company funds, but he had reason to believe that head office would back him up—and he understood from the prime minister that the advance would be temporary. Pressed for repayment, Richard had written a cheque for the full amount from the *Daily Star* . . . on a non-existent account! When the cheque bounced, he had told Miller that he expected the company to contribute that amount to his election campaign.

In his testimony, Richard explicitly denied asking Jean Miller to go to her brother for money. He said that he first found out about the payments from Jim Miller in March 1921 and that he did not know the source of the funds. The package of $5,000 cash that Jean Miller picked up at the Bank of Nova Scotia was a personal donation from Mr. McInnes, he said, an acquaintance of his from Dalhousie Law School.

Walker's eighty-two-page report, released on March 21, confirmed what most people had suspected and many knew to be true. After weaving his way through the contradictions and convolutions of testimony on the payments from the liquor controller, Walker found:

> That Sir Richard Squires realized in August 1920 that money might be obtained for him through Mr. Meaney from the funds of the Liquor Department, and that after his return [from England] he realized that it had been so obtained, and was being so obtained; that he accepted the use and benefit of over $20,000 so obtained with knowledge of their tainted history, and made himself a receiver and an accomplice in Mr. Meaney's wrong.

On the issue of influence peddling by the mining companies, Walker had this to say about the $43,000 from the Dominion Iron and Steel Company:

> To my mind financial assistance from the Company at such a time and under such circumstances would be equally objectionable whether it took the form of accommodation only or of actual cash lent or given. Sir Richard

accepted that help regarding it as a gift, the money was
paid to him and I find that the allegation . . . is proved.

His report was less decisive on the $5,000 parcel procured
by Dominion solicitor H. McInnes, but he cleared the Nova Scotia
Steel and Coal Company of any wrongdoing.

Though I look upon the incident of the $5,000 parcel
with grave suspicion, on the evidence before me I do not
find that the Nova Scotia Company or any of its officials
as such paid any money to Sir Richard Squires.

During the hearings, the allegations against Dr. Campbell
drew as much attention as those against Richard Squires. The
press had already gone out of its way to accuse him of embezzling
government funds and running to Prince Edward Island as a
fugitive from justice. At the inquiry, Campbell's testimony was
straightforward. He said from the beginning that he had nothing
to hide. He took no personal responsibility for relief payments
throughout the districts, which were issued by him on recommendation of the MHAs and the clergy. If he had slipped up, it was
because the demand for relief money was unending and he
was worked to death. In addition, he said the bookkeeping in
his department was lax and informal, which made him careless
in the use of department money for his own expenses. He
admitted he had paid his cab fare from the pit-prop account:
"There was no other place for me to take it."

In a statement that neatly summed up the attitude toward
accountability in government under Squires, Campbell expressed
the view that if ministers were held responsible for overspending
in their departments there would be no one left to run the
government. He also related how he had personally supervised
relief projects around the city, trying to prevent labour unrest,
trying to keep relief workers happy, and combined those trips
with personal canvassing in his district. The pressure of work on
him was crushing, and he had been taking electric shock treatment
for depression for some time.

In his report, Walker was unequivocal about Campbell's behaviour:

> I find that the allegation that Dr. Campbell paid his own private cab fares to a very substantial amount out of the public funds under his control is fully proved. I find that Dr. Campbell improperly used his opportunity as Minister to advance his political prospects and exploited the situation to that end. This in my view was misconduct.

He also found misappropriation and misuse of government funds that had been allocated to the model farm as further misconduct on the part of Campbell. While the inquiry revealed no evidence of misappropriation of relief money, the way it was distributed was, in Walker's words, "slovenly and unbusinesslike and made possible abuses all over the Island of which I cannot think that the staff was ignorant."

Overall, Walker's report was a stark indictment of the Squires regime. It prompted public calls for prosecution of the offenders and reform of government practice. The first week of April, A. B. Morine, practising law and out of politics at the time, gave a masterly overview of the inquiry's work. It was standing room only for his address at Canon Wood Hall in St. John's, where his audience sat spellbound as he went through the report and its implications piece by piece. He praised Walker for his superlative expertise in bringing it all together and called passionately for the complete revamping of the way the government was being run.

In the wake of the inquiry, the Rev. Colonel Thomas Nangle, who had completed his work overseas and was now serving as president of the GWVA, gave a stirring speech to veterans at a jam-packed gathering at the Star Hall. "If the Hollis Walker report has done nothing else it has awakened public morality in Newfoundland," he said. The report "has taken the lid off the pot; we want all the beans spilled and spread to public view."

Walker and his wife preferred not to stay around for the aftershocks of the report. Once the job was done, they left quietly on the express train to Port aux Basques, heading for Halifax and the next transatlantic steamer. As it happened, leaving Newfoundland was no more pleasant than getting there. Crossing the Gulf on the *Kyle*, they were stuck in the ice for two days, couldn't land at North Sydney, and finally made port at Louisburg. (In April, Warren promised a follow-up investigation to the report and invited Walker back to conduct it. He respectfully declined.)

News of the inquiry's report was not long making it into the international press. "Sir Richard Squires is a politically dead man," pronounced the *Halifax Herald*, echoed by the *Montreal Gazette*. Speaking of Squires and Campbell, the *Sydney Post* prophesied that "the political careers of both these men have come to an ignominious end." The *New York Times* even reported on the more explosive revelations coming out of the proceedings. In England, the venerable *Times of London* read Walker's report, shook its head, and frowned:

> It has struck a heavy blow at the Colony's good name; it is an indictment not only of the persons mentioned in the various charges, but of the political morality of large numbers of their fellow-countrymen . . . That it should have been possible to level such accusations against the Prime Minister of a great Dominion of the Crown seems incredible; that it should have been possible to prove them is nothing short of a tragedy.

Richard left Newfoundland soon after the report came out. In Halifax, his first stop, his bold proclamation of innocence earned him a scoffing headline in St. John's: "Squires Tells the World of His Delusion." In Toronto, where a reporter reached him leaving the King Edward Hotel, he delivered more of the same: "The findings were absolutely absurd and contrary to the evidence. From beginning to end it was purely a political affair." (He stopped short of calling it a witch hunt.) He would see that the report was tabled in the House of Assembly, he added, and looked forward to "complete vindication during the debates which will follow.

Moreover, I am certain that as soon as I can get to the country I will lead the Liberals to a victory at the polls and will regain my former position." It's possible he actually believed it.

In St. John's, the FPU members of Warren's governing party pushed for further follow-up to the inquiry. None of them, from Coaker on down, had been implicated in the report. They could hardly be blamed for being high-minded and demanding prosecution of the offenders, or for wanting further investigation into other areas of government corruption—even if it would undermine the very people whose partnership made them members of the government side. The press was behind them, which put Warren in a hard spot. He had written the terms of the inquiry to focus on Richard Squires, knowing that abuse of the Department of the Liquor Controller was widespread and extended to other MHAs. He had in fact commissioned a secret report on that the year before, which he refused to release to Walker. Members of his own party could have been involved—members of the Opposition definitely were (Michael Cashin for one), and they wanted no more prying.

But Warren had little choice—he had to give in to the Unionists or see the governing party split apart. On April 8, the cabinet directed the Department of Justice to proceed with legal action against Squires, Campbell, and Meaney. Warren agreed to launch a further investigation into liquor control and other government departments. The press applauded, but the announcement sent shudders through Warren's Liberals and the ranks of the Opposition, who, congenial up to now, turned sour on him.

On April 17, Richard returned to St. John's from Halifax. On Tuesday, April 22, Warren heard rumblings that some members of his caucus were getting restless with the delay in legal action and were muttering about defecting. He moved at once to have Squires arrested. Richard appeared in court at four o'clock that afternoon, charged with larceny of $22,000, and was released on bail of $40,000. Dr. Campbell was also arraigned, charged with larceny of $400, and released on bail of $4,000. The charge of larceny against John Meaney was $100,000; he, too, was released on bail of $40,000.

Richard Squires was not long exacting his revenge. It took him just two days, in a bold-faced political gambit.

The evening of Tuesday, April 22, Warren held a caucus meeting to prepare for the opening of the House on Thursday. Two members did not show: Richard Cramm, the Liberal Reform member for Bay de Verde and a former law clerk with the Squires firm, and George Jones, the Union member for Twillingate. On Wednesday, the *Evening Telegram* reported that they had left the party. On Thursday, the opening session of the legislature began, as always, with the Speech from the Throne. In the debate that followed, a nervous and agitated Richard Cramm stood up and denounced Warren as "guilty of criminal action." He was ruled out of order but then rose again to move a vote of non-confidence in the government. When the vote was called, A. M. Calpin and Ernest Simmons, both MHAs for Harbour Grace, revealed themselves as two more Warren defectors. They voted in favour, as did the Opposition—and Squires, whose vote was the tie-breaker that toppled the government!

How had he managed to obtain the backing of those four members? Perhaps they were filled with unswerving loyalty. Perhaps they agreed with him that the Hollis Walker inquiry was a set-up to destroy him politically. Then again, Calpin and Simmons had been heard to say that if the government was prepared to pay for their support, the government would get it. Perhaps they, and the other two, made the same offer to Richard Squires. It would surprise no one if Sir Richard took them up on it.

The vote of non-confidence did not shake Warren into resigning. Instead, he obtained a dissolution of the House from Governor Allardyce, set an election for June 2, and tried to regroup. A confused and tangled free-for-all followed, in which alliances seemed to form and reform almost daily. Warren found that he was not on the best of terms with either his own party or the Opposition.

On May 3, at a meeting of Opposition members—those MHAs now defined as anyone opposed to Warren—Dr. Barnes put forward Albert E. Hickman, the regulation-breaking merchant of 1921, as leader of a revived Liberal-Progressive Party. Both Squires and Coaker said they would not run in the next election, but they would support Hickman.

Warren, doing his best but fast approaching the limits of his competence, announced a new cabinet the same day. It included members of the Opposition party, among them St. John's merchant Walter S. Monroe, two former party leaders—W. J. Higgins and John R. Bennett—and one member from the previous cabinet: Minister of Posts and Telegraphs M. E. Hawco. Four days later, Hawco had a change of heart and decided that his future prospects in a Warren government were grim. He resigned, saying that the composition of Warren's cabinet and party was "not of the political faction that I expected it would be."

Hawco's resignation was the death blow for Warren, who could not expect to hold onto his leadership in such an unstable environment. Another call went out to Robert Bond at Whitbourne. Now sixty-seven years old and in declining health, he turned them down one final time. Warren advised Governor Allardyce to send for Coaker to form a ministry. Coaker refused but recommended Hickman, who accepted.

The head-spinning developments were neatly summed up by a droll columnist in the *Evening Telegram* (writing as Pepys Behind the Scenes), who commented: "We might as well be with no Government, seeing how once we did have one in 4 years, and now we have 4 in one year, so that they change about as often as a politician changes his opinion."

There was more change in the offing. At a public rally on May 10 came an overwhelming endorsement of Walter S. Monroe as leader of a new party (calling itself "Liberal-Conservative"— that is, Liberal bordering on Tory, as compared to Liberal-Progressive and Liberal Reform). An unsuccessful candidate for Cashin's party in 1923, Monroe was Dublin-born, with a successful export business in St. John's. An unassuming man of slight build, he had had a brush with government as a member of Warren's four-day cabinet but was otherwise a fresh face in a well-worn field and carrying no extra baggage. He was also an effective antidote to Coaker, the power behind Hickman and still distasteful to the business class. Coaker had once threatened that he would make the grass grow on Water Street, and some of the merchants still thought

Walter S. Monroe, 1871–1952

he might try. The fact that Hickman had placed all three elected members from the Union heartland of Bonavista in his cabinet—and just one member from St. John's—only stoked their fears.

Putting himself forward as "a plain man of business, meaning what I say and saying what I mean," Monroe promised to sweep the government clean and set its finances straight. To make the point that he was fighting as much against the influence of Coaker as against Hickman, he made the bold decision to run in Bonavista, where he had been defeated just the year before.

When the ballots from June 2 were counted, Monroe's Liberal-Conservatives showed a comfortable majority: twenty-five seats to the Liberal-Progressives' ten. Warren ran and was elected as an independent. Monroe and his two running mates took the Bonavista district over the Coaker-backed candidates. Along with a general shift toward a merchant-leaning party, this election saw the tide begin to go out for the FPU as a force in politics.

Coaker did not give up easily. In the by-election that fall to confirm Monroe and W. C. Winsor as members of cabinet, he ran against them again in Bonavista and suffered the humiliation of a personal defeat. After that, he withdrew from politics to focus on the work of the Union enterprises and wintertime travel to warmer climes.

Richard did not run in the election, but he was still part of the action. He lent his endorsement, and that of the *Daily Mail*, to the cause of liberalism and the nine Liberal-leaning candidates he could count on. Some of them ran for Monroe's party, some for Hickman's. Only three were elected, but two of them—the non-confidence mover Richard Cramm and high-ranking Orangeman F. Gordon Bradley—joined Monroe's cabinet. Their presence there gave Richard a direct window into the affairs of government.

He also found the election results satisfying for another reason, as he told his American defence counsel, Merton Lewis:

> Practically all my pursuers were overthrown. Mr. Warren went as an independent candidate to his constituency and was elected, and is an independent with no following whatever. Mr. Foote, a member of the Executive, did not risk a contest and retired from politics. Mr. Winter, the Speaker, representative of Port de Grave District, who was the attorney associated with Mr. Warren, also retired from politics. Mr. Hunt, the other solicitor, also retired. Mr. Cave, Minister of Finance and Customs, Dr. Barnes, Minister of Education, and Mr. Hawco, the Minister of Posts and Telegraphs, were all defeated in their constituencies. The only survivor was the Hon. W. W. Halfyard, and I would regard him as a friend rather than an enemy. I had an outstanding political victory.

Richard A. Squires had been kicked out of politics and was facing criminal prosecution—but in the election results he saw all of his adversaries removed, leaving himself as the real winner. And for him, that was what mattered.

CHAPTER ELEVEN

Watching, Waiting, Scheming
1924–1928

I n a perfect world, the misdeeds of public office holders uncovered by an expert inquiry would be followed by charges, a
trial, and punishment of wrongdoing. And this is what the public
expected after Squires, Meaney, and Campbell were arrested and
charged in April 1924. But the world rarely achieves perfection—
especially when it comes to politics, and more especially when it
came to Richard Squires.

On the sidelines during the 1924 campaign, Richard used
the pages of the *Daily Mail* to begin repairing his image. He
disparaged the Hollis Walker report, spinning the facts into his
own version of events. The paper heaped abuse on Warren (an
"assassin" and a "Judas") for narrowing the terms of reference
of the Hollis Walker commission. In the House of Assembly in
May, Richard Cramm had slammed the inquiry as "a Commission
designed by Mr. Warren to 'get' his former leader." Governor
Allardyce was also complicit in trying to bring down Squires, or
so it was alleged. In a year during which the entire political
process was in chaos, said the *Daily Mail*, the "only attempt to
clean up a political mess was done by Sir Richard Squires,
who, rather than surrender to sinister influences, resigned the

Premiership of Newfoundland." As Richard spun it, he was the victim, maybe even the downtrodden hero, in all of it!

All this noise was not made simply to restore his good name. He was by no means finished with politics and was purposefully sowing seeds of confusion, cultivating a narrative that would favour his return when the time came to step back into the game.

Prime Minister Monroe, first-rate businessman and neophyte politician with all good intentions for government reform, put together a cabinet of familiar faces. Apart from Cramm and Bradley, both ministers without portfolio and friends of Squires, there were few newcomers. John R. Bennett was colonial secretary, W. J. Higgins minister of justice and attorney general, and John C. Crosbie minister of finance and customs. It was unclear how Monroe intended to follow through on his promise of reform with experienced ministers like Bennett and Crosbie—steeped in the tradition of government perks and payoffs—in the fold. William Woodford was back on the front lines as minister of posts and telegraphs and A. B. Morine, the perennial disruptor, came in as minister without portfolio via appointment to the Legislative Council. Morine, in fact, was the brains behind Monroe as his top advisor in the government, and a questionable asset. Not many would disagree with Peter Cashin's assessment of Morine as "the most despised figure in the political history of Newfoundland."

The chaotic events of the spring and the June election over with, the country looked forward to the respite from politics that the long-awaited unveiling of the National War Memorial in St. John's would afford. It was slated for July 1, the eighth anniversary of the battle at Beaumont-Hamel. The monument was the project conceived and executed by Thomas Nangle with the backing of Squires, Coaker, and the veterans' association. Nangle raised money for the sculpture, selected the site, and supervised the monument's design in England. Gerald Whitty of the GWVA handled construction in St. John's and looked after the arrangements for the unveiling ceremony.

What could have been a signature and very public triumph for Richard Squires was wiped out by the unsavoury events preceding it. He played no part in a celebration that went off with style, flair, and a big dose of patriotism. Field Marshal Douglas Haig, commander-in-chief of the British forces in the Battle of the Somme, came to Newfoundland for the occasion. History has been less than kind to Haig, who oversaw the wholesale slaughter of troops under his command, but in 1924 he was the biggest (if not the most popular) celebrity in the Empire. Tall and broad-shouldered, with cropped white hair, a neatly trimmed moustache, and the bearing of a nobleman, Haig projected the very essence of a military commander. St. John's was agog over his visit.

There were many close-up glimpses of the famous field marshal (accompanied by his aide-de-camp Lieutenant Colonel Nangle) during a week crammed with official dinners, lunches, receptions, a garden party, a regatta, and a review of ex-servicemen. Water Street businesses revelled in the hustle of what came to be called "Haig Week": Bon Marche had an exclusive offering of British goods, McMurdo's Drug Store offered special cosmetics so ladies could look their best, Tooton's ran a contest for the best snapshot of Haig. John Bennett's brewery brought out a new product called Haig Ale that became a Newfoundland staple with a shelf life far exceeding the field marshal's visit.

On the day of the unveiling, some twenty thousand people crammed into downtown St. John's, including thousands of veterans brought into the city at the government's expense. Kicking off the event was a giant parade along Water Street led by the mounted police, with brass bands and military platoons and the four companies of the Royal Newfoundland Regiment. Once all were formed up at King's Beach, Haig unveiled the memorial "to the memory of our gallant comrades who gave their lives for King and Country." Dignitaries, society representatives, and citizens came forward with their wreaths until a "great mound" was banked up in front of the monument.

Thanks to the earlier work of Richard Squires and Dr. Arthur

Unveiling of the War Memorial, July 1924

Barnes, Newfoundland's second memorial to the war, the new Memorial University College and Normal School, officially opened the following year. So did Richard and Lena's pet project, the Memorial Park at Beaumont-Hamel, which also featured Haig accompanied by Nangle. Looking back years later, Nangle was clear on where credit lay for the memorials to Newfoundland's fallen soldiers:

> Without Squires' help and encouragement there would be no Beaumont-Hamel Park or War Memorials on the Western Front. And without his backing, you would probably have a Grecian temple on Gibbet Hill as suggested by Gosling or a public lavatory in Beck's Cove, as suggested by John Browning, as a National War Memorial.

After Haig Week ended in July 1924, preliminary hearings for Squires, Meaney, and Campbell got underway, extending into the fall, a replay of sorts of the Hollis Walker inquiry. Witnesses were called and evidence taken, and each case went to a grand jury to determine whether formal charges should be laid. For Campbell, the grand jury upheld one charge of the fraudulent use of $72. That case proceeded to trial and the jury returned a verdict of not guilty. For Meaney, the grand jury returned an indictment of theft of $47,000—but at trial the jury was unable to reach a verdict. Meaney was released again on bail.

The investigation of Richard Squires produced sixty-six charges of larceny. The jurors took less than an hour (Richard said it was ten minutes) to reach the jaw-dropping decision of no indictment. The Crown appealed, citing irregularities in the selection of jurors—could it be that the jury was stacked? No, said the Supreme Court, upholding the selection procedure and the jury's verdict. The result was that on October 13, 1924, Sir Richard Squires left the courtroom with his head high, all charges dropped.

Out of office, out of the House, and now out of trouble . . . for the time being.

In December more allegations came from another quarter— the tax assessor's department. Richard had filed no returns in the six years since income tax had been introduced in 1918. This was, he said, because he was owed money by the government that would reduce his net income and offset taxes payable. But the time had come to pay up; the assessor notified him that his account was going to legal counsel for collection.

The government's lawyer in the tax case was Gordon Bradley, who wrote a courteous but firm demand that Squires submit his returns, or else. Richard eventually filed in August 1925, but the submission form was so badly altered with handwritten amendments as to be useless. He made no remittance and was fined $6,400 for tax evasion. Further fines and court action followed, including the seizure and auction of his Studebaker Light Six. Represented by Howley, Richard delayed and delayed, finally settling up in June 1926.

When he wasn't dealing with these distractions, Richard dabbled at law. His partner, Les Curtis, and student-at-law, Louise Saunders, looked after the day-to-day running of the office, and

Richard indulged his enduring yen for travel. He claimed to have no money to pay his income tax, but even amid the events of 1924 he managed to escape to Canada or the United States for a month here and a few weeks there. At the same time, he was building a new home, Cherry Lodge, on the Midstream estate and clearing additional acreage for farming.

How he could afford this is anyone's guess. After resigning as prime minister in 1923, he was personally not flush with cash, showing $1,297 in the Bank of Nova Scotia and $445 in the Canadian Imperial Bank of Commerce (Lena had $2,411 in the Royal Bank), and the opportunity for lucrative corporate contributions was gone. There were, however, bank accounts in Montreal and New York. How much money was stashed there is unknown, but it could have been substantial, and out of reach of the Newfoundland tax collector. Wherever the funds were coming from, there was money enough for Lena to also spend part of the year in England and to pay for schooling for Elaine and the two older boys, Robert and Richard Jr.

After four years at Crofton Grange preparatory school in Kent, Elaine was struggling and her schoolmistress worried that, feeling pressure to please her parents, she had become anemic and was showing a lack of energy and concentration. Richard and Lena moved her to London to study piano at the Royal College of Music while living at an upscale rooming house for young ladies in Hyde Park. Robert, fifteen, and Richard Jr., two years younger, were also in London by then, at Harrow boarding school. Hilda Brownrigg of St. John's was also nearby, serving as governess for Elaine and the boys. Their correspondence gives us a little glimpse of family relations.

Richard, not given to expressions of affection (even in response to a letter from an eighteen-year-old daughter beginning "Darling Daddy"), instructed Elaine in a businesslike, no-nonsense reply to keep proper account of the expenses for her and the boys (and asked her to transcribe some music for him). "Robert has got his head screwed on alright and is quite clever at saving money,"

Elaine reported to him. "Richard cannot keep money in his own pocket for any length of time. It runs through his fingers like water . . . Mother is always down on me because I am rather strict with the boys. When she is with them she absolutely ruins them, everything under the sun they want, especially Dick, they have only to lift a finger and they have it."

Elaine's sister Rosemary later concurred that Lena was protective of her sons to the detriment of the girls, who "suffered a certain amount of emotional neglect." She felt her mother never got over Jim's death in 1919. Years later, said Rosemary, Lena still mourned his passing, often playing a recording of "Little Boy Blue," a melancholy nineteenth-century poem about a young boy who died, while her tears flowed.

In February 1925, Richard and Lena travelled to the mainland with Norman, seven, and two-year-old Rosemary. Louise Saunders received a letter of concern from their former housemaid Hannah Parrott, now Hannah Smith, married and living in New Perlican, who had seen news of their departure in the paper. "It looked funny to see her take the children this time of year," Hannah wrote, concerned that there might be something wrong. There wasn't; Richard and Lena had just decided on a few months of the high life at the Waldorf-Astoria in New York. Richard sailed from there to London for March and April, taking up residence at the Savoy, leaving Lena in America with the two youngsters.

Richard rejoined them in May and they were all back in St. John's by the beginning of summer. Work was proceeding on the farm at Midstream, with a team of men clearing more land. Elaine, Robert, and Richard Jr. came home on their summer break and, as September approached, Lena escorted them back to England for another year. Richard had Hannah come in from New Perlican to take charge of the country house and the move out of Cherry Lodge back to Rennies Mill Road. She also tended to Norman and Rosemary, especially Norman, who was a handful and needed close supervision. "Library, my bedroom, front bedroom, and any other part of the house in which Norman could make himself troublesome should be locked up," were Richard's instructions. "Norman should go to school as soon as we move out to town."

Hannah stayed until November, while Richard went to Montreal and then New York, where Lena joined him. They were accustomed to the VIP treatment in their travels, but this trip was something special. Richard had a letter of introduction to the manager of the Famous Players movie studios on Long Island that allowed him, as the "Governor of Newfoundland," and Lady Squires to see a picture in the making. Even by today's standards they were having a whirlwind 1925—a pair of globetrotters of their time. Toward the end of the year, Squires and Curtis announced the return of Sir Richard to active practice, available for interviews "by appointment only at the offices of the firm."

Around this time, Richard and Lena transferred their land holdings to a new company, Midstream Realty Ltd., which became their vehicle for mortgage investments and real estate, including their house on Rennies Mill Road. Cherry Lodge, a ranch-style bungalow with a circular drive, was completed as a summer home and the Midstream estate readied for ornamental trees and shrubs. Richard placed a large order with Valley Nurseries, owned by the Tessier family. Apple, plum, and cherry trees, black currant, gooseberry, and raspberry bushes, seven varieties of shrubs and no less than seventeen different tree varieties were to be delivered for planting in the spring of 1926. Two years later, the Tessiers were still trying to collect payment.

They weren't the only suppliers having trouble collecting. Ayre & Sons sent statement after statement to Richard on his account, which he ignored. In 1928, its director, Fred Ayre, finally wrote in frustration:

> Treatment of this nature, we might say, is anything but satisfactory and is not at all fair to us. Such a length of credit is simply absurd, and you must realize this just as well as we do. If we did general business on such princi-

ple, it would be very detrimental to our interests, and we do not quite understand why a legitimate account should receive such treatment at your hands.

Lena had money tied up in shares of the Strong business in Little Bay Islands, but given the dismal the state of the fishery, she had little hope of getting it back. The 1925 and 1926 seasons were so disastrous that fishermen all over the island were trying to sell their schooners and cod traps and leaving in droves for the United States. In early 1927, Richard wrote to her in London: "It appears to be quite impossible to get as much for a quintal of fish as it costs to catch it." The Strong business owed $2,000 to Squires and Curtis and more than $6,000 to Lena personally; their balance sheet at the time showed a loss of $15,000. Ever the optimist, though, Richard concluded his letter on a positive note: "The probabilities for the year are good, and when there is a good

Cherry Lodge

year the profits are great, just as losses are great in a bad year. The difficulty is the carryover period." But if money was tight for them in St. John's, the Squires family were certainly having no trouble paying for first-class travel and accommodation abroad for months at a time, or schooling in England for three children.

Overlying Richard's personal and professional life in these years was his ongoing obsession with politics. At the office, his days were filled receiving political scuttlebutt, as revealed by his diary for 1927. He maintained a wide network of contacts who were plugged into the workings of the government and the Opposition, and into the word on the street. The back door to his office allowed unofficial visitors to come and go unseen—and there were many who did, filling him in on the latest chatter, who were friends and who were foes. He had endless discussions of where alliances lay, who was courting whom, who had it in for certain others, and on and on—the very essence of street-level politics. Richard revelled in it. Someone told him that he'd overheard Errol Munn at the curling club say, "That goddamn crook Squires said Good Day to me on the street but I'm not speaking to the thing." Richard noted that now that he knew about Munn's remark, he would be sure to speak to him again the next time they met, as it was good fun.

In June 1926, the new Newfoundland Hotel opened on Cavendish Square: over a hundred and fifty rooms including two-room and four-room suites, making a classy addition to the business and social life of St. John's. Its plush décor—heavily draped windows, sparkling prismatic chandeliers, rich oriental carpets over hardwood floors edged with marble—soon made it the location of choice for the well-to-do to see and be seen at cocktails, dining, and partying. It also served as a swanky residence for those seeking a carefree place to pass the hard winter months.

Lena spent the winter of 1927 in England, where Norman had started school, and took four-year-old Rosemary with her. Left on his own, Richard closed up Rennies Mill Road and Cherry Lodge, put his car in storage, and moved into "the Hotel." The accommodation was first-class, but the establishment was barely paying its way, and manager Charles Quick was running the food and beverage service on a shoestring. The $1 charged for lunch and $1.50 for dinner did not allow for much variety—certainly not what Richard was used to as a seasoned traveller abroad. As he relayed to Lena:

> You have a consommé for lunch; for dinner you have the same soup under the head of "Beef Broth"; for the following lunch you have the same soup called "Mutton Broth" and that evening you have the same soup, and it is called "Scotch Broth." I was talking to Quick one day in his office and congratulated him upon his being a genius on menus. I enquired the difference in these various soups. He grinned and said I knew altogether too much about Hotel management to please him, but that I had to realize that what he was really doing was running a cheap boarding house on an elaborate scale; that if I wanted a beefsteak occasionally I had better tell the Head Waiter and he would have it looked after, that for regular boarders they did not mind going to that expense occasionally.

Richard coped with the monotonous fare by getting himself invited out to dinner as often as he could, usually at Dr. Campbell's, whose wife was an excellent cook. Campbell was getting over his political bruising and re-establishing his medical practice, and Richard prodded him to get a social life going again as well. When Burns Night at the Hotel came around in January 1927, Richard had space at his table and went to see Campbell at the last minute on the evening of the event.

"Campbell, you and your wife are coming down to Burns Night with me," he announced. "You must go upstairs and get into evening dress and be down at the Hotel by half past ten."

Campbell groused and grumbled but Richard was insistent, as described to Lena:

> After a stormy few minutes I left amidst growls from upstairs, divers and sundry oaths on white shirts and studs, and poor, peaceful Mrs. Campbell fussing around trying to dress up her husband. Mrs. Campbell told me in advance that she did not want to go because she did not have any clothes. Told her I did not care whether she had any clothes or not; that in accordance with Twentieth Century customs, the less she had the better. She must remember that there was a dance and I wanted to see her and her husband dancing together. I went down to the Hotel, just had time enough to get straightened up and get downstairs when they arrived. They had the time of their lives and the next day Campbell was tickled to death with himself.

On Richard's advice, Lena and the children stayed away until well into the spring. "There is nothing to do here in St. John's in the month of March or April, while by remaining in England until after the Easter vacation you can come out and go direct to the country," he wrote. He was especially concerned about Elaine and did not want to risk the embarrassment of having her back in St. John's as a socialite, or, as he put it, turning into "a piece of Newfoundland Hotel boozy driftwood."

Richard made good use of his time while ensconced at the Hotel, where men (yes, still only men) of all political stripes met to talk and make deals. The lunch hour was for keeping up on all the gossip and he was usually there in the thick of it. As 1928 and the next election approached, allies showed up with all kinds of news, encouraging him to get ready for the next campaign. This, of course, is exactly why he was doing all the schmoozing: paving the way to get back in office and exonerate himself. Presumably with a straight face, he assured his cadre that he would not be involved in any buying or selling of political appointments or influence. He had "never been connected with that sort of political business and did not intend to start it now."

This kind of message, credible or not coming from Richard Squires, was nonetheless pertinent in 1927, by which time Prime Minister Monroe was falling short on his promises of clean, solid government and financial accountability. When he breezed into office in 1924, the economy was showing signs of improvement from the desperate conditions of the Squires era. Part of that was attributable to the rush of employment on the Humber development, but the price of fish was also up and that was always good news. To his credit, Monroe's early sessions of parliament produced some progressive legislation. He followed the North American trend in ridding Newfoundland of prohibition (1924), while still restricting the amount of liquor a man (yes, only a man) was able to purchase. The suffrage movement was finally recognized with legislation granting women of twenty-five and older the right to vote and stand for election (1925). Old age pensions were extended to the widows of deceased pensioners that same year. Monroe even managed to rein in government spending—but added to the debt with heavy borrowing for upgrades to the railway and the dry dock and for new road construction.

His efforts toward reform of government practices, however, were faltering. He conducted a sweep of the civil service—but instead of replacing workers with the most capable people, he filled the positions with patronage appointments. Following on the Hollis Walker commission's identification of weakness and corruption in government operations, he ordered an audit of the Customs Department that uncovered gross inefficiencies and crooked dealings in the collection of custom duties, implicating some prominent public figures. Monroe sat on the report for over a year before making it public. When he brought in legislation to revamp the tariff regime, he placed additional duties on imported rope and twine, cigarettes, tobacco, butter, and margarine. These were unpopular moves, putting an added burden on fishing families while benefitting local manufacturers such as the Imperial

Tobacco Company and the Colonial Cordage Company—both of which had Monroe as a major shareholder.

The economic pressure on fishermen and other labourers expressed itself in civil disruption. In May 1926, a group of ninety-odd men from Upper Island Cove went to Harbour Grace demanding extra relief from the relieving officer—Alexander Squires. When he refused, they assaulted him—a man now in his seventies—punching him in the face, smashing his desk, and overturning the stove in his office. They proceeded to Bishop's Cove, where they looted one store, then threatened another in Upper Island Cove. It took a squad of twenty-five constables from St. John's to restore order.

None of this reflected well on the government. Nor had its 1925 repeal of the income tax, which put money back into the economy—but mostly into the pockets of higher earners. In short, Monroe was merely confirming that the people in power were looking after themselves rather than the country or the less affluent, and it led to a sense of cynicism among voters and a rift in his party. The Liberal-Conservatives had come into being for the 1924 election as a rejection of Coaker and a loathing of Squires. It was a party held together not so much by strength of leadership or a commitment to policy (except perhaps enrichment of the wealthy) as by what—or whom—its members were opposed to. They were vulnerable to attack, both from the other side of the House and from opponents on the outside. One of those was Coaker, still stinging after his defeat in Bonavista and nursing his animosity toward Morine, chief counsellor to the prime minister. Coaker found Monroe's pandering to the mon-eyed class deeply offensive and despaired that no form of responsible government could get the country out of its moral and financial morass.

Another opponent of the government was Michael Cashin, which was where the trouble for Monroe really started. Cashin wanted back in the House, and he saw his chance in 1925 when N. J. Vinnicombe, the member for St. John's East, resigned

to become head of the Liquor Board.
Peter Cashin, elected on the Monroe
ticket in 1924, approached the prime
minister on his father's behalf, noti-
fying him that Cashin senior intended
to contest the district. Monroe, however, did not want Michael Cashin
anywhere near the House and refused
to call the by-election. The elder
Cashin was furious and lashed back.
He offered Monroe's own MHAs
bundles of cash to change sides, so
the story went. Inviting W. J. Browne

Peter Cashin, 1890–1977

to his house, he asked: "Why don't you help break up this bad
government we've got?" and promised to make him Speaker of
the House in a new administration. Browne quietly declined.

Peter Cashin also went on the attack, put off by Monroe's
treatment of his father and by the legislation on tariffs and income
tax. He was not one for quiet dissent, which at times made him
look like an oddball and a nuisance. After downing one too many
at the City Club, a private businessmen's retreat on Water Street,
Cashin had a set-to with a few of the members, telling them they
were all bankrupt and not fit to play cards. In the legislature, he
was such a critic of his own party's policies that Monroe told him
if he wanted to oppose the government he should cross to the
other side. In April 1925, he did, and sat as an independent. Five
other MHAs, influenced by Michael Cashin and William Coaker,
followed a year later. This put seventeen members in Opposition,
leaving Monroe with a majority of only two.

Along with Coaker and Peter Cashin, the third prominent
man in opposition to the government was, of course, Richard
Squires. His paper the *Daily Mail* had folded in the fall of 1924,
but by December of the same year there was a new start-up
run by his supporter Richard Hibbs, Liberal member for Fogo.
In its first issue, the *Daily Globe* announced its editorial policy:

"Opposed, politically, from the first page of this and every subsequent issue to the last, to the Monroe Administration, [this paper] supports cheerfully and wholeheartedly the present Liberal Party in Newfoundland and as represented in the Opposition in the House of Assembly."

Harris Mosdell, formerly of the *Daily Mail*, was the *Globe*'s first editor. He was replaced before long by a cocksure young journalist and aspiring politician—J. R. Smallwood—who flailed away at Monroe's government and published a series of articles setting out the principles of liberalism in Newfoundland politics. Smallwood was unimpressed by A. E. Hickman, "one of the most unsuccessful politicians we have ever had at the head of a political party." He remained, however, an unabashed admirer of Sir Richard Squires. The *Globe* published for only a year and a half, closing in 1926 when Smallwood moved to Corner Brook and started the *Humber Herald*, using it in building a campaign to run for the Liberals in the next election.

In 1927, welcome news from London arrived in St. John's: after years of litigation, the Judicial Committee of the Privy Council in Britain had made a determination on Canada's dispute with Newfoundland over the Labrador territory, awarding all 110,000 square miles of it to Newfoundland. This would seem to be ample cause for celebration, but public reaction was underwhelming. Some were elated, seeing it as a windfall. Others saw little value in owning Labrador when there was no means to develop it—sell it, they said, and pay off the public debt. (There is no indication that anyone asked the people who lived there—Innu, Inuit, or others—what they thought. Such was the climate of the times.)

Three years earlier, Monroe had offered Labrador to Quebec for $15 million. He saw the Privy Council decision as a win for Newfoundland—and thus April 1927 seemed finally to be a good time for a by-election in St. John's East (not to mention that Michael Cashin had died suddenly the year before). It should have been a safe bet: Monroe's party had swept the district in 1924. This time, though, with a big campaign push from Peter Cashin, the seat went to the Opposition. The government majority in the House was reduced to one.

Well before the by-election, Monroe had begun making overtures to Hickman about forming a coalition. When Hickman called a caucus meeting to discuss Monroe's offer on a Saturday night in February, he came up against a bloc of disgruntled members. Richard Hibbs dropped into Richard Squires's suite at the Hotel on his way to the meeting, sounding him out about Hickman's leadership. Squires recorded the substance of the meeting in his journal.

"I know Hickman very well and there is not a man in Newfoundland who resents him more than I do," Hibbs began. "If the question of leadership comes up at the meeting, I could say positively that I do not propose to support Hickman to the Polls as leader."

"It's no good to repeat all the things that members of the Opposition usually say about Hickman behind his back," Richard replied.

"What's your advice then?"

"I've been asked that and refused to express an opinion. I have nothing to do with the government and nothing to do with the Opposition. The Opposition members in the House have made fools of themselves, just as the government has. Several Opposition members have offered themselves to me and have been accepted as candidates. As far as this meeting tonight is concerned, I am not concerned what they do; they can all support Hickman if they want to; they can all go to government if they want to—that's their own affair. I am not prepared to have a factional party—a Coaker party or a Roman Catholic party or a Hickman party within the ranks. Every member has to pledge his loyalty to the party and to me as leader. Otherwise, I will not have him as a candidate."

Hibbs then asked him about his general policy.

"I had a program in 1923 that was not touched," Richard replied. "That program would have saved the country from its present disaster. It will be more difficult to handle the situation now, but I am in a position to handle it."

"This is the first streak of light I've seen," said Hibbs. "There's talk of Hickman going across with the government."

"If the members of the Opposition stand firm and decline Hickman's leadership, the best thing he could do is to go across himself," suggested Richard. "If he went over with the government, it would leave the Opposition free. They could select Halfyard or somebody else as House Leader."

Then Richard took a step toward action, albeit behind the scenes: "I will be in town during the Session and would direct their operations, outline questions and bring out necessary facts for a political campaign, prepare amendments, draft necessary legislation, and if necessary write their speeches for them. But to handle a program like that through Hickman," he added, knifing the party's current leader, "would be impossible because he does not have the knowledge of Parliamentary methods or the ability as a speaker and is not prepared to sacrifice the time necessary to put through any program that is laid before him."

Hibbs agreed. "Peter Cashin has taken the position that he would under no circumstances follow Hickman. Many of us have frequently talked about bringing you and Coaker together."

"I was not aware that Coaker and myself have ever been apart," observed Richard disingenuously. "I took it for granted that he proposed to support my party and I would be glad to see him at any time."

Hickman's leadership survived the meeting that night, but Hibbs' reference to Coaker and Cashin proved valuable. Coaker especially would once again be a useful ally to Richard Squires going into an election: he still held sway in the north. But bringing them together would be no easy matter because neither wanted to take the first step.

Smallwood, on good terms with both Squires and Coaker, was unable to convince either to make the first approach until the winter of 1927, when he was in London at work on his book

Coaker of Newfoundland. Early in January, he received a note from Elaine Squires: "Mother would be very pleased if you would have dinner with us on Friday evening." Thus began a friendship with Lena, who took to having Smallwood over to her flat for dinner on Sundays. At the time, she was delving into the occult and invited Smallwood along to some spiritualist meetings. When Coaker, himself an avowed spiritualist, passed through London in the spring on his way home from visiting fish importers in the Mediterranean, Smallwood brought them together, and the two hit it off. Lena then paved the way for a meeting in St. John's between the two former allies, and Coaker came around to join forces with Richard Squires again.

It seemed clear to all of them that if Richard were to lead the Liberals, Hickman had to leave the stage. Back in Newfoundland, Coaker and Smallwood conferred, and Smallwood went to see Hickman at his house on Circular Road. He told him that when the Liberals came to power, they were prepared to give him a seat as government leader in the Legislative Council and get him a knighthood. Hickman stiffly replied that he had no interest in a seat in the upper house, nor any interest in becoming Sir Albert. Smallwood asked what it would take for him to step aside as leader: Would he consider something else? "I want my money back," said Hickman. "I put $23,000 into the party's campaign fund last election, and I'm not going out until I get it back."

Smallwood reported this to Coaker. They had a good chuckle and agreed it wouldn't be a problem to get Hickman out of the way when the time came. Richard, too, laughed when he heard about it, adding:

> You know, Smallwood, Albert Hickman is no politician. He just hasn't got the qualities to make a politician. For one thing, he's totally lacking in any kind of imagination except for business. In here at Midstream, I have some beautiful trees growing, and it's a joy for me to stroll around among them. But if Albert Hickman saw them, he'd be wondering how much lumber he could saw out of them.

In September 1927, after a long, wearisome session of the legislature, navigated without the help of Morine (who was sidelined by illness), Walter Monroe was coming to the end of his rope. As far as his future was concerned, "the rumour factory was working at capacity, or over," said the *Daily News*. The paper rang him up to see what he had to say about his future in politics and found that it was not his intention to lead the Liberal-Conservative Party in the 1928 session of the legislature. The paper commented that although Monroe had borne the responsibility of leadership with dignity and fidelity, "he neither knows, nor desires to know, anything about the mysteries and miseries of political wire pulling." For a man leading a government with a majority of one, this was a serious deficit.

On January 3, 1928, Governor Allardyce sent his quarterly report to the Dominions Office in London. The political situation in Newfoundland, he said, was "kaleidoscopic," and Squires was very much back in the game:

> For several years past Sir Richard Squires has been carrying on an insidious and cleverly organized campaign in the outports, and it is admitted on all sides that he has a very large following. As to whether he would be acceptable as Prime Minister, or, as to whether, if, returned, he would be physically capable of carrying on the duties of the post, the future alone can decide.

In February, Monroe made it official that he would not stand as a candidate in the next election. Once again, the pieces were falling into place for Richard Squires.

CHAPTER TWELVE

Back into the Fray
1928

I n the spring of 1928, Governor Allardyce quietly finished his
term of office and retired to England, no doubt with a sigh of
relief at leaving behind the "kaleidoscopic" jumble that was
politics in Newfoundland. The country was between governors
on May 2, when His Excellency the Administrator, Chief Justice
Sir William Horwood, arrived at the Colonial Building at 3:00
p.m. to open the fifth and final legislative session of Walter
Monroe's government. He inspected an honour guard of the
Constabulary and the CLB, whose band rendered the national
anthem, then proceeded inside to the chambers of the Legislative
Council. As protocol dictated, the Gentleman Usher of the Black
Rod was dispatched to the House of Assembly to summon the
MHAs to the upper house for the Speech from the Throne.

Afterwards, the members filed back into the House, where the
Speaker again read the Throne Speech, followed by the traditional
Address in Reply, delivered that day in fine florid style by W. J.
Browne, seconded by Thomas Power. An overflow crowd filled
the visitors' gallery, drawn not so much by this pro forma speech-
ifying as by the story in that morning's *Daily News* predicting an
imminent split in the ranks of the Opposition.

For once, Opposition Leader Albert Hickman did not disappoint. When his turn came to speak, with an uncharacteristic (and perhaps unintentional) touch of wit, he congratulated the prime minister and the government for having two such able men as Browne and Power propose and second the Address in Reply. "They have selected two of the most long-winded orators on that side of the House," he said, "and they have also selected a lawyer, as they know they wanted somebody to make a good case out of nothing—the Speech from the Throne." Hickman spent a few more minutes trashing the Throne Speech, then delivered his shocker, reading a letter to the Speaker of the House signed by nine members of the Opposition:

> We have the honour to inform you that we have organized a Liberal Legislative group for the more efficient conduct of public business at this session of the Legislature. We support the policy of Liberalism as distinct from Conservatism and propose to work for the liberal cause under the leadership of Sir Richard Squires. We have elected as House Leader for the coming session Mr. W. W. Halfyard, senior member of the Liberal group.

Hickman, appalled at what his own members were doing, went on to say that he would take no responsibility for any "utterances of theirs" and that he had no intention of giving up his position as Leader of the Opposition. It was a bold front, but Richard Squires, without a seat in the House, now had nine members lined up behind him, publicly declared, compared to Hickman's five. Whether he recouped his campaign money or not, Hickman's days as party leader were numbered.

So in May 1928, Richard was out in the open with a base of support in the legislature and ready for the coming election. He had little doubt that Coaker would be onside—six of Hickman's defectors were FPU members, faithful to the Union leader. The Squires campaign was already in action: the Newfoundland Liberal Association had been formed, and the weekly *Liberal*

Press—the party's propaganda organ—had begun publication. Big, bold headlines of Liberal hoopla and disparagement of the Monroe government were a highlight of every issue, always featuring a prominent photo of Sir Richard. In the House of Assembly, Halfyard was the elected leader, but Gordon Bradley took on the role of spokesman for the new Liberal group.

Behind the scenes, Coaker was using Lena's influence, bringing her squarely into the political manoeuvring. "We must be careful," he wrote her from Port Union on May 23, "and above all must secure some R.C. support." He enclosed a letter from veteran Union member W. H. Cave, who was critical of the way Richard was proceeding. "I don't think you better let Sir Richard see Cave's letter. I intend to trust you in such matters, and I feel sure it will be to the benefit of both. We must have Cave, and I leave it to you to plan a meeting between him and Sir Richard. You will know how to bring it about."

Coaker was right to be worried about Roman Catholic support. His own Protestant followers, and those who supported Squires (who was now grand master of the Orange Society for the second time) were limited in appealing to the Catholic districts in the south—"blacklisted" would not be too strong a term. They needed someone like Peter Cashin, a prominent Catholic and president of the affiliated Newfoundland Fishermen's Star of the Sea Association. Cashin, however, was playing it cool, even though Archbishop Roche, thinking Richard Squires would be the next prime minister, was encouraging him to join the Liberals to "look after Catholic interests."

The House of Assembly closed in June, with the election slated for October. In July, government MHAs were rattled when Monroe reiterated his intention to resign before the election, with no one lined up to take his place. W. J. Browne, one of Monroe's more diligent members, rounded up two others, Deputy Speaker John C. Puddester and Thomas Power, to talk about options for a new party leader. What about Fred Alderdice they wondered, Monroe's cousin and party leader in the Legislative Council.

Frederick Alderdice, 1871–1936

Unfortunately, he was not in the best of health. A sports injury had left him physically disabled, missing both feet and one leg; he now suffered from the after-effects of multiple surgeries, which he dulled with several shots of whiskey a day. Still, he had come to Newfoundland from Ireland as a youth and made a go of it in business. He had an air of courtliness about him and had earned a reputation as a man of integrity.

Browne decided to approach him. Alderdice was interested: "This country has been very good to me," he said, "and I am willing to undertake the leadership and to make some return for what I have received since I came here." Browne reported this to Monroe, who was lukewarm—not because he had no confidence in his cousin, but because he didn't want to see him saddled with the burden of the office. After some persuasion, however, he consented to having Alderdice form an interim government to take them up to the election.

In assembling his administration, Frederick Alderdice wanted Cashin—for his Catholic connections, the same reason Coaker and Squires wanted him. W. R. Howley, who had represented Squires at the Hollis Walker inquiry, was already onside with Alderdice, picked to be justice minister. Howley phoned Cashin to ask that he come to see Alderdice at his home on Rennies Mill Road. There, Cashin met Alderdice for the first time and learned he was organizing a new party to do good for the country. Cashin asked who would be in his cabinet. When Alderdice mentioned Monroe, Cashin said he could not be associated with Monroe, who had fired him out of his government.

"You cannot go with Squires," Howley interjected.

"Why?" asked Cashin.

"Because Squires is a crook," replied Howley.

"Well, you defended him, Mr. Howley."

"Yes, I defended him as I would any other crook who engaged me to defend him."

Cashin made no commitment, thanked Alderdice for his time, and left.

He then went to see Richard and agreed to run for the Liberals in the district of Ferryland on condition that he would have a seat in cabinet—the finance portfolio in particular, or so he bragged when reporting all this to Archbishop Roche. To his surprise he found that the mercurial Roche had changed his tune about having him join with Squires and was incensed at the news, practically throwing him out of the bishop's residence on Topsail Road. There would be no Catholic support for Cashin after all; indeed, in his district of Ferryland the Catholic voters would unite against him.

With a new leader in Alderdice and a new party name—the United Newfoundland Party (UNP)—the election campaign was truly underway. The UNP put out a manifesto promising no interference in the fish markets, a study of natural resources, removal of duties on imported fishing gear, encouragement of new industries, and the appointment of women to government boards (women twenty-five or older would vote for the first time in the coming general election). He would deliberately refrain, Alderdice said, from making promises that he couldn't fulfil. "In brief, if elected, my policy shall be a safe and sure administration of government affairs, with fair play to all and favour to none." Sensible enough, though not the stuff to stir souls.

Alderdice recycled the old slogan "Squires can't be trusted," hammering it home again and again in the *Daily News*, where his MHA John Puddester was business manager. And from a different quarter came a popular joke doing the rounds, about a Newfoundlander passing through American immigration in Boston:

"What's your name?" asked the customs officer.

"John Murphy," he said.

"Where are you from?"

"St. John's, Newfoundland."

"What state is that in?"

"Well," said Murphy, "it was in a hell of a state when I left—Sir Richard Squires was in power."

For his part, Richard used his *Liberal Press* to boast of giant rallies and flood tides of Liberal support sweeping the country. He continued to attack the UNP but offered no written manifesto. In a more imaginative move, he sent out copies of a phonograph record to be played in the outports—a stirring seven-and-a-half minute speech extolling the accomplishments of the Liberal Party under Whiteway, Bond, and himself, especially in industrial development, and promising more of the same:

> I *know* that within six months of my resumption of office I can secure industrial development representing an expenditure of not less than two and a half million dollars and more likely three million dollars within a period of two years. I *know* that within a year and a half I can secure an investment of a million and a half dollars for an entirely new industry. I *know* that I can breathe a breath of industrial life into the Gander territory and make it a hive of industry just as surely as the Humber lives and hums today.

The speech ended with an impassioned call to arms: "Hear, then, the call of Newfoundland! Rally to our banner of achievement! The banner of industrial development, the banner of health, education, prosperity, and progress!"

The staid and plodding style of Alderdice must have seemed all the more dim compared to Richard Squires—now forty-eight but sharp, invigorated, and offering better days ahead. He still possessed charm enough to dispel the disgrace of five years ago and there was a grudging admiration for him, for the way he kept his head up and faced down his detractors. Throughout the campaign he made a special appeal to women, a new voting base, with a playful gimmick: giving out large buttons that read "The lady on the other side is requested to vote for Squires for Premier," with a mirror on the flip side. (Smallwood would use the same stunt in his final election campaign in 1971: "Will the lady on the other side please vote Liberal.")

Richard waited until the last minute to choose his district. Smallwood had laid careful plans to run in Humber, where he spent two years building support for himself and Squires. The issue was that, loyalist though Smallwood was, Richard found the man irritating and full of endless chatter. One story goes that, losing patience with Smallwood on a drive to Midstream, Richard had his chauffeur stop the car and put him out on Waterford Bridge Road. Richard did not want him in the House of Assembly. So he wrote to Smallwood a few weeks before election day to say that he was going to run in Humber district himself, and wanted Smallwood as his campaign manager.

Smallwood was crushed. In one swoop all his work and preparation were for nought. He took a long walk out to Mount Moriah to cool off and collect his thoughts. When he came back, he telegraphed Richard: "Not for any other man would I do this but I will step aside and manage your campaign as well."

Richard went to the west coast in the closing days of the campaign for a whirlwind tour of the district, culminating with a rally at the Regent Theatre in Corner Brook on October 28, the eve of the election. When he and Smallwood arrived, they couldn't get through the crowd of people surrounding the building and had to squeeze in through a backstage window. Pushing their way to the front of the platform, Smallwood had to cup his hands around his mouth to make himself heard. "When I introduced Squires," he later wrote, "I had to squirm around behind him, and he squirmed to get in front of me—such was the jam of people. Though his voice was very good, Squires was dog-tired, bone-weary, and his mind befuddled from sheer exhaustion.

It didn't really matter, for it was not his speech but the sheer magic of his person that won the day."

Victory not only in Humber, but in twenty-eight of the forty districts around the country—a solid majority. His cohorts swept in with ease—Coaker in Bonavista East, Bradley in Trinity Centre, Alex Campbell back again in St. John's West, and Mosdell in Fortune Bay—each of them gaining a seat at the cabinet table. Peter Cashin had one of the toughest battles in Ferryland, where the Archbishop had turned the Catholic clergy against him. Even a trusted friend had jumped ship. "My God, Peter, I voted against you—the Monsignor, you know!" she told him on election day. It could be considered a miracle that Cashin got in at all, but he did (by less than a hundred votes) and went into the cabinet as minister of finance and customs. In other districts, Alderdice took St. John's East, but two of his kingmakers, Browne and Power, suffered defeat, as did Richard Cramm in Carbonear. John Puddester was re-elected and became the backbone of the Opposition. Hickman was not in the race, wisely deciding to ditch politics in favour of developing his business.

In 1919, Richard had come to office at the tail end of the prosperous war years only to face governing during the hard times of high unemployment that followed. Ironically, the fall of 1928 found him in similar circumstances. He was elected in a year of good economic prospects, the best since 1919. The cod fishery and seal fishery had recovered, the pulp and paper mills were busy, Bell Island was humming, and there was a new mining operation forging ahead in Buchans. The Newfoundlander "must be wretched of soul and perversely pessimistic who cannot feel a thread of hope that his island home is at last on the up-crest of a wave of development and industrial prosperity it has never before dreamed of," pronounced the *Daily News*.

People dared to hope it was the dawn of a new era.

CHAPTER THIRTEEN

The Last Phase: Part I
1928–1932

D espite the rosy outlook at election time, by the end of 1928 Newfoundland was edging ever closer to the brink of financial ruin. A decade of budget deficits, averaging $2 million annually, had driven the public debt past $86 million, most of it in the form of Newfoundland bonds held by British investors. About $33 million of the total had come from the railway, a black hole for government spending since its inception. The second largest chunk, about $16 million, represented Newfoundland's contribution to the Great War. The debt was so large that interest payments took up nearly half of expenditures every year— and the country was borrowing to pay the interest on money it already owed. This desperate situation rested on the collective shoulders of a population of 270,000 people, a third of them on public relief.

In reality, the question facing the new Squires administration was not whether the country would run out of credit, but just how long it would take. Yet, driven by the Squires election blarney and gusto for development ("I *know* that I can secure industrial development of not less than two and a half million dollars. I *know* that I can secure an investment of a million and a half dollars for an entirely new industry"), the government kept barrelling ahead. The reclusive Robert Bond had seen all the debt and political shenanigans in 1923 and knew what was coming, though he called it five years too soon: "My poor country! The last phase!" Bond had died in 1927, but now Coaker (and others) wondered aloud how any government made up of elected politicians could possibly rescue the country from its financial quagmire.

Thinking in the moment, however, Richard was still exulting in the comeback when he wrote in 1929:

> The facts are that in 1919 I carried the country and became Prime Minister on a vote of two to one. In 1923, at the next General Election I again carried the country, and was confirmed in my office of Prime Minister. In the following year I was overthrown as a result of nego-tiations which took place between a small section of my Party, which desired to get control, and the Opposition. My rivals in my own party and my political opponents realized that there was no possibility of defeating me in the country, and made an attempt to fasten upon me irregularities in connection with campaign funds. The charges laid against me were investigated by a Grand Jury, who, after hearing all the evidence, dismissed the charges, and, in accordance with our English practice, reported "No Bill." The time they took from the conclu-sion of the last item of evidence until they filed to the Court and reported was ten minutes.

> While I was then overthrown so far as public office was concerned, I retained my leadership of the Liberal Party, and when six months ago I led it to the Polls I secured a public victory far in excess of that obtained in 1923. This election of 1928 is consequently the third occasion on which the public has confirmed me as Prime Minister of Newfoundland.

Everything normal, the universe unfolding as it should, back in office, scandals gone.

Another change of office occurred in October 1928, when John Middleton stepped into the role of Governor of Newfoundland. A fifty-eight-year-old Scot, veteran of the British Foreign Service, and a former governor of Mauritius, the Falkland Islands, and Gambia, Middleton was unassuming but stern, possessing "moral excellence," according to the *Newfoundland Quarterly*. Some veteran observers no doubt expected a little enlightened guidance from him.

Enlightened guidance was not a description that fit with Richard Squires, however. "Too aggressive in politics," said W. J. Higgins. "When he started anything in politics he took a hatchet in each hand and chopped through: he ought to have a solid man to control him."

Coaker, as some may have hoped, would not provide that steadying influence as a member of cabinet—he was spending most of his time in Port Union and winters at a new $25,000 Jamaica estate. He was there for the winter of 1928, finding that it worked wonders for his bronchial trouble. His 1929 Christmas message in the *Fishermen's Advocate* showed a man turning sour on Newfoundland politics. He let loose a diatribe against the whole political machine where, regardless of party, service to country was a forgotten ideal. Instead, it was "self and self-interest that continually predominate." The bribing politician "is the most sought after and the most popular for a period" he said, and each new administration was "a little bit worse than its predecessor." He voiced his solution: government by a non-partisan elected commission.

From a high-profile public figure—and a cabinet minister at that—this was remarkable stuff. The cringing within the Liberal Party at his remarks was palpable—and from outside came a torrent of blowback against him and the government as a whole. Richard stayed out of it and, again remarkably, allowed Coaker to remain in the cabinet. But the Union leader's influence and credibility were flagging, and his final attempts to make changes in the fishery would be stymied. In 1930, as chairman of a salt fish commission, Coaker tried to establish new regulations on the culling and marketing of the catch (shades of 1921), but he lacked the support of the prime minister or the party. The regulations died with barely a whimper.

Peter Cashin, the third man in what the *Daily News* dubbed the "unholy alliance" of the election, was wary of Richard Squires's inclination toward shady practice. He was not long in the finance portfolio before discovering that during the election campaign Richard had promised the country's liquor business to the Bronfman family of Montreal in return for a $15,000 contribution. This put Cashin on alert but, a firebrand by nature himself, he was hardly the one to be the steady hand behind Squires. The same could be said of Alex Campbell, whose counsel Richard respected but whose political scruples were as shaky as his own.

But with the Bronfman liquor deal under wraps, Richard began this term as prime minister scandal-free. Inheriting the country's precarious finances amid strong demands for public relief, he carried out a thorough reorganization of government departments—though with no reduction in spending. On the revenue side, he made adjustments to the tariff system and brought back the income tax. On Campbell's advice, he struck an economic commission on unemployment and poor relief, chaired by W. F. Lloyd, that submitted thoughtful proposals on agricultural development and fish exporting and actually created some jobs in road building and lumbering. Given their previous shenanigans, Squires advocating income tax and Campbell pushing relief work caused more than a few smirks in St. John's. Irony aside, these initiatives were admirable—but they had little impact on the overall financial quandary.

It soon became obvious that the prime minister had no new investment lined up for Newfoundland, as promised in the election campaign. But once in office, he did energetically pursue new opportunities for industrial development. This justified extensive travel to the financial centres of New York and London, all on the government tab. In New York in February 1929, he and Lena took an apartment in the heart of Manhattan for the rest of the winter, where they kept up a "dizzying pace" of social engagements. His re-election earned him mention in the society pages of the *New York Times*, as did a reception in Lena's honour given by Mrs. Alton Brooks Parker, society matron and widow of a distinguished judge and former presidential candidate. (Lena in return hosted a luncheon for "the old guard of society" at the Ritz-Carlton.)

Lady Squires shopped and hobnobbed in New York until June, but Richard was back in St. John's for the opening of the House in April. He was still working diligently on industrial development, bragging that he was going to follow up the "Hum on the Humber" by putting the "Gang on the Gander" (and the "Rich in Richard," as they said in St. John's). The Gander prospect drew some interest from the Hearst publishing business in the United States, potentially working in collaboration with the Reids. Richard took Cashin and Coaker to meet with them in New York at the beginning of 1930. The Hearst interests struck an agreement with the Reids and travelled to St. John's that summer for further discussions with the government. Richard didn't like the terms offered, however, and didn't like the Hearst negotiators. The Reids, on the other hand, had suffered financially on the Humber development and were anxious to recoup their losses with a Gander deal—but the project fizzled out. The Reid Newfoundland Company went into receivership the following year.

Gander itself was not off the table for Richard, though, as several airlines were showing interest in Newfoundland as a re-fuelling stop for international airmail service. Richard envisioned a major airport for the area—a good idea, but unfortunately (for him) ahead of its time.

Then came the world-changing events of October 1929. Richard and Lena witnessed the beginning of it first-hand, as they sailed from England to New York on the Cunard liner RMS *Berengaria*. They boarded at Southampton on Saturday, October 19, and were first-class dinner guests of Captain Arthur Rostron for the duration of the voyage. Their table companions included the popular mayor of Wolverhampton, Sir Charles Mander, and his wife, Lady Mander; US diplomat and bon vivant Theodore Marburg and Mrs. Marburg; and American cotton broker Norrie Sellar with his manservant Stephen Cosham. Captain Rostron hosted them all at an ice-breaker reception in his private sitting room prior to Sunday's dinner. The conversation flowed freely, as Rostron's white-starched steward kept their glasses filled, and the lively banter carried on at the dinner table until the coffee and cognac arrived. Richard and Lena lived for occasions like this—high-society chit-chat with influential people. It was a treasured perk of the office of prime minister. The week progressed in the same style. After Tuesday's dinner, Richard stole away to the captain's quarters to lounge with the other men over port and cigars.

And so the crossing proceeded until Thursday, October 24, when word went around the ship that the bottom was dropping out of the stock market. It was the first day of price crashes on the New York Stock Exchange, which soon triggered more dark days of turmoil. The brokerage office (for first-class passengers) on the *Berengaria* was mobbed with panic selling. That night, their last at sea, the mood in the half-empty dining saloon was sombre. Seemingly oblivious to the market chaos, Lady Squires chatted away to a muted table about the heavy calendar of events awaiting her in New York, including opening night at the Metropolitan Opera. She and Richard were not invested in the market and were unaffected by the carnage, but every country in the Western World would soon be—and Newfoundland more than most.

After a few weeks socializing in New York, where the mood was darkened by events on Wall Street, Richard and Lena were ready to come home, just ahead of a Newfoundland disaster of a different sort. On Monday, November 18, a major earthquake under the North Atlantic sent a giant tidal wave into several outports on the Burin Peninsula, washing dozens of homes out to sea and leaving twenty-seven people dead. The tremors were felt in St. John's, but it wasn't until the following Thursday morning that word of the tragedy reached the prime minister's office. Richard responded quickly. By the end of the day, he had an emergency committee in place and a relief ship, the SS *Meigle*, loaded with supplies and a team of first responders, on its way to the stricken communities. It would be Christmas before the work of rebuilding was underway, supported by donations to a relief fund that brought in $182,000 in a few months, a testament to the charity of Newfoundlanders even in hard times.

Chaos in the financial world and disaster on the south coast hung over Newfoundland toward the end of 1929. But for Richard Squires, on the pig's back again after his re-election, things were looking up. Earlier in the year, he had rewarded himself with a new President Eight Studebaker limousine—the finest American automobile on the road—to replace his Pierce Arrow and Studebaker Light Six sedans. Then he bought another yacht. The *Medric*, a two-masted motor vessel, arrived in Bay Roberts from Boston in June. As Christmas approached, he was bringing the new Cherry Lodge at Midstream to completion to replace the house that had been destroyed by fire the year before.

Christmas was family time. In 1929, Robert and young Richard were both home, stories were shared, presents were exchanged, the two dogs—Humber, their treasured purebred Newfoundland, and a white terrier called Peter Pan—romped around the house. After uncertain academic beginnings in England, Robert was enrolled at Memorial University College, where his father found his record to be "quite excellent." Richard Jr. was at Dalhousie, also making high grades and well on the way to Honours degrees in both arts and the law. Rosemary, a sweet child just turned seven who would always be known as Baby, was thrilled at having the two older brothers around. She had just started school that fall—Rockford School at Gower Street United

Church, a little two-room set-up run by a Miss Phillips, educated at Cambridge and catering to young children of the upper class.

Elaine spent Christmas in London, treated with a generous gift of £60 from her father to spend on a vacation of her choosing. Norman, twelve, was also away, at Fernden boarding school in Surrey, where he was having his problems. He was the oldest boy in class but so poorly prepared that the school had him start over in every subject. He could not read fluently and showed a worrisome lack of concentration. Outside class though, Governess Hilda Brownrigg found him "a delightful boy to deal with, having a very happy nature, and always extremely kind and helpful to all the small boys." His father seemed to care little about that but was much concerned about his low level of achievement. "I am looking forward to excellent reports from you at Easter," he wrote. "Robert and Richard are both making good, and I want you to do better, as you are our youngest boy."

This was a time when, having helped Coaker in some backroom manoeuvring before the election, Lena was motivated to move from the sidelines of politics toward the action. Coaker's growing disenchantment with Richard Squires and his policies—and with party politics in general—must have concerned her, especially in light of his traitorous diatribe in the Christmas edition of the *Fishermen's Advocate*. There was danger of a fissure in the governing party between the Squires Liberals and Coaker's Unionists. Perhaps Lena saw the moment as a time for her to show support for Richard and help him to hold the party together. Adding an MHA salary to her income, if only $1,000, plus money for travel expenses, was also not to be overlooked. Whatever her motivation, there were three by-elections coming in the spring and Lena seized on the opportunity to jump in and run for office herself.

But first—another season of the social round in New York. Lena departed in January and Elaine joined her there in March, on her way home from London. The two appeared in the society pages thanks to a reception and dinner held in their honour. In the spring, there was a leap from the social page of the *New York Times* to the local page of the St. John's *Daily News* (albeit anonymously), with word that in the coming by-elections "a lady's name is mentioned in connection with Lewisporte." Richard had knocked aside the Liberal candidate in the district (which included Little Bay Islands) in favour of his wife. At first the move provoked backlash within the party, especially from Coaker's followers, and the idea was shelved. It surfaced again when the date for the by-election was set (May 17), and this time it stuck.

"A Woman in the Field," announced the *Daily News* on April 28, noting it was the first time for a woman running in a general election. The *News* couldn't resist reminding readers of Sir Richard's resistance to the Women's Franchise League in its early years. It gleefully pointed out that the movement also "met no stronger opposition than from the lady who is now exercising the privileges which they won for their sex."

Lena's opponent in the one-member riding was Arch Northcott, a businessman from Harbour Deep and a Beaumont-Hamel veteran. With only a few weeks to canvass the district, she travelled the coast with campaign manager Belle Strong, her brother Will's wife, along with her son Richard, who had come back from Dalhousie at the end of term and was getting a taste of politics on the ground. The two women were a sight, dashing from harbour to harbour in open boats, the candidate sporting the latest New York fashion. Lena met one-on-one with as many voters as she could, avoiding campaign meetings and speechmaking. Sir Richard took care of the oratory in Lewisporte on May 2, at a rally promising a large paper mill for Gander (he was very short on specifics) and a new road from Lewisporte to Boyd's Cove. Lena stayed away from the bluff and bluster. Her campaign message was simple, tasteful, and low-key: "Helena E. Squires, Liberal Candidate, Respectfully requests your Vote and Influence."

Putting herself forward as genuinely concerned and committed to the district, Lena pulled in eighty-one per cent of the vote—an overwhelming endorsement. From the time she was elected, she did show a sincere interest in the welfare of her constituents. Although quiet in the House, she always voted to represent the interests of the people who had put her there. But she did display some spirit on her very first day, when Opposition Leader Alderdice welcomed her with the remark, "I know she will take a large part in government affairs, but hope her actions will never be such as to cause us to name the government a petticoat government."

"Ladies are not wearing them now," came her cheeky reply.

With Lena's election, politics for the Strongs took on the look of a family affair. Lena's cousin Joseph A. Strong, merchant of Fogo, had also been elected a Liberal MHA in 1928. And earlier in the year, Richard had appointed his father-in-law, James Strong, to the Legislative Council, to restore his good name and offer some relief from his financial troubles.

Lena was able to parade her status as a parliamentarian at the 1930 Imperial Conference in London that fall. She and Richard departed New York on September 12 on the liner RMS *Olympic*, Richard having given the *New York Times* his usual sunny commentary on conditions in Newfoundland before departing. In London, their entourage included daughter Elaine, Louise Saunders, and Richard's private secretary, W. J. Carew, all of them booked into the Savoy. Rosemary had also come with them, to be enrolled at Battle Abbey, a prep school in Sussex.

How much impact the Newfoundland contingent had on the conference is hard to know, but Richard had a low profile to begin with. The group arrived at Victoria Station at the same time as James Scullin, popular Labour prime minister of Australia, who found a few thousand well-wishers on hand to greet him. Richard Squires, on the other hand, was spotted walking along the platform alone, unrecognized by the crowd. A tongue-in-cheek writer for the *New York Times* commented that he liked to avoid publicity.

For Lena, London this time far surpassed New York in its

offering of prestigious social events. From the beginning of October, when the conference opened, until the end of November, she was swamped with invitations for teas, luncheons, club events, at-homes, sightseeing outings, and fancy balls, cramming photographic sittings and dress fittings in between. She couldn't possibly attend everything, but some occasions were not to be missed, such as the charity dinner to meet Albert Einstein and George Bernard Shaw. At another affair, she somehow got hold of some frozen Newfoundland salmon for MP and future prime minister Neville Chamberlain. He wrote to thank her on behalf of his luncheon guests, who were, he said, "astonished at the freshness and quality of the fish." Altogether, Lady Helena Squires, MHA, accepted invitations to more than two dozen events over the two months—some attended with Richard, others with Elaine.

Back home post-conference, Lena enjoyed her foray into politics. She loved the work and, like Richard, dealt promptly and sincerely with requests from the less fortunate asking her for money, clothes, food, or jobs. Being an MHA added a new layer to her existing roles as mother, matron, horticulturalist of Midstream, and busy community volunteer. By 1931, she had her own motorcar for getting around. She prevailed upon William Seto Ping, a young Chinese immigrant hired as butler and chauffeur to Sir Richard, for driving lessons. Sharp as she was, Lena was not good behind the wheel. Ping, who went on to become a leader of the Chinese community in Newfoundland, had fond memories of his time at Midstream but often spoke of the nerve-wracking moments in the car giving driving lessons to Lady Squires.

At the Imperial Conference, Richard had been named privy councillor, a distinction according him the title of Right Honourable (not just Honourable) Sir Richard Squires. The favour gave cold comfort to the people of Newfoundland who, along with the rest of North America, were suffering through the unravelling of the economy that had begun with the run on the stock market a year earlier. The crash had wiped out North American investors large and small, taken millions of dollars out of the financial system, dampened industrial output and consumer demand, and put thousands of people out of work. In Newfoundland the aftershock played out on a smaller scale, but it was no less devastating—especially in St. John's, where businesses were laying people off or closing up entirely. The jobless struggled to survive on poor relief—rations of flour, fatback pork, beans, cornmeal, split peas, cocoa, molasses, and a few vegetables. In the outports, things were a little easier: most people owned their homes and had their fish, gardens, and livestock to help stave off the deprivation. But even so, some of the less fortunate were drifting in to St. John's and swelling the ranks of the unemployed.

On returning from London, Richard found a country slipping further into poverty and a government confused, disorganized, and demoralized. Cabinet ministers were out of alignment and had no plan for dealing with the unfolding crisis. The only way to fund relief for the jobless was to borrow. Finance Minister Cashin had managed to squeeze a short-term loan of $1 million out of the Bank of Montreal—but that would have to do until the spring, the time of the annual borrowing exercise to see the government through the next fiscal year.

Despite what he saw all around him, Richard had the happy talk cranked up to full throttle. There was "no real, universal depression," he proclaimed at a Board of Trade luncheon in January 1931. And certainly, for him, there wasn't. With all the family away at school, he and Lena moved into posh quarters at the Hotel for the winter, taking a fifth-floor corner suite overlooking the harbour. In January, they hosted a dinner for Newfoundlanders on the New Year's Honours list. In the first week of February, they threw a gala affair for government MHAs, executive council members and the senior bureaucracy (and their wives)—more than a hundred people dined on fillet of sole and roast turkey, followed by speeches and entertainment. No Depression here.

Just prior to these events, however, toward the end of 1930, Finance Minister Peter Cashin had heard of another unsettling episode involving money and the prime minister. The branch manager at the Bank of Montreal on Water Street had called him aside to ask if he knew anything about $20,000 withdrawn from the government account and transferred to the Bank of Commerce. Cashin did not, but on inquiring at the Department of Finance discovered that the transaction had been approved by an order-in-council. Looking into it further, Cashin found it in the minutes of an executive council meeting, all right, but no minister who had been there had any recollection of it. Cashin brought it up with the prime minister, who told him the money was earmarked for a roads project in Corner Brook and not to worry, it was under the control of the auditor general. How it got into the minutes was unexplained. Cashin later recalled how the episode nagged at him: "I could see now that I was on the road to future trouble."

In the spring of 1931, Cashin went to Montreal to see about Newfoundland's borrowing needs for the new fiscal year. He was full of Squires-like rosy talk about the country, where "employment is available for the people and the future looks good." Prime Minister Squires also took up the theme when the House opened in March—there was "some distress," he said, but "our people are not suffering as are many in other countries . . . We cannot think in terms of destitution." He then proceeded to cut public services and the salaries of civil servants and teachers— while cabinet ministers and MHAs carried on helping themselves to government contracts and other perks of office. Campbell and Mosdell were among them, as was Solicitor General Gordon Bradley, who was billing thousands in legal fees. Shopkeeper Jimmie Bindon (of Three Bees fame and now MHA for St. Mary's) was a major food supplier to government institutions, and Peter Cashin himself had a lucrative contract selling coal to the railway.

Cashin brought down his budget in April, projecting a deficit for 1930–31 approaching $4 million. The half-year interest payment on the public debt, due the end of June, amounted to $2.2 million. This, along with other funding demands, required new borrowing of $8 million. When the country went to the money market, where they had had no trouble selling bonds the year before, there were no takers. Newfoundland's credit had run out.

The news hit the country with a bang. What now? People lined up to take their money out of the Government Savings Bank, businesses were skittish about honouring government cheques. With the June 30 deadline staring them in the face, Cashin and Squires went back to the Bank of Montreal for the $2.2 million interest payment. They were turned down flat.

At this point, Richard decided to approach Canadian Prime Minister R. B. Bennett for help, and here he was successful. Bennett wrote to the Bank of Montreal: "It is the opinion of this Government that it would be very injurious to Canada if New-foundland should make default at this time, and therefore we would appreciate the banks taking such action as would make this event impossible." Four Canadian banks (including the Bank of Montreal) then formed a syndicate to underwrite the loan. In return, Newfoundland agreed to have a commissioner from Great Britain examine its books, make recommendations on balancing the budget, and draw up a plan for long-term financing.

While in Canada working out the details of this loan, Richard took time for a quick exchange of telegrams on domestic matters:

To Lady Squires, St. John's, June 12: RITZ CARLTON MONTREAL SATURDAY. ABUNDANT LOVE. ANDERSON.

From Lady Squires, June 14: SPENDING WEEK IN DISTRICT. GOING HOME FOR SUNDAY. WHEN WILL YOU BE RETURNING. WOULD LIKE TO JOIN YOU BADGER. ANTICIPATING SEVENTEENTH TO BE YOUR LUCKY DAY. MISS SAUNDERS WILL ALWAYS HAVE MY TELEGRAPHIC ADDRESS . . . MUCH LOVE AND ABUNDANT SUCCESS. HELENA.

Possibly a bit frazzled by the events of the day, Richard sent a message to Louise Saunders: WEDDING ANNIVERSARY SOMETIME JUNE. WIRE EXACT DATE.

To Lady Squires, June 17: ABUNDANT LOVE TO YOU AS WE STEP TOGETHER ON THE THRESHOLD OF ANOTHER YEAR ANDERSON

And the reply: TRUST YOU WILL CELEBRATE TODAY'S TWENTY-SIXTH ANNIVERSARY WITH LIGHT HEART ABUNDANT LOVE HELENA.

Turning again to affairs of state, Richard wanted to leave nothing to chance in finding a commissioner to investigate Newfoundland's finances. And so, he (with Lena) took another trip to England. Before they set sail, he sent his requirements to J. H. Thomas, Secretary of State for Dominion Affairs in London:

> I am anxious to secure a man of high financial standing and experience from England—a man who would not only be acceptable to the British Treasury but would be specifically approved of and formally recommended by them.
>
> Success depends in no small measure upon the personality of the man selected because it would be essential for him to be able to work in harmony with our Treasury Board, the Directors of the Newfoundland Savings Bank, our Ministerial Heads and the Deputy Ministers who are in reality the permanent Departmental Heads.

The man Thomas recommended was Sir Percy Thompson, Oxford graduate and deputy chairman of the Board of Inland Revenue, England's tax-gathering service. Exceptional credentials did not come cheap. Thompson asked for remuneration fifty per cent higher than his Inland Revenue salary, plus first-class travel to Newfoundland for himself, his wife, and two daughters. He also wanted John H. Penson, an up-and-comer in the British Treasury, hired as his assistant. It was all agreed to. In addition,

Richard engaged a long-time acquaintance, Robert J. Magor of Montreal, "an outstanding business executive," to oversee the reorganization of public utilities, including the railway, dry dock, and telegraph system.

Richard took his time returning to St. John's, however, where the budget cutbacks had people up in arms against him and the government. It was much more pleasant to be crossing the Atlantic with Lena as old hands and first-class celebrities, again on the *Berengaria*. And to spend September in New York and Montreal while the cabinet faced calls for the government's resignation or outright dismissal.

The absence of the prime minister at such a time was as astounding then as it seems now. Cashin and Mosdell had to go to New York to bring Richard up to date on the developing crisis. They also felt him out on the idea of erasing the public debt by selling Labrador. "Nothing doing," he replied. Then they brought Barnes and Coaker to the States, with an order-in-council authorizing the sale. Still Richard wouldn't budge.

So they went ahead without him.

The four ministers took a formal offer to Ottawa. Newfoundland would sell Labrador to Canada for $110 million, they proposed. According to Cashin, they found Prime Minister Bennett keenly interested. But the timing was wrong for Canada, which had big financial challenges of its own, and the offer was rejected.

Prime Minister Richard Squires finally showed up in St. John's in October, by now intensely unpopular. He was assailed by the press and the public with loud demands that he step aside. He had no intention of doing so, however, while he waited to hear the recommendations of Thompson, Penson, and Magor.

The three found much to comment on, but with very limited sources of revenue available, not much room to act. Thompson was aghast at the way the Treasury functioned—with no real system of control under Deputy Minister John Keating, who had been there for twenty-six years and was cozy with Peter Cashin.

Keating was quickly pensioned off and replaced by Penson, who brought to the position the required expertise, although, according to Cashin, a disturbing lack of personality. Penson took control of the Treasury with no qualms about acting on his own, without even speaking to the minister.

"You know, Mr. Keating," Cashin said to his departing deputy, "you would never be able to get along with these Englishmen, any more than I could."

With expert financial guidance behind it, the government went back to the banking syndicate for a further $2.2 million to pay interest coming due on December 31. Thompson and Magor travelled to Montreal to brief the banks and Penson followed in December. All three were optimistic that Newfoundland's finances were well on the way to turning the corner.

The banks, however, were not convinced. They refused to make the loan. Again Richard asked Bennett to intervene, and on December 29 a loan offer came with twenty-four hours to respond. The conditions were stringent, including a stern warning not to apply for any further credit. The agreement was made. Everyone breathed a little easier going into 1932.

A long-term financial solution was, in fact, beginning to look doable. The next hurdle would be another interest payment, due on June 30. But once that was met, the government had agreed with the banks to apply all revenue to debt service as a priority. The financial advisors expected that next year would bring a balanced budget, the Depression would be ending, and international lenders would again look at Newfoundland debt as a reasonable risk. For the government, there might just be some light at the end of the tunnel.

Or so they thought.

CHAPTER FOURTEEN

The Last Phase: Part II
1932

A t the beginning of 1932, Sir Richard and Lady Squires, shel-
tered in their winter quarters at the Newfoundland Hotel,
were again short of money and feeling the pressure. The ongoing
expansion at Midstream, now a forty-five-acre estate, was a heavy
burden on them, and Richard had added another yacht to the list
of luxuries to maintain. They had been investing large amounts
of money in the Strong business to keep it afloat—$70,000 when
all was said and done—tying up all their available capital. Will
Strong wrote in January asking for $100 to pay on an account
owing. Richard replied: "My wife at the moment has no personal
income to buy a toothbrush, and, as you know, I am at present
myself subject to very considerable financial strain."

His personal finances may have been strained, but Sir Richard had been dipping into government funds, over and above his
$7,500 salary and Lena's pay of $1,000 per session. Cashin knew
about it and, as far as he could see, it was at best unwarranted
and at worst plain and simple larceny.

Percy Thompson caught sight of it, too, in a December 29
minute of the executive council authorizing $15,000 in payments
for legal work on a $10 million lawsuit brought against the

government by the Reids. Included in the amount was a $5,000 payment to Richard Squires. When the *Daily News* reported it, Thompson expressed his displeasure to the prime minister in the restrained, respectful style of British diplomacy:

> In my view the payments which have already been made were at least irregular and I had hoped that on reflection you would have seen fit to arrange for the repayment to the Exchequer of the amount of which it has been deprived . . . I cannot help feeling that at the present juncture when the Government is being credited with initiating and pursuing a campaign of economy and financial reform, a payment of the nature in question made to the Head of the Government cannot but be regarded as highly undesirable.

Peter Cashin, also uneasy about the incident, would be far less restrained or respectful. In late January, John Penson walked into his office to say that he had paid $10,000 to Les Curtis, Squires's law partner, based on an order-in-council. Cashin knew of no such order and concluded that Curtis was getting the money as a front for Richard Squires. That was it, for Cashin. On February 1, he wrote out his resignation, went around and thanked his staff, and cleared out his office. He said nothing publicly, which set the rumour mill going at a fever pitch.

When the House opened on February 4, Cashin stood up to explain: "During the last two months, deliberate falsification of the Minutes of Council has taken place, giving individuals large sums of money, without the direct or indirect knowledge of the members of the Executive Government." Furthermore, he said, a certain government member, despite supporting the income tax legislation, "persistently and brazenly violated the same law by refusing to conform with the regulations and still persists in not making his legitimate returns." There was more to come, he told the House, and he would deal with it later in the session.

Opposition Leader Alderdice rose to say that if he was a member of the government and heard charges like those made by the Honourable Member, he would not wait until later in the session but, "as an innocent man, would be on his feet now to vindicate himself against the charges made." No one on the government benches stirred.

This was all taking place during a bone-chilling winter of unrelenting hardship, with as many as 70,000 Newfoundlanders on relief. There were families in St. John's on the edge of starvation. In early January, Mayor Charles Howlett had walked around the city to see for himself what conditions were like. He went on VOWR to speak about it, pleading for financial assistance for the people he had come across—people like John, a widower of three years. His wife had died of malnutrition and John was trying to look after six young children. Howlett described a scene straight out of Charles Dickens:

> A decent sober labourer, never steadily employed. All the family living in one room of the house, with a table, two chairs, a broken box and a stove lashed together with wire. The melting snow dripping through the roof, rags stuffed in the window to replace two missing panes of glass. Two hollow-eyed, emaciated girls sat on a propped-up couch in torn cotton dresses, the oldest trying to wash a toddler. Two little boys hugged each other for warmth in a tumble-down cot in the corner. They have been without coal or wood for two days, and for food had only a few crusts of bread left by a neighbour. A few more days and a cemetery will solve the problem for one or two of these kids.

There were people like this all over the city, he said, suffering more this winter by the actions of Robert Magor, Richard's "outstanding" businessman friend from Montreal, who had cut dole payments from $1.80 to $1.50 a month with strict rationing. Not only was there not enough to eat, but some of that was barely palatable. The last thing people wanted to hear about with this kind of privation all around them was more tomfoolery at the

House of Assembly. As Sir Percy said, the spectre of well-paid
politicians grabbing extra dollars with thousands going hungry
was "highly undesirable."

More than that, it was highly inflammatory. In January, men
began gathering on street corners here and there—nothing organized, just people talking. Then a citizens' committee emerged,
chaired by James McGrath, an experienced union man who
pleaded with Squires and Magor for higher dole orders so the
poor could buy the food they needed. He got nowhere. A few days
after Cashin's speech in the House, McGrath's committee called
a public meeting, and the crowd sent them on to see Governor
Middleton. He said there was nothing he could do.

Public agitation grew. On February 11, five hundred men and
women gathered outside a dole office in the city's east end, then
marched to the prime minister's office on the ground floor of the
courthouse. The citizen's committee went in to find Richard
Squires at an executive council meeting and refusing to meet them.
So the committee wrote a letter telling him that the people outside
were restless and that committee members could take no responsibility for what might happen if he continued to ignore them.

The crowd dispersed but after lunch strode up Water Street
again, the marchers determined to make their case. The prime
minister was still unavailable, this time in the middle of a party
meeting. Richard kept them waiting for an hour, huddled together
outside, stamping their feet to keep warm, their tempers rising.
Then someone gained entrance to the courthouse through an emergency door at the side and in they all went. Committee members
and a few policemen tried to hold them back, but they smashed
their way through the glass doors of the executive council
chambers, which also served as the prime minister's office. Some
men jumped on the table, sending ink wells and papers flying. As
party members ducked out, the mob confronted Richard, who
took a sharp blow to the jaw. Someone took a picture off the wall
and broke it over his head; the glass cut his hand. Others threatened to tear him to pieces if he didn't increase the dole.

The government news bulletin about the affair said that Richard Squires stood his ground and told the men they could tear him up if they wanted, but there was no way he would consider any changes to the dole under threat of violence. If they were starving it was their own fault, as they were refusing food supplies freely available to them.

There were too few policemen at the courthouse that day to maintain order or make arrests. Superintendent of Constabulary Patrick O'Neill arrived to find Richard in his office, his hand bandaged, blood on his clothes, cornered by men shouting and screaming. O'Neill knew one of the leaders and together they were able to calm the mob and clear them out of the building. After everything quieted down, Richard handed out more dole orders and agreed to an increase in relief payments. He left the premises with his head high—but despite his initial bravado, he had shown that, in fact, he was willing to bend to demands in the face of a display of force.

In the coming days, gangs of unemployed men continued to show up outside the courthouse. They were there again on February 13 and, as Richard was coming down the outside stairs, one of them walked up to him and grabbed the pipe from his mouth. Richard passed on as the man put the pipe in his own mouth and puffed away.

The events of early February put many people on edge—businessmen especially, who had no confidence in the Constabulary to handle the kind of disorder displayed at the courthouse. Storeowners bought extra insurance against damage from rioting. Governor Middleton shared their concern. The previous summer, he had encouraged the inspector general of the Constabulary, Charles Hutchings, to prepare for lawless outbreaks over the winter. He even sent him detailed instructions from the Dominions Office on how to handle public disturbances. Hutchings sent it back, assuring Middleton that he had everything under control. Middleton doubted that, as Hutchings had no police experience— he'd never served in the ranks but had been appointed to the position of inspector general as a lawyer from the Justice Department. "He appeared to remain under a grave misapprehension as to his responsibilities and powers," Middleton reported to London, adding that there were only fifty-five Constabulary members in all of St. John's.

On February 16, a crowd gathered again, this time at the Colonial Building, for the reopening of the House of Assembly, where Cashin was expected to tell all. People filled the visitors' gallery but listened quietly as Cashin spoke. He had plenty to say. He described the details of a financial shell game in which Richard Squires secretly moved some $50,000 of public money around different bank accounts, having it end up in constituency accounts under his control. He told of the prime minister making up false minutes of executive council meetings, one of which authorized payment of $15,000 in legal fees to himself and others (Brian Dunfield, Les Curtis, and Albert Walsh, Speaker of the House). He told of another falsely sanctioned payment to Richard Squires of $5,000 from the reparations account—the "spoils of war" that were earmarked for the benefit of veterans and widows.

There were other accusations, too—the collusion of Secretary of State Arthur Barnes in preparing the false minutes; income tax arrears and illicit earnings of Alex Campbell; a signature forged on a government cheque by the Liberal member for St. Barbe— but the weight of the blame was on Richard Squires.

When the House sat again two days later, Opposition Leader Alderdice presented Cashin's allegations as eleven specific charges and moved for an investigation by a select committee of the House. Richard tried to muddy the waters with arguments that the motion should provide for separate investigation of the individuals involved. He also came at it on another tack: send the charges of falsifying the minutes of council for inquiry by the governor rather than members of the House. His motion, seconded by Barnes and passed by the Liberal majority, was to ask the governor to "enquire fully into the charges . . . and to inform the House as to whether or not Your Excellency was deceived or induced by such deception to sign the Minutes in question."

This caused a pause in the action. While the governor made his inquiry, Richard, briefly taking Cashin's place as finance minister, brought in the budget for 1932–33. It had been crafted by Thompson and Penson, with the strict directives from the banks hanging over them. The budget was tax and slash all the way: income tax went up, along with the sales tax on imports. Even though many people were close to starvation, the budget slapped extra duties on basic foodstuffs such as flour, butter, eggs, and tea. There were further cuts to civil service salaries, including twenty-five per cent for cabinet ministers. The pensions of war veterans and their widows and orphans were reduced, though the outcry against this measure was so strong it was later rescinded.

To oversee all the changes, Richard proposed to appoint a shopkeeper and all-round congenial fellow, Jimmie Bindon, as minister of finance. Not surprisingly, this alarmed Percy Thompson. "Mr. Bindon, for whom personally Mr. Penson and I have the greatest respect, is not competent to undertake the post of Finance Minister," he told Richard. "Mr. Bindon should definitely be precluded from interfering in any way with the conduct of financial business." Richard made him finance minister anyway.

The budget was heartless, perhaps necessarily so, and Richard lost three party members because of it, including Minister without Portfolio Harris Mosdell. They all crossed the floor to sit as independents. Nonetheless, Richard still had the numbers to push the budget through the House on March 22. That same day Middleton presented his report on the falsification of executive council minutes. It was not so much the conclusions of an inquiry (he had held no hearings nor called any witnesses) as a dry discourse on the constitutional basis of the executive council and its relation to the Assembly, along with a detailed description of how the minutes of the meetings were recorded and confirmed. Middleton described how the official minutes came to him for approval within a few days of each meeting. The minutes were read again at the beginning of the next meeting, which he invariably followed on his copy. There was no variance in the two versions for the time period covered in Cashin's charges. "I have the honour to inform you," Middleton concluded, "that there has not been any falsification of the said Minutes and that I have not been deceived or induced by deception to sign the said Minutes."

The answer to any question can depend on how the question is framed. In this case, to the benefit of Richard Squires, the governor's report neatly skirted the relevant issue. Cashin had charged that the minutes did not reflect what happened in cabinet meetings—not that they were changed after the governor had approved them. The fact that Middleton, in his pedantic way, found the official minutes to be the same from one meeting to the next might have been reassuring, but it was irrelevant. In any event, Richard came out of the governor's inquiry untainted, as far as the record showed. How many believed there was no wrongdoing was another matter. At least one Liberal cabinet minister, P. J. Lewis, did not. He became the fifth party member to jump ship.

The public was outraged at Middleton's report. The scheming, smooth-talking Richard Squires was off the hook again! Another citizens' group called an open meeting in the Majestic Theatre on April 4, to determine if Cashin's charges could be dealt with properly. About two thousand people showed up for this one, with thousands more listening on the radio at home or over loudspeakers at the LSPU Hall. They resolved to make an orderly procession to the Colonial Building the next day to present a petition for the House to investigate Cashin's charges without delay. As they reassembled at lunchtime on a chilly, misty April 5, one of their leaders, lawyer Harry Winter, took the microphone to remind them that this was to be a peaceful and law-abiding demonstration. At two o'clock they set out on a winding route to get to Military Road, marching behind the Guards band and a colour party of veterans carrying the Union Jack. Downtown businesses gave their staff the day off and more protesters—men, women, and a few children—joined the parade from the sidelines, swelling the ranks to thirty-five hundred.

The day of the riot, April 5, 1932

The grounds of Colonial Building were already packed with spectators anxious to see the outcome of the citizens' group's petition. The arriving parade brought the size of the crowd to an estimated ten thousand people. There was a heavy police presence—heavy for St. John's—between forty-five and fifty constables plus four mounted policemen under the command of Hutchings and O'Neill. The delegation from the Majestic meeting, including Harry Winter and Rev. W. E. Godfrey of St. Thomas' Anglican Church, waited for half an hour while the public galleries inside filled up. Then they were taken in past the tightly guarded entrance, the doors barred shut behind them, and onto the floor of the House with their petition. There was a long delay while the honourable members debated how to handle the matter, the muttering and shuffling of the crowd outside growing louder all the while. The delegation waited uneasily, then took their leave, still with no decision on the petition. When a disturbance arose in the gallery shortly after, the Speaker adjourned the proceedings.

The disturbance in the gallery was nothing compared to what was brewing outside. While the committee was in the House, a few minor skirmishes had occurred with the mounted policemen, one of whom had his cape torn off. The agitation was quashed when the band struck up the national anthem, which brought the men in the crowd to attention with heads bared. After the delegation emerged to report no action on the part of the government, Winter asked the protesters to go back to the Majestic for a full account of the Assembly proceedings. A large section of the crowd fell in behind the band as it moved off, but some stayed put on the steps of the building. Egged on by a few ruffians, they tried to push their way through the bolted doors, which were reinforced by a phalanx of policemen inside the building. Eventually they smashed through a panel of the door, and the police used the opening to wield their batons on anyone who came near. O'Neill went out to try to calm the crowd. The mob, infuriated by the police clubbing, piled onto the doors. At this, the bolts were drawn, and on Hutchings's orders, the force rushed out, swinging their batons left and right, striking protesters and spectators alike. Several people had to be taken across the road to O'Mara's Drug Store for treatment of head injuries, among them a ten-year-old child.

The ill-conceived police sortie sparked further uproar among the crowd still on the Colonial Building grounds. Some men ripped palings off a fence and rushed a different entrance on the ground floor. A gang of youths pelted the building with rocks and bricks, breaking windows and splintering sashes. The mounted policemen tried to break up the crowd by riding round and round the building at full gallop. They were knocked off their horses and attacked with stones and palings, sending two to the hospital and the other two scrambling back to police headquarters. Soon after, the mob broke into the ground floor of the building, gaining access to the small apartment of Miss Ella Morris, the House librarian, and the quarters occupied by the caretaker Ryall's family. Their rooms were ransacked, furniture demolished, books and papers strewn outside. Some young people lugged Ella Morris's piano into Bannerman Park, where a crowd of boys and girls gathered round singing "We Won't Go Home until Morning" and "The Gang's All Here." When they tired of that, they trashed the piano and took pieces as souvenirs.

And so the afternoon wore on. Most of the MHAs were allowed to leave the building, but the crowd demanded Richard Squires's resignation and, after the violent attacks by the police, also Inspector General Hutchings's. Richard took refuge in the Speaker's room adjacent to the Assembly, along with Hutchings, newly minted Finance Minister Jimmie Bindon, Lena, and, by his own account, J. R. Smallwood. The windows were heavily draped, blunting the force of the rocks and bricks coming through. Hutchings, who carried a cane, used it to part the drapes gingerly from time to time to see what was going on outside.

Cashin and Coaker came in at one point, spoke to Richard, and got his promise to resign. Cashin went outside and announced this to the mob, then he and Coaker left to speak to the governor about the resignation. Coaker proposed the formation of a national government with Alderdice as premier. There was no word from Hutchings, though he ordered the police to put away their batons. Still the crowd hung around.

Just after dark, at around seven o'clock, Reverend Godfrey called for some volunteers to come inside for a special mission. L. E. Emerson, a member of the Opposition, felt some responsibility for the rioting and wanted to get the prime minister to safety. He knocked on the door of the Speaker's room. Smallwood related what happened next.

"Are you there, Sir Richard? Are you there?" he asked. "We have come to escort you out."

No response.

"We're afraid they may set fire to the building—you'd better let us take you out."

It was Lena Squires who answered. "You should have thought of that when you people got up this parade."

"My God, are you there too, Lady Squires? You'll simply have to come out with us."

"I'll never leave," she snapped.

Lena had been nicked by a flying object and Smallwood whispered to her husband that he should make her go, which he did. She made her escape with her face bandaged. Then the volunteers came back for Richard. He removed his glasses, someone gave him a cap to pull down low over his head, and he went out, surrounded by Godfrey's helpers. They got him through the front door, down the steps toward Bannerman Road, and almost to a waiting car. Without his glasses, however, Richard was nearly blind and he tripped over some fallen fencing. Someone spotted him and the cry went up.

"Squires is here! Drown the bastard! Throw him in the harbour!"

"Don't do that," a woman shouted; "he'll pollute the waters. Take him outside the Narrows."

The crowd jostled Richard about for an hour as his phalanx tried to make it through the gate to Military Road. Superintendent O'Neill and several clergymen, along with familiar St. John's street character "Tommy Toe," did their best to protect him, all the time appealing for order. Finally they were able to gain passage down Colonial Street, across from the legislature. On passing number 66, a man beckoned: "Come in here, Sir Richard." Richard ducked in, leaving the crowd waiting at the front of the house while one of the clergymen escorted him through the backyard to a house on Bannerman Street. There, taximan Ernest G. Reid was waiting to ferry him away into the night.

Nettie White, one of the servant girls staying with Richard and Lena at the Newfoundland Hotel, recalled the night of the riot:

> I wouldn't [wasn't] up there that night—I was home
> I know, I wouldn't out anywhere. They had like a riot
> up there and they were all after Sir Richard. My dear, he

came home and the policeman with him—coming down the lane the crowds tore his coat. He came with his coat all torn up where they got hold of him.

Smallwood and Bindon slipped out through a broken window shortly after Richard left. Hutchings changed clothes and was able to make it home, reportedly in a state of collapse. A police guard was stationed at his house. Downtown, the looting had started. Ex-servicemen were pressed into duty for overnight patrols, but roaming vandals broke into two liquor stores and smashed in the display windows of several shops along New Gower Street. Just before midnight, the last of the police left the Colonial Building, and quiet returned to a badly scarred seat of government.

The next day, the country was horrified at the spectacle of the legislature's broken windows and by all that had transpired. The events of April 5 left a terrible blot on Newfoundland, a place not given to such outbursts of violence.

Bad as the riot was, some press reports made it worse. Richard and Lena's friends in New York opened the *Times* of April 6 to the headline "NEWFOUNDLAND MOB WRECKS ASSEMBLY, FORCES PREMIER OUT." The story that followed began:

Following a turbulent day in which an infuriated mob of 10,000 persons besieged and wrecked the Newfoundland legislative building and completely demoralized the police and other civil forces, Sir Richard Squires, Prime Minister of Britain's oldest colony, was beaten and trampled on this evening until he promised to resign.

The St. John's papers were a little more restrained (and accurate), but the image of "a seething mob of ten thousand people massed outside the legislature" became part of history, lingering like a bad hangover.

A few weeks after the event, thirty-eight members of the citizen's committee that had organized the march to Colonial Building went on the record to tell how the riot unfolded:

The outbreak that occurred, the destruction of property

and the other acts of lawlessness that followed during that night and the next day, were all the work of a very small and irresponsible number, most of them youths and boys. Very few of them were in the actual procession; the rest had assembled before it arrived, and thus were enabled, when the agitation began, to force their way up the steps of the House in front of the genuine petitioners. Irritated by an unfortunate delay on the part of the House in admitting the deputation and in receiving and debating the petition, this small and lawless element became restive and noisy. In the extremely difficult circumstances the police, in their endeavour to preserve order, angered them further, and in a few minutes they resorted to violence, with the result that everyone now knows.

Some said that the business elite had aroused the protesters in order to get rid of Richard Squires. Peter Cashin laid blame on Opposition member John C. Puddester—who had been unrelenting in his attacks on the government—saying he had spotted a few of his tough operatives "rummed up" at the forefront of the violence. Harry Winter implicated Richard himself:

> Certain well-known and disreputable heelers of his party were recognized in the crowd gathered on the steps: all they needed to do was to simulate sympathy with his antagonists, particularly the war veterans, and egg them on in every way possible. Many of the windows of the House were broken by youths and boys carrying stones in sacks for that very purpose, and there was little difficulty later in tracing back that particular vandalism to Squires and his henchmen.

Why would Richard Squires go to such improbable lengths to intensify an uprising against himself? In a desperate attempt to gain favour with the public by painting himself as a martyr, said Winter. The way things were going, he had few other choices and little to lose. He added:

The simple truth, and the most charitable interpretation of his behaviour from the beginning of that parliamentary session, is that he was quite unbalanced and hardly to be held responsible. Possessed as he was by an insatiable love of power for its own sake and frustrated by the rapidly diminishing means of exercising it, he was driven to desperation. If I were alone in that opinion, I should not think of expressing it, but I am not.

The consensus was that the flashpoint for the rioting started with a small group of undesirables—allegiance undetermined—who were there for that very purpose.

The morning after the riot, Richard was out and about, all cleaned up and ready for business. As usual he stopped first at his law office in the Bank of Nova Scotia, then had his chauffeur, Tom Crossman, drop him at the prime minister's office in the courthouse and wait for him at the curb. Still full of himself, Richard showed his bruises from the night before to the staff and declared, "I'll be damned if I resign." By the time he left, a few hundred people had gathered around his car. He walked right through the crowd, smiling left and right, and no one laid a hand on him. That evening he was spotted at the Colonial Building, leaving his car to run up the steps and in the front door, appearing little the worse for wear. Unbalanced? Maybe. But beaten? Never.

In the aftermath, the organizers of the rally sent a deputation to Governor Middleton demanding that the prime minister resign or be dismissed. "It's the resignation of Squires or bloodshed," Harry Winter warned him. Middleton countered that the resignation of Richard Squires was a matter to be left to him to decide, but any criminal act of his would be punished according to the law.

A few more uneasy days passed with an occasional break-in, usually for liquor. Middleton did not ask Richard to resign but did move ahead with enlarging the Constabulary, proposing an additional one hundred constables and seven more mounted policemen. Richard agreed and brought the proposal to an executive council meeting. Thompson and Penson were opposed (because of the cost) but the proposal passed. Uniforms were made up in a hurry, and a larger Constabulary, supported by close to a thousand war veterans ("special constables"), saw order restored in the city. Middleton also requested a visit by the British warship HMS *Dragon*, whose appearance coming through the Narrows on April 12 had a calming effect.

Repairs to the Colonial Building took two weeks (and $10,000). The House reopened for business on April 19. There had been no indication that Richard Squires was about to resign, but the Liberal caucus voted for an election—and soon. Upon opening, the House struck a select committee to deal with the citizens' petition. Richard announced the raising of $1.5 million toward the debt payment due in June, from Imperial Oil Ltd. In return, they wanted a fifteen-year monopoly on the sale of petroleum products in Newfoundland. He also made much talk about a scheme to build a paper mill in St. George's Bay. That slipped to the side, as did any action on the citizens' petition of April 5, when the legislative session ended on April 30. The election was set for June 11.

This time, Richard went into the campaign with a losing hand. If he had been hoping for a sympathy vote after the rioting, there was none. His support was at rock bottom. Members of his party continued to creep away, with more defections and retirements. Five MHAs had already deserted; in May they were followed by Barnes, Halfyard, and Hibbs, sliding into well-paying government jobs. Coaker announced he was leaving politics and would run only on a policy of government by commission, if his health allowed.

Richard published a fourteen-page manifesto pushing his government's achievement of financial stability (at least in the form of no default on the debt), the civil service reorganization and, of course, industrial development. He blamed the "insidious Tory foe" for creating havoc at home and discrediting the country's "strong financial position" with international money markets. He said he would repay the country's debt and produce a balanced budget. He promised schemes of development just waiting to be deployed, on hold only because of the Depression. Given the circumstances, it all amounted to empty twaddle and the people knew it.

Alderdice promised an inquiry to look into the idea of governance by commission but said that, if elected, his government would take no final decision without first going to the people. As far as the election was concerned, it really made little difference what Alderdice said or didn't say. The voters had simply had it with Richard Squires. Alderdice's United Newfoundland Party won by a landslide: twenty-four seats to the Liberals' two— Gordon Bradley in Humber and Roland Starkes in Green Bay. Mosdell went in as an independent, unopposed.

Among those joining Richard on the road to defeat were J. R. Smallwood, whose timing for his first election attempt proved impeccably bad, and old cronies Richard Cramm and Alex Campbell. Lady Squires saw the end of a brief parliamentary career, though she came respectably close to keeping her seat. Sharing the victory with Alderdice were Harry Winter and his brother Alex, and the persistent W. J. Browne, back for another swing at it.

Popular GWVA organizer Harold Mitchell ran against Richard in Trinity South, part of his old district, where he had connections going back to his early days in politics. In New Perlican, home of the Squires's housekeeper, Hannah Parrott Smith, one family kept a bedroom dedicated solely for the use of Sir Richard, a modest version of the royal suite at Government House. District headquarters for the election was the Fishermen's Hall in Heart's Content, which had a large chalkboard set up on the front of the building to record the returns. Richard was there for the final count on June 13: Mitchell 2,365, Squires 1,686.

Richard Squires was ungracious in defeat. When the final figures were posted, he emerged from the hall and climbed into his car. As chauffeur Tom Crossman slowly edged through the jeering crowd, Sir Richard turned around, thumbed his nose at them all, pulled down the blind, and drove away into his political twilight.

CHAPTER FIFTEEN

Citizen Squires
1932–1940

The new government took office on June 28. Frederick Alderdice assumed the dual roles of prime minister and minister of finance, with a cabinet that included John C. Puddester, Harry Winter, W. J. Browne, and Harold Mitchell—reputable men for the most part, facing an unenviable task. They inherited the same set of problems that had burdened Richard Squires, though without the accrued resentment that had dogged his administration. Thompson and Penson, working in the background during the tumult of 1932, found funds to go with the $1.5 million Richard had obtained from Imperial Oil and met the debt payment on July 1. But the country's books were still way out of balance as the Depression ground on. The revenue was simply not there to cover demands on government services, including the cost of poor relief.

Prime Minister Alderdice reneged on his pre-election promises to examine the idea of government by commission and to investigate the charges against Squires and Barnes. Instead, he focussed on the country's financial dilemma. In July he imposed further cuts on the public service, followed by another round in September, resulting in savings of nearly $600,000. He also tightened the dole regulations to clamp down on abuse.

Public discontent simmered on with scattered flare-ups, both in St. John's and outside the city, especially in Conception Bay North. On July 25, there was another day of rioting in St. John's, with businesses ransacked and eighteen men arrested. In September came more unrest, this time in Carbonear and Spaniard's Bay, where stores were looted and merchants beaten. The number of arrests outstripped the capacity of the penitentiary; the government refitted one of its coastal boats, the SS *Meigle*, as a prison ship, anchored in St. John's harbour to handle the overflow.

Reducing spending as much as he dared, Alderdice still could see no way to meet the debt payment at the end of the year. He reasoned that the only option was to default on the full payment, to go to the holders of the country's debt and tell them, as he put it, "We have done our best, but unfortunately our best is not good enough, and we must ask you to take what we have to give you." Accordingly, he drafted a notice to bondholders that Newfoundland would reduce interest payments to one-quarter of the normal rate for the next four years, offering an increased rate on a sliding scale after that, and notified the British government of his intentions.

"We are greatly disturbed by your telegram," came the response. "We cannot too strongly emphasize our view that the action proposed would be regarded as unacceptable by holders of debt in United States, Canada, and United Kingdom." No part of the Empire had failed to meet its obligations to external creditors, said London, and Britain wanted no default by Newfoundland. Nor did Canada, fearing repercussions on its own credit. So, in December, Canada and Britain advanced a joint loan of $1.25 million to Newfoundland, with the condition that Britain appoint a commission "to examine into the future of Newfoundland and in particular to report on the financial situation and prospects of the Dominion and what measures may be necessary to secure its financial stability." Alderdice accepted the terms.

The three-man commission—representing Britain, Canada,

and Newfoundland—began hearings in St. John's in March 1933. It was headed by Scottish lawyer W. W. MacKenzie (Baron Amulree), flanked by Canadian bankers C. A. Magrath and Sir William Stavert, an insolvency expert who was Newfoundland's nominee.

For his part, Sir Richard Squires lay low as these events unfolded. Shattered by his own defeat and the election results from around the country, he simply collapsed. "It was my mother who kept things together after that," Rosemary recalled. "My father never completely regained his health. He had lost everything—his health, his career, his money."

Still, Sir Richard did not, could not, disappear completely from sight. He remained Leader of the Liberal Party, what was left of it. In March 1933, when a by-election was called in the district of Port de Grave, he decided that the party should contest it. Loyalist Richard Cramm put his name forward and Squires went out with him on the campaign trail. Cramm lost, and Richard showing his face again aroused concern that he was not beyond attempting a comeback. But he was, for now at least.

After the by-election, he settled into a quiet routine with occasional attendance at his law office, which now had J. B. McEvoy and Louise Saunders added to the name, along with Les Curtis.

The Amulree commission held closed hearings in St. John's to examine Newfoundland's finances and just about every other aspect of its affairs, as it turned out. Though not much was made of it in the report, the commission did hear further evidence of the unbounded ingenuity of Richard Squires in squeezing money from the office of prime minister. D. R. Thistle, former accountant at the *Daily Star* appointed by Richard to the position of King's Printer, testified that the prime minister had demanded a kickback of ten per cent of his salary as payment for his largesse, a custom Thistle said was his "daily practice."

The Amulree report went to the British House of Commons on October 4, 1933. Six weeks later it reached St. John's—a sweeping analysis of the state of the country and a harsh indictment of its record of governance. "Politics," it said, "have come to be regarded as an unclean thing which no self-respecting man should touch; the very word 'politician' is virtually a term of abuse which carries with it a suggestion of crookedness and sharp practice." Moreover, and without naming names, it noted that "the spoils system has for years been in full force in Newfoundland," where it is considered "quite fair, whilst one's party is in power, to make what one can for oneself and one's friends."

As a cure for this "misgovernment" of the country, the commission recommended that "until such time as Newfoundland may become self-supporting again . . . full legislative and executive power be vested in the Governor acting on the advice of a specially created Commission of Government over which His Excellency would preside." The commission would have six members appointed by the Crown: three from Newfoundland and three from the United Kingdom.

Prime Minister Alderdice stood fully behind the Amulree report, abandoning his pledge to make no decision on government by commission without a plebiscite. He convened the House on November 27 and railroaded through the legislation enacting its recommendations in less than a week. Newfoundlanders' fatigue with politics was so deep that they accepted the loss of responsible government with barely a murmur.

One objection came from Coaker, voicing irritation over the notion of an appointed, rather than elected, commission. And from left field (in this case, Toronto), A. B. Morine wrote that, under the proposed Commission of Government, Newfoundland "would become, to all intents and purposes, as colonies were when they were mere appendages of the Kingdom, even worse than they were in the United States of America before the Revolution of 1776." And Richard Squires, perhaps out of patriotism, perhaps out of despair that the door to another comeback was quickly closing, roused himself to register his own disapproval. He made no public pronouncements, but quietly lobbied highly placed people of influence. On November 28, 1933, he presented his concerns in person to the new governor, Sir David Murray Anderson, a British admiral brought out of retirement to see the country through its time of transition. He also dispatched a lengthy cable to Secretary of State for the Dominions J. H. Thomas, requesting that Thomas share it with Foreign Secretary Sir John Simon, Prime Minister Ramsay MacDonald, and the private secretary to the King. His statement began:

> Permit us to record on behalf of Newfoundlanders both at home and throughout Empire against degradation of this country below that of any ordinary crown colony with introduction of principle obsolete in Empire for centuries of taxation without even minority representation of those taxed.

Richard objected to the speedy passage of the Amulree commission's recommendations through the House when not more than one per cent of the people had the opportunity to consider the report. He questioned the impartiality of the commissioners in seeking to gain popular support for their recommendations by holding out the prospect of increased public service salaries and war pensions and lower taxes. He predicted that when the people learn "they have been constitutionally betrayed by their elected representatives they will feel and express resentment as loyal and devoted subjects of the King should do when fundamental principles of British rule have been violated."

Thomas replied via Governor Anderson, telling Richard that "insofar as your criticism relates to the procedure adopted by the Government and Legislature in considering the Royal Commission's recommendations, the matter . . . is fully in accord with constitutional practice. I am also to inform you that His Majesty's Government in Great Britain wish to dissociate themselves entirely from your criticism of the impartiality of the Royal Commission." In desperation, Richard and Lena wrote to an aging Lord Beaverbrook, who replied with sympathy but no suggestion that he would take any action on their behalf. The empty responses to his pleadings made it painfully obvious that Sir Richard's political capital was severely depleted, at home and abroad.

And so, on the afternoon of February 16, 1934, in the ballroom of the Newfoundland Hotel, the country of Newfoundland relinquished responsible government in favour of government by commission. Frederick Alderdice, described by Governor Anderson as "thoroughly honest in matters of finance," was appointed as one of Newfoundland's three commissioners. The other two were senior cabinet minister John C. Puddester ("probably 75% honest and can be kept in check," said Anderson) and W. R. Howley, Richard's erstwhile defence counsel, the requisite Catholic appointee. Their British counterparts, already settled comfortably in private suites at the Hotel, were Sir John Hope Simpson (retired from the Indian civil service), E. N. R. Trentham (Sir Percy Thomson's successor as financial advisor to the Newfoundland government), and a sharp, fiercely opinionated, and impetuous former bureaucrat and businessman, Thomas Lodge, the odd man on deck.

From the very first days of the commission, the Englishmen took charge. They outdid the Newfoundland members in competence, experience, and diligence for the task, had personal connections with their overseers in London, and possessed the well-honed British disposition of superiority toward colonials. Generally speaking, the Newfoundland commissioners followed their direction, offering consultation and advice—which was sometimes taken, often not.

The new government went right to work with a fierce bureaucratic efficiency, reorganizing government departments, grouping them into more effective units, each under the direction of an individual commissioner. In their first year, they financed a land settlement program for St. John's men who had the gumption to go out of the city and reclaim land for farming in the Markland area near Whitbourne. They built cottage hospitals in major outports and founded the Newfoundland Rangers, a rural police force modelled on the Royal Canadian Mounted Police. While these efforts met with popular approval, their modus operandi—cloaked in bureaucratic secrecy with no accountability to an electorate—did not. Transparency was not in the commissioners' playbook; their speeches and communiqués were as much platitudinous pronouncements as factual reports.

The English commissioners wasted no energy trying to endear themselves to the St. John's elite or to marginalized former politicians, let alone the lesser folk. Thomas Lodge especially—arrogant, abrasive, and impatient for action—won few friends in the capital city. So, despite the public's initial acceptance, signs of opposition were not long coming, from people such as Peter Cashin and John T. Meaney (still the political hustler).

Richard Squires stayed out of sight, wintering in Jamaica with Lena during the time of transfer of power in February 1934. In March, Lady Hope Simpson, living in the former Squires suite at the Newfoundland Hotel, shared this gossip:

> Mrs. Lodge has just been in to tell us the latest news: the Squireses—the villain and villainess-in-chief of this place—are coming back from Jamaica, where they have been hatching plots, & will be coming to call on us. Mr. Lodge says he will not receive them. John says we will have to, as he, Sir Richard Squires, is a Privy Councillor, & we are official.

There was more: "I believe they are a very clever couple but horribly unscrupulous and have piled up enormous fortunes for themselves at the expense of their country. They attracted followers by paying them liberally out of public resources. He was nearly as possible pitched into the harbour during the riots." Not far from accurate—except for the "enormous fortunes." Richard and Lena were, in fact, by this time struggling to scrape by.

In May, their son Robert came home from Harvard Business School finding his father "a lot better than he was 6 months ago and should recover completely with luck." He was driving his car again, a good sign, and getting his yacht *Medric* in Harbour Grace ready for charter over the summer. His law practice was not doing well, however, and Richard was giving up his two rooms at the office. The working farm at Midstream did provide an income, albeit a small one. The same was true of the Squires's stake in the Strong business—a lot of money tied up with little or no return. Richard worried about being able to afford another college year for Norman in England. He was still sending money to Elaine while she looked for work in London. Robert left St. John's in June to join her, working off his passage in the ship's galley. They were both virtually penniless, depending on money from home, £10 here, £30 there, to keep them going. Robert was finally able to sign on as a low-paid clerk at the Pigs Marketing Board, but Elaine bounced around from job to job, including a role in a motion picture. She took heart from a fortune teller's prediction that she would be marrying a wealthy man within the year.

In St. John's, with some help from Rudolph Cochius, Lena was doing what she could with the landscaping at Midstream, setting the prettiest of flower beds and ornamental shrubs to border the driveway to Cherry Lodge. After breakfast in bed served by one of the housemaids, she spent hours at a time tending the flowers. Richard's trees—Lombardy poplar, linden, beech, maple, chestnut, sycamore, laburnum, hawthorn, pine, and cedar, now growing to maturity—added a majesty to the sweeping lawns, as did his lines of rose bushes. Throughout the 1930s, Lena would regularly host summer picnics on the grounds of Cherry Lodge for the Grace Hospital Auxiliary, where she served as president, and for other women's groups. In June 1935, a large gathering of ladies visiting from the Loyal Orange Benevolent Association Grand Lodge of British North America enjoyed a grand afternoon at Midstream estate.

Lena also brought in a number of young outport women as domestic staff during these lean years. She trained them to be cooks, housemaids, and nursemaids, then sent them on to work at the homes of the well-to-do in St. John's, including Government House. Sometimes she was able to place them in clerical jobs. She also took in unmarried expectant mothers at Cherry Lodge, to help them through their pregnancy.

Richard kept his social contacts to a minimum. Despite (or perhaps because of) the checkered past they shared, he did stay in touch with John Meaney, now a correspondent for the international press and on his way to election to the St. John's City Council, who started a new newspaper, the *Newfoundlander*, in October 1934. "Dedicated to the Restoration of Self Government," the publication proclaimed, and it was filled with hard-nosed content blasting the government and individual commissioners. Meaney also tried to organize a group called the Representative Government League of Newfoundland. His paper folded after a few months due to lack of advertising. The Commission of Government certainly had offered it none and apparently had threatened to hold back patronage to anyone who did.

In December 1934, the family learned of the passing of eighty-two-year-old Alexander Squires at his home in Harbour Grace. Unconventional to the end, Alexander had fallen out with the church in his final years over his insistence on chewing and spitting tobacco during the service. He was denied burial in the United Church cemetery as a result, relegated instead to a spot on the southern shore of the harbour.

Alexander's death came as a surprise to Richard, as his father had seemed quite fit on a recent visit there. "I was so impressed by his manner, the firmness of his voice and a handshake abnormally strong, that I came back from the car to see him again," he wrote to Robert, who was closer to Alexander than any of the grandchildren.

"Harbour Grace is no more," Robert wrote wistfully in his diary. "No more trips around the Bay . . . Grandfather has not had an easy life. What he had he earned, but his losses were great. But whether he lost or won he was honest to the last. He paid one hundred cents on the dollar every time and although his worldly returns may have been small his spiritual gains and accomplishments and satisfactions must have made up the difference."

Richard's own health showed gradual improvement as 1935 got underway. "From the general tone of the letters from home it looks as though things are beginning to straighten up again after the lapse of the last couple of years," Robert wrote in his journal. "Some definite political situation will develop which may prove very advantageous if handled with a clear head. Daddy's letters are in truth of the old form and it is certainly a wonderful feeling to feel that the old form is returning in full strength."

Richard and Lena managed to pull together enough money for a vacation that winter in Canada and the United States. And on their return to Newfoundland, Richard did indeed find a definite political situation developing. It had nothing to do with him, but it did reinforce the government's suspicion of him as a potential rabble-rouser that needed watching. The unemployed of St. John's—still trying to feed their families on a bare subsistence of rations and dole—had banded together under the leadership of Pierce Power, a rugged, clever, twenty-four-year-old labourer from the Southside, just home from working in British Columbia. Like Richard Squires, Pierce Power had a magnetic personality that energized an audience and attracted people in droves. In May 1935, riled up by Power, a thousand of them paraded to the Colonial Building, where the police force—now enlarged to one hundred—waited on the steps. Rioting erupted and the police charged. Commissioner Hope Simpson, with a certain degree of smugness, wrote to his son that "the crowd ran like rabbits and all was over in two minutes." But not before Power and others, both men and women, were brutally clubbed.

As in 1932, nightfall brought looting to the downtown. Unlike in 1932, however, the police quickly took control, which Hope Simpson was also pleased to share with his son:

> There was a riot in 1932 when the Inspector General of Police was confined in the parliament building (my office) for several hours—he was in terror—and the police did

not know what to do and shut themselves into the office also . . . But we have a new chief of police, and the men have been properly trained and are proud of themselves. Now the whole of the mob has a very wholesome respect for the police, and the town generally feels very much happier than it did.

Englishman Peter D. H. Dunn, working in St. John's as an advisor to the Customs Department, offered the observation that disgruntled political elements were "exploiting the present economic troubles for all they were worth and meeting with considerable success." The most dangerous of these was Sir Richard Squires, he said, who was thought to have a shadow government in place, though Dunn felt that he would not come into the open just yet. "His most likely course of action would be to foment disaffection by the underground methods of which he is a master."

No doubt the Commission of Government had serious concerns—bordering on paranoia—about Squires, given his reputation for scheming and his track record of rousing the public to his cause. But the times had changed. Richard had no real following, no press to give him a public bullhorn, no money to fund a campaign, and seemingly no connection with any of the various "take back the government" movements that arose in the wake of the 1935 riot. The commissioners thought he was hard at work behind the scenes, trying to incite rioting, preparing to burst forth in opposition when the time was right. But it was a myth—none of the opposition movements had any truck with Sir Richard Squires.

The only action of the "master fomenter of disaffection," as Peter Dunn called him, was to surface occasionally with a speech here and there (mostly to Orange Lodges), though he did involve himself in some unrest among the settlers at Markland in the spring of 1936. These appearances drew little interest from the public, though they may have continued to feed the commissioners' suspicions. Richard turned some heads in Canada with a comment in 1936 while travelling to sessions of the Grand Orange

Lodge. "Native Newfoundlanders," he remarked—and it was reported in St. John's—"have less constitutional importance than the negro population of many of Britain's overseas possessions."

Richard's troubled finances persisted through the decade. Robert came back from London in October 1935 to find the family home on Rennies Mill Road leased out and Richard, Lena, and Rosemary living in a rented house at 19 Gower Street, their situation looking "pretty precarious." Robert took an office in the Board of Trade building and went to work to put the family's interests in Midstream, the Strong business, and their real estate and mortgage investments in order, all of which were in a "pretty unhealthy state." The family assets also included the yacht *Medric* and a coastal freighter (the *Earl of Devon*, acquired somewhere along the way), both of which were offered for charter in the warmer months. At Midstream they were about to lose their farmer, with no replacement in sight.

Elaine, recovering from surgery and unfit for work, soon followed Robert back from London and moved into Cherry Lodge. The whole family was there for Christmas in 1935.

Squires family at Midstream, Christmas 1935: Norman, Robert, Rosemary, Richard Jr., Elaine

Richard Jr., fluent in French, was attached to a Montreal law firm, preparing to join his father's practice in St. John's; Norman was home for the holidays from his first year at Dalhousie. After Christmas the family shut down the farm for the winter; Richard Jr. and Norman returned to Canada, and Lena left for New York. She stayed until April.

During these dark days, Rosemary Squires remained especially close to her father. When she was home from boarding school, she brought him his meals and got him to eat. She would sometimes sit quietly on the stairs, watching him at his desk, or accompany him as he tended his prized rose garden. He was still, in her words, a deeply religious man who never lost his faith— though in a new twist, in 1936 he (and Lena) drew inspiration from consultations with Rexford Kendrick, a New York astrologer who advised Richard that he could look forward to a surprise return to high government office before 1942.

Richard's fighting side resurfaced in May 1936, when a festering problem with the Strong family came to a head. Will Strong and his half-brother Hubert were running James Strong Ltd., the sprawling but unstable business in Little Bay Islands. The two of them came to St. John's for a meeting of the company shareholders, sitting down with Richard, Robert, and a lawyer representing Lena in Will's suite at the Crosbie Hotel. Will, once a solid rock of a man, was feeble and ailing. It was Hubert, four-teen years younger, who set the tone for the meeting. He flew into Richard, accusing him of cheating James Strong out of shares of the company in order to gain control. "Mean and grasping" was the way Robert described the outburst, but he was, after all, trying to protect the Squires family interests. As the meeting wore on, the air grew thick with abuse flying in both directions.

The fact was that Richard had (in his and Lena's name) taken more than fifty-one per cent of the company in return for the $70,000 in advances they had made when, in his view, the business was worth no more than $50,000. But no matter the reason, he was now in control and he intended to stay there. Before the

James Strong premises, 1939

meeting ended, the company hired Robert Squires to be their representative in St. John's. Discussions renewed in the same vein in August when Richard arrived at Little Bay Islands aboard the *Medric* for a follow-up meeting that included James Strong, now eighty-six. Will was too sick to be involved (he died before the month was over), but Hubert kept up his hostility toward Richard, who made it clear he was going to keep control of the company until the cash advances were repaid. The business stumbled on. James Strong died three years later, his estate, including shares in the company, valued at a modest $4,200.

On the political front, three years into government by commission, Richard maintained a low public profile but was still trying to exert influence through official channels. He went to Government House in January 1936 to bid goodbye to Governor Anderson, leaving at the end of the month, who according to Richard received him with "studied contempt." Regardless, Richard launched into a familiar rant about the state of the government. It was dictatorial, oppressive, and corrupt, he told

Anderson. People were afraid to speak out for fear of retribution, patronage was rampant, the commissioners were buying off their opponents. Peter Cashin was going around bragging that he could get any government job he wanted just by promising to keep quiet. With the exception of Lodge, he said, none of the current commissioners were worth their salt, and he was certain that, if he were to go to the people himself with a political party, he could beat them ninety-five to five.

Squires on the *Medric*, ca. 1935

Richard was back at Government House in February, for a luncheon hosted by the new governor, Sir Humphrey Walwyn. Flamboyant, pompous, with a shirt stuffed full of self-importance, Walwyn was another naval man, good entertainment for the public but a serious headache for the appointed government. He was not long falling out with the commissioners, once he discovered they were the ones actually in charge of the country. Richard, however, thought it an advantage to be in his good graces. When Walwyn made an official visit to Harbour Grace in June, with as much pomp and circumstance as he could muster, Richard arranged a cruise for him around the harbour on the *Medric*. "Squires is a clever fellow," murmured Hope Simpson when he learned of it.

Bolstered by the good omens of the astrological signs from New York, Richard cranked up his backroom attack on Commission of Government, now taking his case to London, to the office of Malcolm MacDonald, the youthful secretary of state for Dominion affairs. Richard arrived in May of 1937, full of himself, as MacDonald recalled: "I do not remember ever having the pleasure of conversing with Sir Richard Squires, but he greeted me as though we were old bosom friends and proceeded to make the most flattering remarks about myself." Getting down to business, Richard told him that England's position in Newfoundland was quickly deteriorating. The people were now openly critical of the Commission of Government, which he thought was clearly incapable of performing its task. According to MacDonald's notes, the conversation continued in this vein:

> "No one could expect that an Admiral who had never set eyes on the island before and two or three civil servants from India or elsewhere could know anything about Newfoundland, its people or its problems," Squires told me.

> I begged to differ, pointing out that the Empire had been run successfully for generations by sending out members of the public service who had no personal knowledge of foreign parts. "I do not see why an arrangement which worked well elsewhere should be incapable of working in Newfoundland."

> "We Newfoundlanders deeply resent having our franchise taken away from us," replied Squires.

> "No one has taken the franchise away from Newfoundlanders except themselves," I shot back. "The Legislature in St. John's petitioned His Majesty to suspend the constitution under which they enjoyed the right to vote, and His Majesty took the action which the people of Newfoundland of their own volition begged him to take."

Richard argued that the petition to His Majesty had never represented the desire of Newfoundlanders, coming from a legislature out of touch with the electorate, and it could not be said that the petition expressed the view of the people because it had never been submitted to a referendum.

"Not so," I said, reminding him that the whole point of representative government is that the popularly elected representatives of the people in legislatures should express their will.

"I understand how you feel compelled to hold that view over here," Squires replied, "but it is not the right view! I represent ninety per cent of the people of Newfoundland. The position is by no means hopeless, and I would like to sit down with you to devise a programme to carry out with their approval."

I patiently pointed out that working out a programme was the business of Commission of Government and I was not prepared to discuss it with anyone else behind their backs.

After Richard left, MacDonald noted that he had seemed a bit unsettled by the refusal to accept without rejoinder his various contentions. "When he first entered the room, he had remarked on the joy it was to him to see a young man holding high office," he wrote. "I cannot help feeling that the father of this joy was the hope that youth and inexperience would prove putty in his hands."

At a second meeting, Richard said he was not looking for a return to responsible government, but as Leader of the Opposition he wanted a modification of Commission of Government to ensure close touch with public opinion. "I have been quiet for the last three years and have always refused to do anything which might embarrass the Commission, but I can remain quiet no longer."

MacDonald concluded that "altogether the interview was as unsatisfactory to Sir Richard Squires as it was to us. He got no change out of us, and, on the other hand, we were not able to influence him at all in a direction away from his self-appointed post of Leader of the Opposition. I have not the slightest doubt that he now intends to do as much mischief as he can." Perhaps, but that would only be possible if there was some substance behind Richard's bluster. There wasn't. He still had no organized following, despite his outrageous claim to be Leader of the Opposition representing ninety per cent of the people. It was pure bluff.

By 1938, when opposition to Commission of Government was intensifying, the wind was out of Richard's sails. There was a widespread public outcry that year after the commissioners allowed Bowater (operators of the Corner Brook mill) to back away from an agreement to build a paper mill at Gander, even though the company had gained major timber concessions in the area. An opportune time to unite and empower opposition forces, but Richard Squires uttered not one peep. He stayed out of sight, even avoiding the state funeral of Sir William Coaker in November. His days of influence and his energy to reclaim them were gone.

He was heard from again, though, early in 1939, when the *Daily Express* of London sent their star reporter out to Newfoundland to see what all the upheaval was about. Morley Richards toured the country for two months and published a series of articles highly critical of Commission of Government. He arranged to meet with Squires, out of the public eye but as opinionated as ever. The interview painted an image of a distracted and diminished has-been:

> He is a lonely man now, little seen in public life. He talked to me for six hours . . . he is highly strung and at times his left shoulder twitches up and down. He filled his pipe many times, but his gestures threw the tobacco out again. He never lit it.

> "We have no finesse," he told me angrily. "We are the same breed without your 200 years of regimented living. So you send out charming, highly paid English gentlemen to govern us—men who think according to rules we

know nothing about. These men have the social graces. We are men of action. We do not want pleasant parties at Government House. You have become our overlord and reduced this island to serfdom. Why are you making us hate you?"

Cynical, jaded, consigned to bristling from the sidelines, Richard got away with Lena on a cross-Canada trip as Supreme Grand Master of the Loyal Orange Association Grand Lodge that spring—their final time venturing abroad together. It happened that King George VI and Queen Elizabeth were on a royal tour of Canada at the same time. Hospitalized in Winnipeg with lung congestion, Richard issued a statement saying, in part:

> Those of us who live in the oldest part of the British Empire, where we are at the moment in a state of suspended animation politically, are naturally very unhappy not being able to express ourselves from a governmental point of view. Our case is very similar to the American colonies in that we have taxation without representation.

He offered the suggestion that the occasion of the royal tour should be recognized by Newfoundland joining into confederation with Canada.

Approaching the long, dark shadows of his life, Richard was housebound by the fall, diagnosed with congestive heart failure and under the care of two nurses. He was too weak to leave his bed, so they had him set up in the library at Rennies Mill Road. In March 1940, as the end neared, the family was called together. Richard spoke to each of his children individually. Rosemary was in her first year at Memorial. When her turn came to go into his room, Richard told her (rather coldly) that there would not be enough insurance money to support her after he died—what there was would have to go to her mother and Elaine, who was still not able to work. He expected Rosemary to go out and find a job and try to make it on her own.

Sir Richard Anderson Squires died in the early morning hours of March 26, 1940, surrounded by his family and his books. His body lay at home for visitation for one day. Rosemary in particular agonized at his passing. She had always felt she had not lived up to her father's expectations. Her proudest achievement was to be named a school prefect in her final year at Battle Abbey, rare for a girl from the colonies. In her private goodbye, while his body lay in the library, she stole into the room and folded her prefect pin into her father's hand.

On March 27, Sir Richard received the honour of a full state funeral. Rosemary, once taunted by her friends about a mob threatening to throw her father in the harbour, was astounded at size of the crowd that turned up on Rennies Mill Road to accompany the body to a simple funeral service at Cochrane Street Church, where Les Curtis's father, the Rev. Levi Curtis, delivered the eulogy. Afterwards, on a chilly, windy afternoon, a long procession of dignitaries, government officials, and representatives of the military, the municipal council, Memorial University College, and community organizations, as well as members of the general public, trudged westward through flurries of snow to the General Protestant Cemetery on Waterford Bridge Road, Richard Squires's final resting place.

On the evening of his death, radios all over the country tuned in to *The Barrelman* program on VONF to hear Joseph Smallwood's fifteen-minute tribute, rambling but effusive and heartfelt:

> In sheer intellectual power he stood out head and shoulders above all his contemporaries, above all the public men of this country during his adult life. He had not only a tireless brain, a brain which he could, and so often did, subject to simply terrific pressure and burdens—pressure and burdens that would kill any ordinary man—in addition to that terrific brain power he had a truly remarkable, truly astonishing, iron will, an implacable control over his own mind, a power of determination over his own personality and movement, which were such almost as would frighten you.

And Smallwood spoke of a Richard Squires that not everyone knew:

> It was perhaps inevitable that a man so brilliant, with such a dynamic and mesmeric personality, should appear perhaps hard and cold. But underneath that exterior, as I have such good reason to know, was a man of kindly and generous impulses and instincts. He had a feeling for beauty, beauty of nature and beauty of human personality. He was generous to a positive fault, money never meant a thing to him, except for what it could accomplish. In this town and country today there are many hundreds who have felt the benefits of his generosity with money. He would never see a man stuck, whether that man were friend or foe.

The *Twillingate Sun*, far less partisan and passionate than Smallwood, allowed that as a lawyer, politician, leader, and organizer, Richard Squires had many fine qualities. Damning him with faint praise, the paper observed that whatever Sir Richard was, he was no worse than any other politician: "His efforts for the welfare of his country cannot be overlooked whatever his faults, and whether little or many, politics finds them all in everyone engaged therein."

———

On a still, crisp day in the hard sunshine of late December 2020, Sir Richard's grandson Robert Squires took me to see his gravesite at the General Protestant Cemetery in St. John's. The ground was bare; the gravel crunched on the walkway as we neared the oversize granite headstone marking the family plot, SQUIRES etched boldly across the front. "The Rt. Hon. Sir Richard Anderson Squires" and "Helena E. Strong" and their dates are inscribed underneath, and a one-line epitaph—"He loved God and the people and attempted to serve both"—along the bottom.

On the monument's side are the names and dates of Baby Madeline and James Alexander Squires, and on the back Elaine, Robert Holloway Squires, and his son Richard James, brother of the man standing next to me—this last addition made in 2017. Rosemary's ashes are here too, Robert tells me, though her name is not yet on the stone.

We linger for a while, chatting about the family. Then Robert says something quite telling about Sir Richard's extraordinary celebrity in Newfoundland: "You know, it wasn't until Elaine passed away and Rosemary came down that the family arranged to have all the engravings put on the headstone. Before that, it had only SQUIRES and the epitaph along the bottom. Father often said that Grandmother, Lady Squires, felt that was all that was needed on the headstone—because everyone knew Squires."

AFTERWORD

Sir Richard Anderson Squires left an estate valued at $53,600 after assets of $75,700 were balanced against liabilities of $22,100. The bulk of his assets were a combination of shares in Midstream Realty Ltd. and James Strong Ltd. (totalling $19,800) and book debt ($50,400). He had cash in the bank of $43. He left it all to Lena.

At the time of his passing, his five surviving children—Elaine (thirty-four), Robert (thirty), Richard Jr. (twenty-eight), Norman (twenty-two), and Rosemary (seventeen)—all lived in St. John's. Robert, who married Alice Butt a month later, took charge of Midstream, developing it into a full-fledged productive farm with hens, pigs, and fifty head of dairy cattle, turning out a variety of produce. Solid and dependable, he moved into the original owner's house (Lena would spend her summers at Cherry Lodge). For a time, Robert also acted as agent for James Strong Ltd., though under Hubert's management the company never regained the success enjoyed in its glory days. When fresh-fish processing came on the scene, Hubert stubbornly hung on as a salt fish producer. The business eventually went insolvent, scaling back to a general store in Little Bay Islands.

Norman Squires, carefree and outgoing, volunteered for the Newfoundland Militia at the beginning of the Second World War, rising to the rank of Captain, then joining the Canadian army in 1944. His older brother Richard, after several years at his father's law firm, enlisted with the Canadians in the fall of 1940. He went through officer training at Camp Borden in Ontario, reaching the rank of lieutenant. In 1941, Richard married Jean Parsons in St. John's before going overseas with the Canadian Armoured Corps. He was killed in June 1942 during a training manoeuvre at Headley Down in England; he had just turned thirty-one. Richard's death was a harsh blow to the family. He had been an honours graduate who showed promise in the law and was a good public speaker—the natural heir to his father's legal and political legacy.

Elaine struggled after her father's death. Unable to work because of illness, she began wintering in Tucson, Arizona, along with her mother. In 1943, a little later than the London fortune teller had predicted, she married Daubeney Drury, scion of an English military family of some means. He, too, had a lingering illness, contracted as a prisoner during the First World War. The couple moved around in search of a salubrious climate, living for a few months in Victoria, British Columbia, then in Nassau, where Daubeney's brother, Captain Vyvyan Drury, served as aide-de-camp to the Duke of Windsor, governor of the Bahamas.

Daubeney died in Nassau in the spring of 1946, and Elaine returned to the swaying palms, saguaro cactus, and desert climate of Tucson. Her mother visited in the wintertime—installing herself as a grand dame of Tucson society, where titled ladies were a novelty. In her formidable style, Lena extolled the qualities of life in Newfoundland and made sure everyone knew the proper pronunciation of the country's name ("equal emphasis on each syllable"). She involved herself in a number of community groups, including the American Red Cross. Occasionally, she visited her old social circle in New York. In Newfoundland, after confederation with Canada, Premier J. R. Smallwood had her elected as the first president of the Women's Liberal Association. Lady Squires represented the province at a national Liberal conference in Ottawa in 1950.

Rosemary grew into an affable young woman. She spent a year at the University of Toronto and stayed with her mother at

Cherry Lodge the following summer. Her teenage friends were both enchanted and intimidated by Lady Squires—by her aristocratic bearing, her wit, and her ability to put them in their place with a few well-chosen words.

In the mid-1940s, Lena sold the Rennies Mill Road house and auctioned off the contents. Rosemary went to Victoria (perhaps at Elaine's suggestion), where she found secretarial work with the Canadian navy. She later moved to Montreal, marrying George Mersereau, an insurance salesman, in 1952.

Lady Squires alternated between living at Cherry Lodge and the Balsam Hotel on Barnes Road. Robert's two young boys, Robert Jr. and Richard, lived on the farm but went to school at Prince of Wales Collegiate and lunched with Lena from time to time. They remembered her as distant and aloof; she didn't talk much and never played with them. As Rosemary observed, Lena was not much interested in children once they passed the baby stage.

In 1956, once her winter trips to Tucson were no longer viable, Lena moved to Toronto to be close to Hannah Smith, her devoted housemaid of fifty years earlier. She lived out her final years with dementia, in a nursing home a short walk from Hannah, who cared for her until her death in 1959 at the age of eighty-one.

By that time, Midstream was no longer in the family. Robert had wound down the farm, bringing in some revenue by selling building lots from the property and renting out the farmhouse and Cherry Lodge to Americans from Pepperrell Air Force Base. In 1956, most of the estate was expropriated by the City of St. John's for the expansion of Bowring Park. Robert shared the proceeds of $250,000 with his siblings. He moved his own family to a multi-unit house at 37 Topsail Road, where they were living at the time of his death from cancer in 1961 at age fifty-one. As this book was written, the name Midstream Manor still hung over the front door.

After his time in the Canadian army, Norman emigrated to Massachusetts, married, started a family, and worked in the hotel business as a maître d'. A happy-go-lucky fellow, he moved back to St. John's with his wife, Frances Ross, in the early 1970s. Through family connections with William Seto Ping, the former Midstream butler, he took over a Chinese restaurant on Harvey Road. The business failed after a year or two. Norman ran a second restaurant in Bay Roberts before returning to the States. He died of cancer in Hyannis, Massachusetts, in 1977, aged sixty.

In 1971, Elaine suffered a stroke in Tucson that left her partly paralyzed, forcing a move into a nursing home. She passed away ten years later at seventy-five. Rosemary was seventy-two when she died in Ottawa in 1995, after a long career in community service.

SOURCES

THE SQUIRES PAPERS

This book would not have been possible without access to the collected papers of Sir Richard Anderson Squires.

In 1950, one year after Confederation and ten years after Sir Richard's death, Robert H. Squires, his eldest son and keeper of Midstream, the family estate, was convalescing at the sanatorium in St. John's. His son, Robert A. Squires, told me in an interview (December 12, 2016) that his father had phoned in to Midstream one day to say, "Joe Smallwood is sending someone for Sir Richard's files. They're in the barn, in the loft, and would you make sure they get whatever they want."

Smallwood stored the collection in the basement of Canada House, his St. John's residence during his early tenure as premier of Newfoundland. He spent years going through the papers, a pastime every night before bedtime and "a joy to engage in," as he related in his book *Newfoundland Miscellany* (Newfoundland Book Publishers, 1978, p. 167). Smallwood saved what he thought should be saved and destroyed what he thought should be destroyed.

In 1992, the collection (or what remained of it) was moved to Memorial University. Smallwood said he took three tons of material from the Squires barn. What showed up at Memorial's Centre for Newfoundland Studies was less than a ton—7.5 linear metres, to be exact—suggesting that Smallwood might have destroyed a lot more than he kept. Still, what remains is a large collection and it offers glimpses into Richard Squires's personal and professional life. It was invaluable in putting together this biography.

We'll never know what Smallwood decided to get rid of, but the greatest gap in the collection is in some ways the most valuable information on a man's life—his personal diaries. Somewhere between Canada House and Memorial University, they all disappeared.

Or almost all. There are two diaries among the Squires papers, both slim volumes from his student years, but that is it. We know there were others, and we know it from a curious source. Among the papers of William J. Browne housed at The Rooms Provincial Archives (file MG864.111) is correspondence from an unnamed person in Montreal who had come into possession of four of Richard Squires's diaries from the 1920s and '30s. He recorded portions on a series of reel-to-reel tapes and sent the recordings to Browne, knowing that they were an important part of Newfoundland history. Browne had them transcribed—and they offer a highly detailed description of Squires's daily life. The man told Browne that Smallwood had the rest. What became of them remains a mystery.

OTHER SOURCES

In order to let the story unfold without interruption, I have not footnoted specific sources in the text. Instead, you will find sourcing notes below for pertinent information in the same sequence as the information occurs in the book. Key words from the text are also highlighted to assist with identifying the source of the information.

I consulted a wide range of sources, including generally recognized historical references such as the *Encyclopedia of Newfoundland and Labrador*, the *Dictionary of Canadian Biography*, Smallwood's *Books of Newfoundland*, newspapers of the time, websites such as heritage.nf.ca, and books on the history of Newfoundland and Labrador, as listed in the Bibliography.

Particularly useful was the access kindly granted to the papers and photographs in the private collections of Robert A. Squires and the late Richard J. Squires, grandsons of Sir Richard.

I have been as thorough as possible in giving the source of specific items of information, particularly direct quotes, but the decision as to what is listed and what is not was mine alone, as are any errors that may occur.

ABBREVIATIONS

ASC	Archives and Special Collections, Memorial University	
	HSC	Helena Squires Collection, ASC
	RBC	Robert Bond Collection, ASC
	RSC	Richard Squires Collection, ASC
CNS	Centre for Newfoundland Studies, Memorial University	
ENL	*Encyclopedia of Newfoundland and Labrador*	
PLC	Proceedings of the Legislative Council	

PRL Provincial Reference Library, A. C. Hunter Library, Arts and
     Culture Centre
RDNL Registry of Deeds, Newfoundland and Labrador
TRPA The Rooms Provincial Archives

CHAPTER ONE

Robert A. Squires of St. John's provided **genealogical information** on the Gregory Squires family; additional details of **births, deaths, and marriages** came from the Gert Crosbie and Mildred Howard lists in the Newfoundland Collection, A. C. Hunter Library, St. John's.

The **description of Harbour Grace** and its amenities comes primarily from *Lovell's Province of Newfoundland Directory* for 1871. I pieced together **Alexander Squires's business activities** in Harbour Grace from various issues of the *Harbor Grace Standard*, beginning February 14, 1874.

I am indebted to Augustus G. Lilly, K.C., for documentation on **Richard Anderson** from the Minutes of the Supreme Court Northern District Circuit at Harbour Grace (RPA, GN 5/2/B/1), provided in emails of March and April 2019. The **will** of Richard Anderson is at http://ngb.chebucto.org/Wills/anderson-richard-4-131.shtml.

The **letter from Sidney Squires** to Alexander dated July 30, 1880, is in the private collection of Robert A. Squires.

Information about **Anderson's boyhood** (and Sarah Comer) are from various sources, including Robert A. Squires's files, and the *Harbor Grace Standard*. Anderson's **letters to his father** are from the private collection of Robert A. Squires. His **scholastic achievements** in Harbour Grace come from various issues of the *Harbor Grace Standard*, as do his **father's efforts at agriculture** and his attempts at **political office**.

Information on Anderson's public speaking efforts comes from the Robert A. Squires collection. His activities in the **summer of 1896**, including his friendship with Alfred Seymour and his first term at **Methodist College**, are described in his diary of that year (RSC 1.01.001). His diary of 1897 is in the HSC at ASC (uncatalogued).

For background information on **Robert E. Holloway** and Methodist College, I relied on Ruby L. Gough's masterful *Robert Edwards Holloway: Newfoundland Educator, Scientist, Photographer, 1874–1904* and *Above All Price: The United Church College Residence, St. John's, Newfoundland* compiled by Garfield Fizzard. **Holloway's notes to** Alexander Squires and to Anderson are in the Robert A. Squires collection.

The 1897 **mortgage to John Squires** is at RDNL v 16, f 374. The quote on Lena and Anderson's **courtship** comes from "Memories of Helena Squires," the 1990 recollections of her daughter Rosemary Mersereau (CNS).

CHAPTER TWO

I obtained background information on **Little Bay Islands** from "Little Bay Islands. Past, Present and Future: An Historical Review" in *Little Bay Islands U.C. School Magazine* 1942 at CNS. **James Strong**'s background comes from ENL and handwritten notes by H. L. Strong, Maritime History Archive, MUN, file MF-039. Jill Marshall kindly provided genealogical details on the **Strong family.**

Robert **Holloway's visit** to Little Bay Islands is referred to in Ruby Gough's *Holloway* (p. 147).

Information on Lena's attendance at **Mount Allison Ladies' College** and her whereabouts in 1904 was provided by David Mawhinney, Archivist, Mount Allison University. I found a general description of life at the college during Lena's time in Raymond Clare Archibald's *Historical Notes on the Education of Women at Mount Allison 1854–1954*, a digital copy of which was provided by David Mawhinney.

Anderson's standing in his **final law exams** I obtained from Law School Lists, Faculty of Law Calendar 1902–03, Dalhousie University.

Information on **Richard and Lena's activities** in their early St. John's years comes from various issues of the *Evening Telegram* and *Harbor Grace Standard* 1904–09.

Particulars of **Richard**'s defence of Walter Hart are in the *Evening Telegram* of September 14, 1907.

Richard and Lena's various **mortgage and real estate investments** are on record at RDNL. Information on the **Harbour Grace Agricultural Society** is at CNS.

CHAPTER THREE

The evolving **relationship between Bond and Morris** is detailed in my 2017 book *Robert Bond: The Greatest Newfoundlander*. The Hants Harbour incident between **Squires and Gushue** is in the October 5, 1908, issue of the *Evening Telegram*.

E. B. Foran described the 1908 election cliffhanger **results in Harbour Grace** in his article "Battle of the Giants: Bond and Morris" in Volume 3 of Smallwood's *Book of Newfoundland* (pp. 153–70).

Peter **Cashin**'s description of his father is in Peter Cashin, *My Fight for New-foundland* (p. xxvi).

Richard's maiden speech is in the *Daily News* of March 16, 1910. The reaction of **Shoal Harbour** to his comments on the railway lands is in the *Evening Telegram* of April 8, 1910. The reaction from **Elliston** is in a letter in the issue of October 21, 1911, and the reaction from **British Harbour** is in a letter published in the issue of May 15, 1912.

You can find Squires's comments on the **men from Elliston** looking for money in RSC 2.08.003.

P. K. Devine's **description of Coaker** is in "Memories of the F.P.U. in the Early Days of Its Organization" in Coaker's *Twenty Years of the Fishermen's Protective Union of Newfoundland from 1909–1929* (p. 141).

Correspondence from Richard to Coaker, October 23, 1909, is in ASC, COLL-009, 10.03.070, and Richard's **account with Morris** in dissolving their partnership is in file 3.04.002.

The **Charlotte Butler case** is described in the *Evening Telegram* of March 1–2, 1912. The *Evening Telegram* of August 8, 1911, outlines Richard's involvement with the **Motor Association**.

I obtained information on Lena's enrollment at **Emerson College** in email communications from Archives and Special Collections, Emerson College, in March and May 2017. The quote on **Lena's diction** is from Mersereau's "Memories." Additional information about Lena Squires is from various editions of the *Evening Telegram*.

The information about **Armine Gosling** and the **Ladies Reading Room** comes from Margot Duley's "The Radius of Her Influence for Good: The Rise and Triumph of the Women's Suffrage Movement in Newfoundland 1909–1925," in editor Linda Kealey's *Pursuing Equality: Historical Perspectives on Women in Newfoundland and Labrador*.

The *Evening Telegram* of February 8, 1915, reported Lena Squires's address to the **current events club**. The information on Rabindranath Tagore is from http://www.nobelprize.org/nobel_prizes/literature/laureates/1913/ (accessed July 3, 2017).

Information on **Sarah Comer's passing** comes from Robert A. Squires and an obituary in the *Harbor Grace Standard*, July 4, 1913. The yacht is referenced in the *Evening Telegram* issue of August 12, 1913. Further details on the boat are in letters to Dr. Kean and George Gulliford (RSC 2.12.012).

Information about the **1913 election campaigning** appears in various issues of the *Evening Telegram*.

CHAPTER FOUR

Coaker's remark in the House is cited in S. J. R. Noel's *Politics in Newfoundland* (p. 118). The question of FPU members dining at Government House is related in Davidson's diary (TRPA, MG 136.5).

Comments by the *Newfoundland Quarterly* on Richard's appointment are in the April 1914 issue (p. 15).

Coaker's log of his trip to the seal hunt is in *Newfoundland and Labrador Studies* vol. 25 (2), 2010. The quotes from the commission of inquiry report are cited in Patrick O'Flaherty's *Lost Country: The Rise and Fall of Newfoundland 1843–1933* (p. 269).

Richard's correspondence with Elisha Button, Aaron Smith and Sons, and the Harbour Grace supporter is in RSC 2.12.010/011 and 2.13.003.

For background and details about the events involved in Newfoundland's war effort, included throughout this chapter, I relied on G. W. L. Nicholson's classic *The Fighting Newfoundlander: A History of the Royal Newfoundland Regiment* and more recent papers by Mike O'Brien and Chris Martin which appeared in *Essays on the Great War: Papers Published in Newfoundland and Labrador Studies* (ed. Christopher A. Sharpe et al). Davidson's comment on Richard's speech is from his diary entry of August 12, 1914, and his comment on the formation and powers of the Patriotic Association from December 9, 1914 (TRPA, MG 136.5).

Richard's lacklustre participation in the war effort comes from a letter from "An Old Time Liberal" in the *Evening Telegram* of September 24, 1919, and his patriotic speech to the Loyal Orange Association ladies is from the *Evening Telegram* of February 25, 1915.

Rockwell Kent wrote of his time in Brigus in *It's Me O Lord: The Autobiography of Rockwell Kent*. See also "Newfoundland's Famous 'German Spy': Rockwell Kent" in J. R. Smallwood's *Newfoundland Miscellany*. Richard's involvement with Kent is in RSC 2.11.005.

The service record of Norman Wheatley Strong (including the telegram about his death) is in the regimental records of the Royal Newfoundland Regiment at TRPA, St. John's.

Richard refers to the death of infant daughter Madeline in correspondence with J. W. James, June 16, 1916 (RSC 2.13.006).

Squires's comments on the Salvation Army are in PLC, March 28, 1916.

Richard's family habits and the state of the house in Harbour Grace are relayed in letters to his father June 21, 1915, and May 29, 1917 (RSC 1.05.001). The handing out of five-cent pieces is mentioned in a letter from

Allen Squires to Lady Helena Squires of March 8, 1957 (Robert A. Squires collection). The **Squires children in Little Bay Islands** are in a photograph provided by Carolyn Molson.

Books from Richard's **personal library** are in the possession of Robert A. Squires. Richard's book-lover comment is from a letter to Thomas Nangle of January 12, 1923 (file 12.04.00, RSC).

The 1916 interaction with Cochius comes from correspondence in RSC 12.04.003.

Richard's comments **welcoming Governor Harris** are in PLC, 1918 (pp. 28–29).

CHAPTER FIVE

The *Evening Telegram* of January 18, 1918, notes Richard's **re-entry into law practice.** Harry Winter wrote about **working with Squires** in his memoir in the *Newfoundland Quarterly*, Vol. 72 (2), winter 1976 (pp. 17–18).

Information in this chapter on the **financial difficulties** of the *Daily Star* and *Morning Post* comes from various documents and correspondence with Richard Squires in RSC 2.13–2.16 and 4.01–4.02. Mosdell's **resignation letter** (September 7, 1917) is in RSC 4.02.002. **Judith Taylor's** letter to Squires of February 9, 1918, is in RSC 4.02.003, as is Squires's memo about his meeting with her.

Richard's remarks on the **state of the railway** are in PLC, 1919 (pp. 49–50).

Crosbie's comment about closing down the *Star* comes from an affidavit of Edward Earles in June 1918 (RSC 2.15.006). The **order-in-council** is in RSC 4.01.010. The subsequent **court action** and reaction of **Governor Harris** are outlined in correspondence of October 5, 1918, between Richard and W. U. Tilley (RSC 4.02.008) and Richard to W. R. Howley of January 12, 1919 (RSC 4.02.010).

Coaker's **comments on the conscription** issue are from the *Fishermen's Advocate*, October 19, 1932. Richard commented on conscription in PLC, 1918 (p. 52). The Squires-Coaker **libel case** is described in the *Evening Telegram* of June 13, 1918.

The letter to Henry Squires on the **death of James** (May 16, 1919) is in RSC 2.16.005. Correspondence from Alexander Squires on the death of James (February 10, 1919) and Richard's reply (February 14, 1919) are in RSC 1.05.003.

A letter to Thomas MacKinson (May 3, 1919), containing information on the **fire at Fruitland** and the house rental is in RSC 1.05.003, and the letter concerning payment for the house (March 31, 1920) are in RSC 1.05.004. The **Handley-Page** arrangement is in the letter of May 16, 1919, from Richard to Henry Squires.

Bond's refusal to get back into politics is in RBC 3.38.003 (Bond to John St. John, April 9, 1919). **Richard's comments** on the uncertain government are in a letter of April 17, 1919, to Elisha Button (RSC 2.13.012).

The *Daily News* account of the **non-confidence motion** is in the issue of May 21, 1919. Squires's **May 20 letter** was to Alan Benson of Clarenville (RSC 2.13.012).

The **Coaker inkwell** story is described in the *Daily News* of May 28, 1919, and by Peter Cashin in *My Fight* (p. 4).

Richard's **memo to Mosdell** (June 28, 1919) and Mosdell's reply are in RSC 2.16.006. **Judith Taylor**'s letter of July 19, 1919, is in RSC 4.02. 015, as is James Sellers's comments to Richard of the same date. Judith Taylor's letter to Squires of October 31, 1919, is in RSC 4.02.017.

CHAPTER SIX

Richard's description of his **rise to power** is from a letter to P. M. Newman of Pennsylvania, January 12, 1920 (RSC 2.17.001).

The remarks from the *Twillingate Sun* are reprinted in the *Evening Telegram* of August 7, 1919. The formation of the Liberal Reform Party is described in the *St. John's Daily Star* (August 22, 1919) and the *Evening Telegram* (August 23, 1919).

Richard's **meeting with Bond** and its aftermath are described in correspondence between Bond and H. E. Cowan, and Bond and R. Callahan (RBC 3.38.004). The *Daily News* report on the formation of the **Liberal Reform Party** is in the issue of August 23, 1919.

Richard's **letter to Coaker** of August 23, 1919, is in the William Coaker Collection at ASC (10.03.070). For information on the **agreement between Richard and Coaker**, see Ian D. H. McDonald's *"To Each His Own"* (p. 81), and Edward Roberts's incisive 2006 thesis "Nothing Venture, Nothing Have: Mr. Coaker's Regulations," footnote 113 (CNS). Richard's **commitment to Meaney** is in RSC 2.16.006 (September 26, 1919). The **Squires manifesto** is in the *Morning Post*, October 13, 1919.

The Crosbie **"kiss my ass"** incident is described in a telegram from Mosdell to James MacDonnell (October 16, 1919) in RSC 2.16.010 and in the *Morning Post* and the *Evening Telegram* of October 17, 1919.

The *Telegram* story about **Mosdell's liquor scrips** and the **fundraising meetings** at Squires's house is in the issue of October 16, 1919. The letter from **Methodist College fundraisers** appeared in the issue of October 27.

Governor Harris's **description of the election** is in GN 1/1/17 (Box 28), Harris to Milner, November 14, 1919 (TRPA).

Richard's comments on **opposition in Trinity Bay** are in a letter to Charles Pollett, New Harbour, November 8, 1919 (RSC 2.16.11). James **MacDonnell's break with Squires** is described in the *Evening Telegram* of November 19, 1919.

The *Evening Telegram* of November 26, 1919, tells of **Lena's involvement** with the maternity hospital campaign, and her involvement with the Women's Patriotic Association committee is in the issue of May 19, 1920.

My description of the **Woodford affair** is based primarily on the transcript of the Royal Commission hearings, July 7 to September 2, 1919, a copy of which is in RSC 15.01.001.

The arrangement between **John Meaney and Richard Kelly** is referred to in correspondence from Meaney to Richard dated June 9 and June 26, 1920 (RSC 2.17.006). The **Woodford affidavit** is in the *Evening Telegram*, March 25, 1920. The commission decision is from the *Evening Telegram* of May 2, 1921 (quoting the *Twillingate Sun*).

CHAPTER SEVEN

Mosdell's despairing question is in a letter to Squires of April 9, 1920 (RSC 4.02.021).

D. R. **Thistle's correspondence** (May 15, 1920) is in RSC 4.02.024. I estimated Richard and Lena's **real estate and mortgage investments** from records at RDNL. Richard's comment on his own **financial situation** is from a speech in the House of Assembly (*Daily Star*, March 31, 1921).

Louise Saunders was admitted as a student-at-law, articled to Squires and Winter, in January 1919 (the *Evening Telegram*, January 29, 1919).

The saga of **Richard and the Bell Island mining companies**, and the **advances from John Meaney**, comes from evidence given at the Hollis Walker inquiry of 1924, the transcript of which is at TRPA (GN 126).

Meaney's **relieved comment to Squires** is in a letter of December 7, 1920 (RSC 2.17.011).

The **Smallwood quote** is from his *The New Newfoundland* (p. 16). **Coaker's words** of praise come from his address at the FPU Annual Convention, November 23, 1922, as contained in his *Twenty Years*.

The **Cashin-Squires exchange** in the House was described by J. R. Smallwood on *The Barrelman* radio program; the script is at ASC, COLL-028, 1.01.041 (May 1940). Harris's comment on **Richard's optimism** is in a dispatch to the Colonial Office, London, on September 26, 1921 (GN 1/ 1/7, Box 29, TRPA).

Richard's interview with the *Daily Mail* was reprinted in the *Evening Telegram*, September 4, 1920.

The **note from Morris** (August 11, 1920) is in RSC 2.34.004/.

For the information about **Thomas Nangle's work and the War Memorial** I relied largely on Gary Browne and Darrin McGrath's *Soldier Priest in the Killing Fields of Europe*; the quotes are taken from that publication, except Richard's comments to the *Newfoundland Quarterly*, which appeared in the issue of December 1920.

Richard's meeting with the **Beaumont-Hamel widow** is described in the *Evening Telegram* of June 19, 1920.

The primary source for information about **Coaker's fishery regulations** was Edward Roberts's "Nothing Venture" (see Chapter Six notes). Coaker's comments at the **fish exporters conference** are in the *Evening Telegram* of September 6, 1920.

Richard's comments on the regulations were reported by Harris to Milner in a dispatch dated December 23, 1919 (GN 1/1/7, TRPA).

Minutes of the Squires and Harris **meeting with the fish exporters** on January 4, 1921, are in MG 73 (Board of Trade), Box 69, File 13 at TRPA. **Coaker's speech** on the removal of the regulations is in the *Daily Star* of April 19, 1921.

CHAPTER EIGHT

Richard's **letter to Edward Morris** of January 12, 1921, is in RSC 2. 18.001.

I obtained background material on **the Reids and the railway** from James Hiller's 1981 monograph *The Newfoundland Railway 1881–1949*, published by the Newfoundland Historical Society, and *A History of the Newfoundland Railway* by A. R. Penney and F. T. Kennedy. The **ouster of W. D. Reid** is documented in the Reid Newfoundland Company papers at TRPA (MG 17, Box 53 and 54).

Richard's comment about his value as a **reference for employment with the Reids** is from a letter to John Crawley of May 28, 1921 (RSC 2.18.005). **R. C. Morgan's resignation letter** to H. D. Reid is in RSC 2.18.009.

The comments by Governor Harris on the **finances of the colony** are in dispatches to the Colonial Office, London, on January 22 and May 28, 1921 (GN 1/1/7, Box 29, TRPA). **Crosbie's assessment** is in the *Daily Star* of April 16, 1921.

The **expenditure and deficit** quoted for 1920–21 comes from a note to Richard Squires from the auditor general dated December 8, 1921 (RSC 2.18.012). The **deficit figures** for the following two years and the **total debt** are from Noel, *Politics* (p. 152). **Coaker's comment** on economic conditions is from *Twenty Years* (p. 284).

The letter from **Richard to Smallwood** (November 2, 1921) is in RSC 2.18.011.

Information on the **James Strong business** is from a letter from Strong to Pincock, April 7, 1928 (courtesy of Carolyn Molson), and on the **White company** in a letter of April 27, 1922, from William White to Richard Squires (RSC 2.19.003).

Governor Harris's comments on the events of May 1921 are in GN 1/1/7, Box 29 at TRPA.

The specifications of **Road De Luxe** are in a memo to Squires from the auditor general's office dated December 12, 1921 (RSC 2.18.012).

The account of the **Women's Suffrage League's meeting** with Richard is in the *Daily News* of August 18, 1921. **Coaker's comment** on women's suffrage is in *Twenty Years* ("Trip to Europe, winter of 1920"). **Richard's remark in London** was reported in the *Daily News* of September 5, 1922.

Smallwood's comments on Coaker at this time are in *Twenty Years* (pp. 392–93).

Coaker's New York experience is in *Twenty Years* (p. 293).

The description of the **pit-prop program** comes from the Hollis Walker inquiry report in the *Daily News* (March 21, 1924). W. B. Jennings's **comments on Campbell** are in a letter to Richard of February 26, 1921 (RSC 2.18.002). Campbell's **words on political opponents** are in a letter to Richard of May 3, 1921 (RSC 2.18.005).

Jean Miller's **supply of wine** is mentioned by former office boy John Pearce in a conversation with Richard of November 16, 1924 (RSC 2.21.011). Les Curtis talked about the **state of affairs at the law office** in his testimony at the Hollis Walker inquiry, January 10, 1924.

Crosbie's claim of **buying his KCMG** is reported by Michael Harris in *Rare Ambition* (p. 79).

Richard's appearance before the **House of Representatives finance committee** in Washington is described in the *Evening Telegram* of September 26, 1921.

Information on Richard and Meaney travelling to **Montreal and New York** in 1921–22 comes from Meaney's testimony of January 24 and 25, 1924, at the Hollis Walker inquiry. Squires's comments on **campaign contributions** are from his testimony of January 17 (GN 126.23).

Campbell's cable to Richard of January 1, 1922, is in RSC 2.19.001, as is **Warren's telegram** of January 10, 1922. **James Strong's letter** to Richard on the Humber deal (February 22, 1922) is in RSC 2.19.002 and Richard's reply is in RSC 2.19.003.

The **Newfoundland Club dinner** in London is in the *Newfoundland Quarterly* of December 1922.

Warren's note to Richard on the **sale of Labrador** (November 23, 1922) is in RSC 2.19.011.

The account of the trip by **Jim Miller and John Meaney to Montreal** in 1922, and Richard's participation, is from their testimony at the Hollis Walker inquiry (Miller on January 21, Meaney on January 24 and 25). **Jean Miller** told about the promise of $5,000 from Richard in her testimony (as Jean Harsant) on January 25.

CHAPTER NINE

Richard described his negotiation with Besco on reopening the mines in the *Evening Telegram* (February 15, 1923). A letter from Jim Miller to Meaney (March 6, 1923, RSC 2.20.009) contains his **wife's threat.**

James Hiller gives the **details of the Humber deal** in "The Politics of Newsprint: The Newfoundland Pulp and Paper Industry, 1915–1939" in *Acadiensis* 19. 2, 1990 (pp. 3–39).

The cable of **support from Nangle** and friends (February 20, 1923) is in RSC 12.04.008. Richard's **letter to Mosdell** on the new newspaper, dated January 24, 1923, is in RSC 2.20.001.

Richard's meeting with **Browne and Bindon** is described by Browne in his *Eighty-Four Years a Newfoundlander: Memoirs of William J. Browne Vol. 1, 1897-1949* (p. 360). Richard's comments on Harbour Main district are in a letter to P. J. Griffin (March 21, 1923) in RSC 2.20.024.

The **telegram to James Strong** about money owed is dated March 23, 1923 (RSC 2.20.026). Strong's reply of March 24 is in RSC 2.20.027, and a follow-up telegram from Richard of March 26 is in RSC 2.20.029. The reorganization of the Strong business is described in Strong's letter to Pincock, April 7, 1928.

Richard's "maximum pressure" comment to Bonia is from a letter of March 31, 1923 (RSC 2.20.034). His letter to P. J. Summers on "terrorist tactics" is dated April 30, 1923, and is in RSC 2.20.065.

S. J. R. Noel's quote on pump-priming is from his *Politics* (p. 157). The complaint of Cashin's behaviour on polling day was from Harry Tansley (May 4, 1923, "To Whom It May Concern," RSC 2.20.070).

The *Evening Telegram* issues of May 16 and June 6 talk about the controversial reappointment of Campbell and the resentment of Hawco and Downey. Cashin's and Walsh's charges in the House are taken from O'Flaherty's *Lost Country* (p. 318).

Constable Byrne's June 19 report on the break-in at Meaney's office is in RSC 2.20.099, as is Meaney's letter to Richard (June 25). See also Richard's June 20 letter firing Harris O'Keefe (TRPA GN8, Box 20, 8.208).

The *Evening Telegram* of July 7, 1923, contains information on the early July cabinet meeting.

Warren's July 22 letter to Richard is in RSC 2.20.100, as is Richard's letter of resignation. The circumstances surrounding Warren's resignation are in the transcript of the Hollis Walker inquiry, February 4, 1924, 4:30–5:00 pm. Richard's meeting with Warren and his terms of resignation are in the transcript of January 17, 3:30–4:00.

Harry Winter described the FPU members' attempt to recruit him as party leader in his *Newfoundland Quarterly* memoir (72.2, winter 1976).

Campbell's call for an inquiry is in the *Evening Telegram* of August 17, 1923.

Richard's comment on his return from Little Bay Islands is in a letter of August 2 to A. H. Salter (RSC 2.20.101). The comment to the Montreal press is in the *Evening Telegram* of August 17, 1923, and his comment to an acquaintance ("no impairment of health or vigour") in a letter of August 4 to R. W. Steele (RSC 2.20.101).

Richard's remarks to a Toronto reporter are in the *Evening Telegram* of August 28, 1923, and his comments while in the United States are in the issue of October 13.

The rejection of Richard's request regarding the Imperial Conference is in a letter from Warren of September 12, 1923 (RSC 2.20.102). Lena's participation in the health conference is reported in the *Evening Telegram* of June 1, 1923.

I obtained information on Richard's purchase of the **land in the Waterford Valley** from RDNL (v83 f497, v83 f504, v96 f486).

A brief account of **Warren's involvement in the Imperial Conference** is in the *Newfoundland Quarterly* of December 1923. Warren's comments to Halfyard on Richard's behaviour in London is from a letter of September 28, 1923, quoted in Noel, *Politics* (p. 162).

The *Evening Telegram* **quote** is from the edition of December 31, 1923.

CHAPTER TEN

For the **weather in St John's,** see the letter of January 5, 1924, from Richard to "Gush" (RSC 2.21.001). **Coaker's comment** on Squires is from his report at the FPU Annual Convention, 1923, in *Twenty Years* (p. 223). **Smallwood's quote** about him is from his *Coaker of Newfoundland* (p. 74); his comment on Squires handling his money was made to Robert A. Squires, as told to me in an interview of December 27, 2016.

W. J. **Browne's quotes** on the St. John's judges and Walker are from his diary (entry of January 10, 1924), found at http://brownepapers.com. The **terms of the inquiry** are described by Noel in *Politics* (pp. 162–63). The issue of **Warren's phrasing** of the question concerning the Department of the Liquor Controller is discussed by R. M. Elliott in "Newfoundland Politics in the 1920s: The Genesis and Significance of the Hollis Walker Enquiry," in *Newfoundland in the Nineteenth and Twentieth Centuries* (Hiller and Neary, eds.).

My references to the proceedings of the **Hollis Walker inquiry** come from the transcript at TRPA GN 126. A copy of his report (Newfoundland Commission 1924) is at ASC.

Morine's presentation on the report is in the *Evening Telegram* of April 4 and 5, 1924. **Nangle's comments** are in the issue of April 16.

Reaction of the **Canadian papers** is reprinted in the issue of April 1. The *New York Times* reported on the inquiry on January 20, 29, and 31 and February 9, 1924. The quote from the *Times of London* is cited in Noel, *Politics* (p. 170, footnote 45).

Richard's remarks to the **Toronto reporter** were in the *Evening Telegram* of April 21, 1924. The post-inquiry **political machinations,** including the salient quotes, come from Noel's *Politics* (pp. 170–79) and O'Flaherty's *Lost Country* (pp. 323–28).

The **court appearances** of Squires, Campbell, and Meaney are reported in the *Evening Telegram* of April 24. The "Pepys behind the Scenes" comment is from May 8.

Richard's **letter to Merton Lewis** dated June 26, 1924, is in RSC 2. 21.006.

CHAPTER ELEVEN

The quotes from the *Daily Mail* are in the issues of May 23 and May 31, 1924. Peter **Cashin's assessment of Morine** is in *My Fight* (p. 37).

The activities of **Haig Week** in St. John's are described in the *Evening Telegram* issues of that week. **Thomas Nangle** gave credit to Richard and talked about his dispute with Archbishop Roche in a letter to J. R. Smallwood of November 22, 1965, filed in the Thomas Nangle Collection (COLL-308, Box 1) at ASC.

The **charges to the grand jury** on Squires, Campbell, and Meaney are in the *Evening Telegram* of October 9, 1924. Subsequent issues cover the decision on Squires (October 14) and the trials of Campbell (October 22) and Meaney (November 22).

The notice to Richard from the **tax assessor** and correspondence from **Bradley** are in RSC 2.21.012. The **fine for tax evasion** is reported in the *Evening Telegram* of December 3, 1925, and the final **court judgement** releasing Richard from default is in the issue of June 13, 1926.

The **Squires bank balances** are in a letter to Richard from Louise Saunders dated September 29, 1923 (RSC 2.20.102).

Information on the **Squires children in England** comes from various files in their names in HSC. Elaine's condition at Crofton Grange is in a July 28, 1923, letter from Lyster to Lady Squires (2.01.009). Elaine's letter to "Daddy" of December 8, 1924, is in 2.01.001, as is Richard's letter to Elaine (December 9, 1924). Elaine gave her assessment of brothers Robert and Richard in a letter to "Daddy" dated January 11, 1925 (2.01.001). **Rosemary's comment** about Lena is from "Memories."

The **letter from Hannah Smith** to Louise Saunders (February 22, 1925) is in RSC 2.22.02, and **Richard's correspondence** with Hannah (September 1, 1925) is in RSC 2.22.009.

The letter of introduction to **Famous Players** studios (October 28, 1925) is in RSC 2.22.010. The advertisement announcing Richard's **return to law practice** is in various issues of the *Evening Telegram* in November 1925. The order for **trees and shrubs** from Valley Nurseries, dated December 21, 1925, is in RSC 2.22.012. The letter from **Fred Ayre** (April 2, 1928) is in RSC 2.25.001.

Richard's **political manoeuvrings of 1927** are recorded in his diary of that year (TRPA, MG 864.111). The **Errol Munn comment** is from March 4.

Richard's comments to Lena on the **Strong business**, his description of the fare at the **Newfoundland Hotel**, and the information about **Burns Night** are from "Notes to Lady Squires" in RSC (3.01.001), which also contain his comments on Lena and Elaine moving back to St. John's.

The **assault on Alexander Squires** is in the *Evening Telegram* of May 7, 1926.

W. J. Browne's **encounter with Michael Cashin** is described in *Eighty-Four Years* (p. 147). The incident of **Peter Cashin at the City Club** is in Richard's 1927 diary (January 18). The first issue of the *Globe* was December 16, 1924.

Smallwood's **description of Hickman** is from *I Chose Canada* (pp. 153–54). **Hibbs's meeting with Richard** was on February 26, 1927. I have reconstructed the conversation based on Squires's detailed notes on the meeting, recorded in his diary.

The January 4, 1927, **note from Elaine Squires** to Smallwood is from the Smallwood Collection (COLL-285) at ASC (1.11.005). Smallwood described getting **Lena Squires and Coaker** together in London in *I Chose Canada* (p. 160). His **meeting with Hickman**, and Richard's comments on it, are on page 159.

The *Daily News* **assessment of Monroe** is in the issue of September 19, 1927. **Allardyce's report** of January 3, 1928 (secret), is in GN/1/1 (Box 34) at TRPA.

CHAPTER TWELVE

The **opening of the legislature**, the Speech from the Throne, and Hickman's speech are in the *Daily News* of May 3, 1928. The formation of the **Newfoundland Liberal Association** is described in the first edition of the *Liberal Press*, April 14, 1928. This and subsequent issues are at the PRL, Arts and Culture Centre, St. John's.

Coaker's correspondence with Lena Squires is included in the Squires Diary (TRPA, MG 864.111). Cashin's **conversation with Archbishop Roche** is in *My Fight* (p. 61).

The meeting of **Browne et al. with Alderdice** is in *Eighty-Four Years* (p. 160). Cashin's **meeting with Alderdice and Howley** is in *My Fight* (p. 62), and his subsequent meeting with Roche is on page 63.

Alderdice's manifesto is in the October 9, 1928, edition of the *Daily News*. The **joke** about the state of Newfoundland is in *Eighty-Four Years* (p. 163). Richard's **phonograph speech** is in the personal collection of the author. The Squires and Smallwood **mirror buttons** are described in the *Free Press*, v. 1 (24), 1971 (PRL).

Smallwood describes the **Squires campaign in Humber** in *I Chose Canada* (pp. 170–71). The anecdote about **Smallwood on Waterford Bridge Road** is from the Robert A. Squires interview, December 27, 2016. The quote about **voting against Cashin** is in *My Fight* (p. 68). The *Daily News* quote is from September 10, 1928.

CHAPTER THIRTEEN

I estimated Newfoundland's **public debt** from data contained in the *Newfoundland Royal Commission Report* of 1933, Appendix F. The **budget deficits** are taken from the same report (p. 47). The **war debt** is from a letter from the auditor general to Richard Squires of February 24, 1921 (RSC 12.04.019), though the *Newfoundland Royal Commission Report* gives it as just under $13 million.

The **Robert Bond quote** is from a letter to George Bond of March 3, 1923 (RBC 1.02.033). Richard's outline of **the decade's events** is from a letter of May 10, 1929, to Martin J. Teigan (RSC 2.26.003). There is a **brief biography of John Middleton** in the *Newfoundland Quarterly*, July 1931 (p. 214).

The comment of **W. J. Higgins** is quoted in Richard's diary (March 4, 1927) at TRPA (MG864.111). The reputed cost of **Coaker's Jamaica estate** is in the *Evening Telegram* of October 22, 1928. **Coaker's Christmas message** is in the *Fishermen's Advocate*, December 27, 1929.

The **Bronfman donation** is reported in *My Fight* (pp. 75–76). O'Flaherty describes the **early days of the Squires government** in *Lost Country* (pp. 347–50).

Richard and Lena's 1929 **activities in New York** are mentioned in the *New York Times* of February 14, February 27, and April 19, and the New York *Daily News* of April 19. The **meeting with Hearst interests** is in the issue of January 24, 1930.

The **"Rich in Richard"** saying was told to me by Richard J. Squires in an interview of December 27, 2016. Sir Richard's pursuit of the **airline business for Gander** is told by Robert C. Stone in *A Gentlemen's Agreement*.

Richard and Lena's **voyage on the *Berengaria*** is noted in Paul Knapp's *The Berengaria Exchange*. The story of the **1929 tsunami** and its aftermath has been told by Linden MacIntyre in *The Wake*.

Information on the **new Studebaker** comes from a May 15, 1929, letter from Richard to his son Richard Jr., in an unlabelled folder in Box 4 of HSC. The *Daily News* (June 25, 1929) reported on the purchase of **the *Medric*.** The letter to Richard Jr. also contains information on the Squires children during **Christmas of 1929.** Additional **information on Norman** is in a letter from Brownrigg to Richard Squires dated October 2, 1931 (RSC 2.28.010). Richard's letter to Norman of December 24, 1929, is in an unlabelled folder, Box 4 of HSC.

The *New York Times* noted **engagements involving Lena and Elaine** in the issues of March 13 and 18, 1930. The **by-election note** in the *Daily News* appeared on April 16. I learned about **Lena's campaigning with Belle** (Haddon) Strong from Carolyn Molson (personal email, January 26, 2017). The *Daily News* comments on **Lady Squires and Alderdice's remarks** in the House of Assembly are in the issues of May 20 and 29, 1930, respectively.

Richard's arrival in London is described in the *New York Times* of September 25, 1930. Information on **Lena's social calendar** at the Imperial Conference is in 1.02.026 and 1.02.027 of HSC. Information on **William Seto Ping** comes from a conversation with his son William (February 9, 2021).

The upbeat statement of Squires to the **Board of Trade** comes from O'Flaherty's *Lost Country* (p. 362). The **dinner at the Newfoundland Hotel** of January 19, 1931, is described in the *Newfoundland Quarterly* (April 1931) and the February 3 dinner in the *Daily News* of February 4, 1931.

Peter Cashin's account of Squires's withdrawal from the **Bank of Montreal** is in *My Fight* (p. 79). **Cashin's comments in Montreal** are from *Lost Country* (p. 363), as are Richard's **comments in the House** in March (p. 363) and the information on **government members' largesse** (p. 365). The quote from **R. B. Bennett's letter** to the Bank of Montreal is from Noel's *Politics* (p. 191).

The **telegrams between Richard and Lena** are in RSC 2.28.006.007. **Richard's letter to J. H. Thomas** (July 11, 1931) is in RSC 2.28.007 and **Thompson's acceptance** in 2.28.008. *Lost Country* describes the **visits of Cashin and Mosdell to New York**, followed by Barnes and Coaker, and the offer to **sell Labrador** (pp. 371–72).

Cashin's account of **Penson and Keating** is from *My Fight* (pp. 84–85). I obtained information on the **loan application** of late 1931 and **Bennett's intervention** from Noel's *Politics* (pp. 194–96) and O'Flaherty's *Lost Country* (pp. 373–74); the **optimistic outlook** of January 1932 is described by O'Flaherty on page 376.

CHAPTER FOURTEEN

The **$70,000 advanced to the Strong business** is confirmed in an entry of May 19, 1936, in the diary of Robert H. Squires (private collection of Robert A. Squires). Richard's **letter to Will Strong** of January 18, 1932, is in RSC 2.29.001, as is **Thompson's letter** to Richard of January 15.

Peter Cashin described the circumstances surrounding his **decision to resign** in *My Fight* (pp. 89–90). **Cashin's statement in the House** of Assembly of February 4, 1932, and other quotes from legislative proceedings for 1932 come from *The Debates of the Newfoundland Legislature 1932* (James Hiller, ed.).

Mayor Howlett's statement is a condensed version of the case of John, taken from his VOWR appeal as printed in the *Evening Telegram* of January 6, 1932.

My account of the **disturbance of February 11** and the **pipe anecdote** of February 13 is based on several sources: Melvin Baker's article "Governor Sir John Middleton's Memorandum on the 1932 St. John's Riot," *Newfoundland and Labrador Studies*, 34.1, 2019, (pp. 131–57); the *New York Times*, February 12, 1932; and the government bulletin of February 13 (RSC 2.29.002). **Middleton's attempt to prepare for rioting** and his quote describing Inspector Hutchings are in Baker's "Memorandum" article.

Cashin's accusations in the House of February 16 and the events that followed, including quotes, are based on the accounts in Noel's *Politics* (pp. 198–201) and O'Flaherty's *Lost Country* (pp. 379–82). Thompson gave his **assessment of Bindon** in a March 7, 1932, memo to Richard (RSC 2.29.003).

I based my account of the events of **April 4, the April 5 riot, and the aftermath** on reports in the *Evening Telegram*, the *Daily News*, and the *New York Times*, a file of newspaper clippings held by Robert A. Squires, and Baker's *Memorandum*, as well as Smallwood's recollections in *I Chose Canada* (pp. 176–79) and Smallwood's 1983 interview with Rob Pitt, posted online in the Digital Archives Initiative at MUN (Smallwood Interview 10B).

The **Nettie White quote** is from "Recollections" by Eliza Reeve, a term paper for English 3420, Memorial University, 1980 (CNS). The **"seething mob"** quote is from Noel's *Politics* (p. 201). The **statement of the citizen's committee** is in Hiller's *Debates*. Peter Cashin's **allegation against Puddester** is in *My Fight* (pp. 90–91). **Harry Winter's comments** are from his *Newfoundland Quarterly* memoir (72.2, winter 1976).

Squires's election manifesto is at CNS. The account of **Squires in Heart's Content** comes from the unpublished memoir of Hudson Davis, a resident at the time, in the private collection of the author.

CHAPTER FIFTEEN

Alderdice's quote on **debt repayment** is from O'Flaherty's *Lost Country* (pp. 390–91). **Britain's response** to his default proposal is from Noel, *Politics* (p. 207), as are the terms of the **Amulree commission** (p. 209).

Rosemary's comments are from "Memories."

Quotes from the *Newfoundland* **Royal Commission** *Report* are from pages 86–87 and 197.

D. R. Thistle's testimony is reported in *Lost Country* (p. 397). **Morine's comments** are in the *Globe*, November 24 and 25; the quote is from November 24.

Richard's cable to Thomas dated November 30 is from the Robert A. Squires private collection, as are **Anderson's reply** of December 7 and the correspondence with **Lord Beaverbrook**.

The quotes describing **Alderdice and Puddester** are from December 1933 correspondence of Governor Anderson to Sir Edward Harding, Dominions Office, as contained in Noel's *Politics* (p. 222).

Lady Hope Simpson's comments on the Squireses are from Peter Neary (ed.), *White Tie and Decorations* (p. 55).

Descriptions of the **Squires family activities** in 1934, including quotes, are from the diary of Robert H. Squires (Robert A. Squires collection) and from Rosemary Mersereau's "Memories."

Issues of Meaney's **Newfoundlander** are at PRL.

Richard's remarks and those of Robert H. Squires on the **death of Alexander** are from Robert's diary (January 1, 1935). Alexander's **falling out with the church** comes from my interview with Robert A. Squires, December 27, 2016.

The story of **Pierce Power** is told by Carmelita McGrath in "Dole and Desperate Measures: Life in the Great Depression in Newfoundland" and Kathryn Welbourn in "Pierce Power and the Riot of 1935," both contained in *Newfoundland and Labrador Adult Basic Education Social History Series* (Book 4), Writers' Alliance of Newfoundland and Labrador, 1996. **Hope Simpson's comments** on the 1935 riot are in *White Tie* (p. 152).

Peter Dunn's comments on Squires are in Noel's *Politics* (pp. 234–45). Squires's **"negro" comment** appeared in the *Daily News* of June 30, 1936. **Kendrick's astrological reports** are in RSC 2.32.001 and 2.32.002.

The **meetings with the Strongs** in May and August 1936 are described in the Robert H. Squires diary. Richard's **meeting with Governor Anderson** (January 17, 1936) is detailed in his diary excerpt in MG 864.111 at TRPA. Hope Simpson's **"clever fellow" remark** is in *White Tie* (p. 315).

I have reconstructed the conversations between **Richard and Malcolm MacDonald** from MacDonald's notes of their meetings (RSC 12.27.001). The **Morley Richards interview** appeared in the London *Daily Express*, March 31, 1939. Richard's **statement from Winnipeg** is in the *Daily News* of May 23, 1939.

Rosemary's recollections of events surrounding her father's death come from her private writings, kindly provided by her daughter, Elaine Wilson.

I have distilled Smallwood's lengthy *Barrelman* **tribute** from the script of the program (ASC Coll-028 1.01.028).

Richard Squires's obituary and funeral are reported in the *Daily News* of March 28 and 27, 1940. The tribute from the *Twillingate Sun* is in the issue of March 30, 1940.

AFTERWORD

The will of Sir Richard Squires (March 7, 1940) is at the Registry of the Supreme Court, St. John's.

Much of the **family information** in this section comes from interviews with Robert A. Squires (December 12, 2016, and December 29, 2020) and Robert A. and Richard J. Squires (December 27, 2016).

I obtained information on **Lady Squires and the Drurys** in Tucson, and the **death of Norman Squires,** from various issues of the *Arizona Daily Star* in the 1940s and '50s, in particular the issue of September 8, 1951, at the Tucson Family History Center. Additional details come from an undated affidavit of Elaine Squires Drury provided by Elaine Wilson and from Rosemary Mersereau's "Memories."

Daubeney Drury's death was reported in the *Montreal Gazette* of April 19, 1946. The **Midstream Realty** transactions can be found at RDNL.

PHOTO SOURCES

p. 148 William R. Warren, 1879–1927, *findagrave.com*

p. 165 Walter S. Monroe, 1871–1952, *findagrave.com*

p. 170 Unveiling of the War Memorial, July 1924, *en.Wikipedia.org*

p. 175 Cherry Lodge, *Courtesy Robert A. Squires*

p. 181 Peter Cashin, 1890–1977, *Who's Who 1930*

p. 190 Frederick Alderdice, 1871–1936, *Wikitree.com*

p. 220 The day of the riot, April 5, 1932, *TRPA, A 19-21*

p. 240 Squires family at Midstream, Christmas 1935, *Courtesy Robert A. Squires*

p. 242 James Strong premises, 1939, *Courtesy Carolyn Molson*

p. 243 Squires on *Medric*, ca. 1935, *Courtesy Robert A. Squires*

BIBLIOGRAPHY

Archibald, Raymond Clare. *Historical Notes on the Education of Women at Mount Allison 1854–1954*. Mount Allison University: The Centennial Committee, 1954.

Baker, Melvin, and Peter Neary. *Joseph Roberts Smallwood: Masthead Newfoundlander 1900–1949*. McGill-Queen's University Press, 2021.

Browne, Gary, and Darrin McGrath. *Soldier Priest in the Killing Fields of Europe*. St. John's: DRC Publishing, 2006.

Browne, William J. *Eighty-Four Years a Newfoundlander: Memoirs of William J. Browne Vol. 1, 1897–1949*. St. John's: Dicks and Company, 1981.

Cadigan, Sean. *Death on Two Fronts: National Tragedies and the Fate of Democracy in Newfoundland, 1914–1934*. Penguin Random House Canada, 2013.

Cashin, Peter. *My Fight for Newfoundland*. Edited by Edward Roberts. St. John's: Flanker Press, 2012.

Coaker, W. F. (compiler). *Twenty Years of the Fishermen's Protective Union of Newfoundland from 1909–1929*. St. John's: Advocate Publishing Co. Ltd., 1930.

Fizzard, Garfield (compiler). *Above All Price: The Story of the United Church College Residence, St. John's, Newfoundland*. St. John's: UCCR Reunion Committee, 2002.

Gough, Ruby L. *Robert Edwards Holloway: Newfoundland Educator, Scientist, Photographer, 1874–1904*. McGill-Queen's University Press, 2005.

Harris, Michael. *Rare Ambition: The Crosbies of Newfoundland*. Viking Press, 1992.

Hiller, James K. *Robert Bond: A Political History*. St. John's: ISER Books, 2019.

Hiller, James K. (ed.). *The Debates of the Newfoundland Legislature 1932*. St. John's: Queen's Printer, 2010.

Hiller, James, and Peter Neary (eds.). *Newfoundland in the Nineteenth and Twentieth Centuries: Essays in Interpretation*. Toronto: University of Toronto Press, 1980.

Kealey, Linda (ed.). *Pursuing Equality: Historical Perspectives on Women in Newfoundland and Labrador*. St. John's: ISER Books, 1993.

Kent, Rockwell. *It's Me O Lord: The Autobiography of Rockwell Kent*. New York: Dodd, Mead & Company, 1955.

Knapp, Paul. *The Berengaria Exchange*. New York: The Dial Press, 1972.

McDonald, Ian D. H. *To Each His Own: William Coaker and the Fishermen's Protective Union in Newfoundland Politics, 1908–1925*. Edited by James K. Hiller. St. John's: Institute of Social and Economic Research (MUN), 1987.

MacIntyre, Linden. *The Wake: The Deadly Legacy of a Newfoundland Tsunami*. HarperCollins, 2019.

Neary, Peter (ed.). *White Tie and Decorations: Sir John and Lady Hope Simpson in Newfoundland, 1934–1936*. Toronto: University of Toronto Press, 1996.

Nicholson, G. W. L. *The Fighting Newfoundlander: A History of the Royal Newfoundland Regiment*. McGill-Queen's University Press, 1964.

Noel, S. J. R. *Politics in Newfoundland*. Toronto: University of Toronto Press, 1971.

O'Flaherty, Patrick. *Lost Country: The Rise and Fall of Newfoundland 1843–1933*. St. John's: Long Beach Press, 2005.

Penney, A. R., and F. T. Kennedy. *History of the Newfoundland Railway*. St. John's: Harry Cuff Publications Ltd., 2003.

Rowe, Ted. *Robert Bond, The Greatest Newfoundlander*. St. John's: Creative Book Publishing, 2017.

Sharpe, Christopher A., P. Whitney Lackenbauer, Helene Staveley, Robert J. Harding, Mike O'Brien, Sonja Boon, Melvin Baker, Peter Neary, Maarten Gerritsen, and Chris Martin. *Essays on the Great War: Papers Published in Newfoundland and Labrador Studies*. Edited by James Feehan. St. John's: Faculty of Arts Publications (MUN), 2014.

Smallwood, J. R. *Coaker of Newfoundland: The Man Who Led the Deep-Sea Fishermen to Political Power*. London: Labour Publishing Co., 1927.

———. *I Chose Canada: The Memoirs of the Honourable Joseph R. "Joey" Smallwood* (Vol. 1). Toronto: Macmillan, 1973.

———. *The New Newfoundland*. New York: The Macmillan Company, 1931.

———. *Newfoundland Miscellany*. St. John's: Newfoundland Book Publishers, 1978.

Stone, Robert C. *A Gentlemen's Agreement*. Boulder Books, 2015.

INDEX

Page numbers in *italics* denote photographs.

TED ROWE grew up in Heart's Content, Newfoundland and Labrador. He is a graduate of Memorial University, Dalhousie University, and the University of Western Ontario. After teaching at Memorial in the 1970s, he had a thirty-year career in real estate and has been active in a number of community organizations. Along the way he and his wife Maureen raised five sons. He is the author of *Connecting the Continents: Heart's Content and the Atlantic Cable* and *Heroes & Rogues and the Story of Heart's Content*, a community history of Heart's Content. His biography *Robert Bond: The Greatest Newfoundlander* was shortlisted for the Shaughnessy Cohen Prize for Political Writing by the Writer's Trust of Canada in 2018.In his spare time he travels, plays music, and enjoys good food and wine.